Building Moral Communities
Through Educational Drama

Contemporary Studies in Social and Policy Issues in Education:
The David C. Anchin Series
(formerly Social and Policy Issues in Education:
The David C. Anchin Center Series)
Kathryn M. Borman, Series Editor

Building Moral Communities Through Educational Drama

edited by

Betty Jane Wagner
Roosevelt University

 Ablex Publishing Corporation
Stamford, Connecticut
London, England

Printed in the United States of America

Library of Congress Cataloging-in-Publication Data

Building moral communities through educational drama / by Betty Jane Wagner.
    p. cm.—(Contemporary studies in social and policy issues in education)
    Includes bibliographical references and index.
    ISBN 1-56750-401-9 (cloth)—ISBN 1-56750-402-7 (pbk.)
    1. Moral education. 2. Drama in education. 3. Conflict management—Study and teaching. I. Wagner, Betty Jane. II. Series.
LC375.B85   1999
370.11′4—dc21   98-28975
                                                             CIP

Ablex Publishing Corporation
100 Prospect Street
P.O. Box 811
Stamford, Connecticut 06904-0811

Published in the U.K. and Europe by:
JAI Press Ltd.
38 Tavistock Street
Covent Garden
London WC2E 7PB
England

To my mother, Pearl Brown, a child elocutionist,
who raised me on her dramatic readings and, at 101,
still lets me role-play the child in the drama of our family

Contents

Introduction

Betty Jane Wagner
Roosevelt University

I f you ask teachers what their overriding concerns are as professionals, the most common response has something to do with the breakdown in morality among their students. Not only do they relate personal encounters with an increasing number of young people who are witnessing or engaging in cheating or dishonest interactions, violent acts, drug or alcohol abuse, and irresponsible sexual behavior, but they will point to an attitude change they find disturbing. Their students have difficulty imagining the consequences of their actions and all too often seem not to care about the impact their behavior has on others. Far too many are underparented and spend precious few hours engaging cooperatively in mutual tasks with significant adults. Except for peer groups or gangs, too many young persons are left to fend for themselves without appropriate role models who have the time and commitment to help them grow into responsible adults. They seldom confront moral dilemmas in a context that illumines issues and provides an opportunity for reflection and guidance. One of the more powerful ways teachers and community leaders can fill this gap in adult modeling is through educational or improvisational drama.

The first time I became aware of the power of drama as a way to build moral communities was in Evanston, Illinois, when I watched the internationally renowned drama teacher Dorothy Heathcote conduct dramas. I remember vividly the first day I found myself in her presence. She awakened in me something that has been bubbling ever since. Splashing into my ordered thinking with a left-handed paddle, her boat was not headed just toward a new teaching gimmick, but rather toward a truth beyond mere facts where the moral waters stirred are deep within.

Why did I enroll in Heathcote's class in the first place? Simply because her three-week course at Northwestern University in Evanston that summer of 1971 was one that fit neatly into my babysitter's schedule. The course title, "Drama in Education," sounded mildly intriguing. On the first day of class, I locked my bike, climbed three flights of stairs, and scrunched myself past a roaring fan and a row of seated students in a hot, far-too-small, top floor room in the Methodist Church. After I slid as noiselessly as possible onto one of the metal folding chairs and schlepped my bike bag on the floor beneath me, I checked my watch. Was I late? No. It was ten of eight. Class had not begun. Yet, there in front of me, as if the class had been going on for hours, was this teacher, her brown sleeveless cotton gown with its tiny flowers sweeping the floor, her arresting eyes riveted on the student in front of her, her arms flung wide, telling about a recent drama she had led. Had I missed something? Of course I had. Even before my bare thighs had had time to warm up the welcoming cool of the metal beneath me, I knew this was going to be no ordinary summer class. I was seated before an electric presence. At that point, I expected to be challenged; I did not yet realize the power of Heathcote's work to awaken our ethical sensibilities.

There is a primitive element in Heathcote's work that simplifies and focuses attention. She quickly cuts to the essence of an experience, to its solid dwelling place within our bodies. Before we know what is happening, however, we are in the throes of an agonizing moral dilemma.

For example, I saw her lead a group of eight- and nine-year-olds into wrestling with the challenge of how to become a community of strong-spirited and ethical human beings. She began by having them consider this sentence, which she had written on the blackboard: "A nation is as strong as the spirit of its people."

She gently invited them to consider the meaning of those words. When one boy said that a nation was strong because it could defend itself in a war, she mirrored his idea back to him with these words: "You are saying a nation's strength lies in guns." This implication surprised the child, and he began to back pedal. Instead of contradicting the boy, Heathcote magnified his utterance to show the meaning behind his words. She listens intently and takes seriously any contribution a child makes to either a discussion or a drama. But then she quickly moves beyond the child's initial sortie and takes the discussion or the drama into the realm of implications and ethical considerations.

Here is another example: When a group of teenagers decided they wanted to do a drama about killing a bad guy, she started the drama with the dead body lying in front of the students. They were invited to improvise the family in mourning, remembering all the good things they could about the deceased. Suddenly, the students were plunged into a consideration of the consequences of their act of murder. Before long, killing the person who posed a threat to them did not seem like so simple a solution.

In this book, we present many other examples of the way drama can bring about effective character education. It includes a group of studies and reports that show what happens when drama in education is used to deepen understanding of human affairs and of the moral dilemmas in literature and history, to foster growth in interpersonal relations, to develop writing ability, and to help teachers grow.

EDUCATIONAL DRAMA

The studies reported here all employ informal or improvisational drama. This type of drama has come to be termed drama in education (DIE), or process drama—that is, drama at the service of the participants themselves, not primarily to prepare a play to present to an audience. The purpose of DIE is to educate. We have included in this book activities in which participants work together to improvise a fictional encounter in order to understand something better. The ways in which the fictional encounter is set up differs, however. For example, Peter Smagorinsky and Paula Salvio report on invitations to students to respond to a piece of literature by improvising and role-playing; in Jennifer Lynn Wolf and Shirley Brice Heath's study, the students develop their own script, largely through improvisation and successive trials; in Holly Giffin and Kathleen Yaffe's chapter, the situation is set up by the leader and a teacher in role; I report on the way Dorothy Heathcote as a teacher in role helps children create a drama set in a medieval monastery through assuming the roles of monks; and Joe Norris shows how he deliberately sets up invitations to drama to help his adult students gain insight on teaching and the curriculum.

Before the term "drama in education" came into use, largely due to the influence of Dorothy Heathcote, classroom teachers, especially in the elementary schools in the United States, directed what they called creative drama or creative dramatics lessons. Most of the studies reported in Chapter 3 are in the creative dramatics tradition, as creative drama was originally termed. Creative drama had the same goal as drama in education, as can be seen by this definition, presented by The Children's Theater Association of America in 1972: "An improvisational, process-centered, non-exhibitional form of drama in which participants are guided by a leader to imagine, enact, and reflect upon the human experience." Participants improvise the action and dialogue to explore content, "using elements of drama to give form and meaning to the experience. The primary purpose of creative drama is to foster personality growth and to facilitate learning of the participants rather than to train actors for the stage" (Davis & Behm, 1978, p. 10). Brian Way describes the goal of this type of drama as leading "the inquirer to moments of direct experience, transcending mere knowledge, enriching the imagination, possibly touching the heart and soul as well as the mind" (Way, 1972, p. 1). Joe Norris uses the term *creative drama* for the work he does with college and graduate school students. Both creative drama and DIE are something all children can do and benefit from, not just those who might have a natural gift for theatrical performance.

Both creative drama and drama in education always involve role-playing, which is a problematic term because it can mean anything from simply improvising a dialogue in a simulated situation in which the participants "play" themselves as they discuss and solve a problem, to assuming a role in a full-scale improvised drama in the drama-in-education tradition. In traditional conflict-resolution simulations, participants role-play themselves in a directly analogous way. By contrast, in a DIE session, the conflict is indirectly presented. For example, in a traditional conflict-resolution exercise two children role-play a situation in which one of them is instructed to grab the other's pencil, and then they are encouraged to role-play to solve the problem this poses for the other person. Working in the drama in education manner, Giffin and Yaffe make it clear that they are not advocating simply role-playing a simulation of a conflict. Instead, the leader is conducting a full-scale drama, in which the children play roles that are very different from their everyday selves. They are thrust into the position of the experts in an imaginary village who can help solve the problems posed by the teacher in role. It is he who is causing the problem, not one of them.

In this book, except in my study of the effect of role-playing on persuasive letters (Chapter 8), all of the role-playing is set in an imagined world. The goal in these improvisational dramas is to transform students' understanding of human dilemmas and conflicts, rather than to provide simple practice in how to solve social problems. Both creative drama and drama in education strive to achieve distance from the participants' real-life situations so participants feel freer to explore alternatives. Thus, this kind of drama is never simply a rehearsal for a real-world interaction. Students create an imagined world that on the surface may seem very different from real life. In this setting, they may come to empathize with other people and internalize alternative points of view.

Although creative drama and DIE share common goals, there are some differences between them. In creative drama, the action is often suggested by a story, poem, original idea, or music provided by the child or adult. It may include pantomime (movement, gestures, and facial expressions without the use of words), improvisation, or role-playing, and usually has a beginning, middle, and end. Students typically dramatize or pantomime a story or poem, the plot or substance of which is known in advance, or enact a scene that is not actually included in the story but could be. The field of creative drama is evolving, but enacting a story is still its center. In contrast, drama in education or process drama practitioners usually begin with an area of the curriculum that is difficult for the students. If a text is used, it is only a starting point for a transformation of a text, exploring the spaces between episodes in an account to create an imagined world that illumines not only the text, but the world it represents.

Both creative drama and DIE focus on exploring how an experience might feel to the participants. In DIE, however, there is less emphasis on story and character development and more emphasis on problem solving or living through a particular moment in time. Through ritual, dramatic encounters, pantomime, *tableaux vivants*, writing in role, and reflection, participants enter the lives of imagined characters and play out their responses to challenges and crises. Experienced teachers of DIE often initiate or move the drama along by assuming a role themselves, and heighten the tension by challenging the participants to respond to dilemmas in authentic and believable ways. The aim is to explore a particular experience through a nonlinear layering of episodes which cumulatively extends and enriches the fictional context (O'Neill, 1994).

The emphasis in DIE is learning *through* drama—for example, exploring the world in which a novel is set, understanding a historical event, experiencing conflicts between different cultural groups, or capturing the feel of other walks of life. DIE enables participants—either during the drama itself or after the drama in a reflection and discussion—to look at reality through fantasy and to see below the surface of actions to their meaning.

Drama is powerful because its unique balance of thought and feeling makes learning enjoyable, exciting, challenging, and relevant to real-life concerns. Participants work imaginatively in role to construct contexts and events. In the process, they learn to build a collective belief in the imagined situation and to explore issues, alternate courses of action, relationships among people, and the emotional subtext of encounters with others. This type of drama is a mode of interpretive thinking. The drama is generated through a perceived need to explore a problem or a dilemma and thus serves a heuristic function in learning the subject matter and in the development of the oral and written language of the participants. Participants are testing hypotheses, inviting supposition, and experiencing the art of logical argument. As they experience the perspectives of various roles, not only do they see the world from another viewpoint and develop empathy, but they broaden their understanding.

Participants in a drama are instrumental in creating an event. Simultaneously, they are playwrights, actors, audience, and critics. When they stop the drama to assess its effectiveness, they reflect on the implications of their actions. Because the classroom atmosphere during a drama is one of exploration and playfulness, participants are less likely to reach premature closure or hasty solutions. In their effort to understand or make sense of a certain imagined situation, they have to use all their previous knowledge and experience—physical, cognitive, intuitive, and emotional. Often, students discover responses in themselves that are unexpected and more mature than even they realized they were capable of.

Drama is a mental state. "The essential nature of the dramatic medium is a liberating act of imagination,...a dual consciousness in which the real and fictional worlds are held together in the mind" (O'Neill, 1995, p. 159). Because profound learning is that which fuses both thinking and feeling, the lessons children take from drama in education are likely to stay with them. They are assimilating material in a way that is natural and relevant (Rice & Sisk, 1980).

OVERVIEW OF THIS BOOK

Most of the studies you find in this book are of teachers or other drama directors who employ informal or improvisational drama with the goal of enhancing the understanding of self and others, improving the social interactions of a group, and giving birth to deeper insight into human affairs, particularly those involving conflict. The teenagers in Jennifer Lynn Wolf and Shirley Brice Heath's study in Chapter 4 do plan to perform the improvisational drama they create, but what they learn about solving conflicts along the way is what matters to them.

I use the term *educational drama* to highlight its goal toward transforming its participants rather than entertaining an audience and to encompass both creative drama and DIE.

Unlike theater-as-performance, educational drama is more democratic. The differences in the skill level of the participants is not highlighted, as when auditioning for roles in an intended performance for an audience. Instead, educational drama becomes a way to learn about life, and all the roles the participants assume become part of the drama. If a person is not quite up to the responsibility the drama thrusts upon him or her, the rest of the group have to figure out how to help or take over a needed function, just as in real life. Through informal educational drama, "students catch brief glimpses of each other's inner thus enhancing understanding" (Garcia, 1996, p. 9). Teachers also catch these glimpses and in the process grow themselves as facilitators of student learning. Even after years of teaching, informal drama teachers grow personally and professionally as they repeatedly enter into ever new and fresh experiences themselves while engaging in classroom drama. They improvise and improve along with their students.

The chapters in this book may be read in any order. They are grouped together in each section according to the type of effects of drama that were looked at, but the instructional strategies described could easily have other outcomes as well. Consequently, in any of these chapters, teachers of all subjects or age levels may find techniques they want to use. In each chapter, leaders are using drama to benefit all persons, not just those who might have a natural talent for theatrical performance.

In Part I of this book, chapters by Peter Smagorinsky, Paula Salvio, and Karen Hume and Gordon Wells show how teenagers and adults can respond through drama at a deeper level to the moral issues presented in literature or in historical events, how they can learn to speak and write with a greater awareness of audience, and how they can develop a more solid understanding of why persons behave as they do. Improvisational drama is not magic, but in the hands of a skillful teacher it can be a powerful tool for learning about the world of human interactions, which is the world that literature reflects and that history records.

Smagorinsky's methodology (Chapter 1) is to ground an analysis and discussion of dramatic enactment in response to literature in a Vygotskian perspective of the dynamics of individual psychological growth as participation in a social drama. He analyzes the dramatic response of a group of students in a drug and alcohol rehabilitation facility, to the moral dilemma presented in William Carlos Williams' short story, "The Use of Force." As he roots his analysis in Vygotsky's theoretical framework, he makes explicit the relationship between drama's function of regulating and mediating emotions and the development of personality through dramatic tension. His lens is the critical literary theory of reader response and Vygotsky's view of the relationship between art and personality.

In Chapter 2, Salvio, using Bertolt Brecht's dramaturgy, shows how adult teachers respond to Edwidge Danticat's *Krik? Krak!*, a collection of testimonial stories that viscerally present Haitian life under the terrorism of the Tonton Macoutes. In a moving account, Salvio shows how the teachers used their own bodies as the medium for response, engaging physically, emotionally, and morally with the text. In the process, they learned that coming to understand the emotional world of another person is often a painful process of self-discovery. The teachers chose among three theatrical conventions to stage their response to *Krik? Krak!*: montage, context building, and reflective action, each of which Salvio describes in detail.

Salvio not only describes what she did, but also analyzes her interaction with others, and her reflections in action as she made in-process decisions while conducting her lessons. Through the lens of critical social feminist theory, she analyzes the reasons for her decisions and examines her assumptions. Salvio is a reflective practitioner. What she communicates is a powerful sense of a lived experience.

In Chapter 3, the methodology is collaborative action research. Hume, a teacher of sixth, seventh, and eighth grades, and Wells, a university professor, observe, describe, analyze, and interpret the effect of a short drama on the building of the Canadian railway, led by David Booth, and another on the bomb dropped on Hiroshima, led by Karen Hume. They are both challenged by a group of students who were disinterested in history. Through the drama the class becomes engaged and curious, and this helps Hume build the ethos of a classroom community of inquiry.

The three chapters in Part II convincingly show how drama helps young people deal with conflicts, develop a more positive image of themselves, become more socially aware, and understand moral dilemmas presented in their own emerging group-constructed drama. In the first two chapters are descriptive studies by Jennifer Lynn Wolf and Shirley Brice Heath, and by Holly Giffin and Kathleen Yaffe. The third chapter is a review of quantitative studies on drama's effect on attitudes, behavior, and moral reasoning. As students role-play and reflect on their drama, they have an opportunity to clarify their attitudes and see the consequences of certain types of action; in the process, they can develop higher ethical and moral standards of behavior. They also gain much-needed experience to face issues and solve problems in imaginative and creative ways—problems including interpersonal tangles that spring up in the process of putting on a play. As a result, the social health of a whole group is improved.

In Chapter 4, Wolf and Heath present a comparison of conflict-resolution strategies with stages of creating a drama, using as their cases two groups of teenagers who have come together to make a drama. Wolf and Heath show how the conflicts teenagers face as they create, plan, try out roles, and rehearse a play of their own making can provide a potent force for the development of conflict-resolution skills. Wolf and Heath describe and analyze the interactions of two groups. Both are inner-city youth at high risk for drug use, dropping out of school, crime, etc.; both groups volunteer to come together to create a play they will later perform, and both are facilitated by a trained drama teacher. One meets during school in an elective class to develop a play to take on tour; the other meets after school to work up a performance to take throughout the city to school and community events. In both settings adults and teens work together in a mutually dependent collaboration. The material for the play comes from the troubled lives of the young participants. Their diversity and lack of interpersonal skills create tensions and conflicts, but the focus on a mutually agreed-upon goal forces conflict resolution, thus forging genuine community. In the process of getting ready for and developing an original play, teenagers learn essential strategies not only for play production, but also for academic performance in school and for the management of their often chaotic lives.

Giffin and Yaffe also use a case-study methodology to present and analyze a classroom drama that is conducted in order to improve the social behavior of second graders. Through use of a modified "mantle of the expert" strategy developed by Dorothy Heathcote, Yaffe helps children understand the problems posed by persons who either do not listen and respond to the needs of others or who take things that do not belong to them. Throughout the drama, children learn conflict-resolution skills.

In both of the studies in chapters 4 and 5, the researchers compare conflict resolution with drama, and both find some interesting parallels. In each study, we see how role-playing in drama can provide a powerful rehearsal for conflict-resolution in real life.

John Carroll (1996) sees case study as "the research methodology that most clearly fits the special conditions of drama." Because drama by its very nature is "a negotiated group at form," it "is a non-reproducible experience" (p. 77).

> The participants within a drama in education session or series of sessions create a unique set of social relationships that becomes a single unit of experience capable of analysis and study. Because of the complexity of the interactions, the whole creative sequence needs to be studied and not just aspects of variables within it. These characteristics are also aspects of a case study methodology [Hartfield, 1982] and provide a close fit for drama researchers to follow. The case study honours the agency of the participants and sees them as experts not just a source of data for analysis. (p. 77)

In Chapter 6, I review a large number of studies of drama in the classroom, showing its effects on student attitudes, social behavior, and moral reasoning. Most of these studies are quantitative or quasi-experimental in methodology because the research questions call for an assessment of the *effects* of drama, rather than a close analysis of the drama itself. This methodology is appropriate because the audience for much of this research is composed of policy makers and those who control school or community budgets, and they want to know what good can come out of drama lessons. As Johnny Saldaña and Lin Wright (1996) put it, in "the generally skeptical social climate of today,...those with power to distribute funds and mandate programs demand justification and accountability. Research has the potential...to serve as an agent for advocacy—to show decision makers that drama and theatre for youth 'works'" (p. 129).

In Part III, we show how improvisational drama can help children come to value the world of written records, as well as to build a conversational context for written persuasion and develop their skill as context-sensitive writers. In Chapter 7, using a case-study methodology, I show how Dorothy Heathcote conducted a drama with a group of American 9- to 13-year-olds. She raised to consciousness an awareness of the importance of the written word and deepened the children's commitment to preserving historically important written documents. The setting of the drama was a monastery in the time of King Arthur. I describe in detail how the children in role as monks come to value an "ancient" scroll (actually one created by the adult teachers who were watching the drama) they find hidden in a tree. In my analysis, I show how many of the characteristics of effective drama are also those of good writing.

In Chapter 8, I present the results of a quasi-experimental interventionist study, with groups of fourth and eighth graders, of the effect of role-playing on persuasive writing. Children who role-play before writing write letters that show a significantly greater awareness of and empathy with an audience. Using a counterbalanced design comparing role-playing with a lesson consisting of a discussion and presentation of models, and with no instruction, I showed that role-playing significantly ($p <$ .003) improves persuasive letter writing.

Finally, in Part IV, the late Richard Courtney and Joe Norris show how improvisational drama can benefit preservice or practicing teachers. In addition, Courtney's Chapter 9 traces the research he has done over his long and distinguished career as a drama educator. He couches his retrospective in the political context in which drama educators strive to make a case for their art. His method of presentation is primarily memoir within a historical context.

Norris, in Chapter 10, shows how future and practicing teachers can be introduced to the effectiveness of drama in education (what he terms *creative drama*); Norris engages his students in drama from the first day of a graduate class. He anchors his discussion in the logocentrism of language, pointing out how the concept of *play* is subordinated to the concept of *work* in our society, to the detriment of all of the arts. Norris's chapter is resonant with fully elaborated descriptive examples of drama that he conducts in his graduate classes. His chapter is an essay, not an analysis. Because Norris perceives drama as I do—as an instructional medium with the power to change hearts as well as minds—his chapter makes a fitting climax to this collection on drama as a medium for moral development.

The studies presented in the chapters of this book represent different research methodologies and modes of presentation. This is appropriate at the end of this century when we are in the throes of a paradigm shift from quantitative to qualitative method, not only in drama research, but in educational and social science investigation as well (Saldaña & Wright, 1996).

WHY EDUCATIONAL DRAMA?

Today's students are swimming in an ocean of facts. As more of them are linked to the World Wide Web, online chat rooms, and e-mail, as well as to print sources, they are constantly in touch with more information than was available to the entire educational enterprise not a generation ago. The total amount of information in the world *doubles* every 18 months. There is no way any person can begin to keep up with more than a tiny fraction of what's out there. It goes without saying that an infinity of factoids does not add up to wisdom, or to the kind of knowledge that provides guidance for making choices. Information is at best only the grist for thinking, acting, and reflecting on our actions. As Michael Heim puts it, "With a mind-set fixed in information...we become mentally poorer in overall meaning. We get into the habit of clinging to knowledge bits and lose our feel for the wisdom behind knowledge" (Heim, 1993, p. 9). An informed person is not necessarily more moral—a wise person is.

We only make temporal and eternal questions clear by making choices and seeing what happens. Invectives, directives, and sermons from others are comparatively ineffective in changing our outlook. The beauty of improvisational drama in education is that participants can make ill-advised choices and see what happens—without real-life consequences. To find their choices have landed them in a worse mess than they were in before is to learn in a way that has the power to lead to wisdom.

Drama involves choice making at several different levels. First, participants must assume a role and decide who they are and what stance they are taking to the action of the drama. In so doing, they are trying out versions of themselves and their possibilities without committing themselves permanently, as in real life. When the drama is over, they can reflect on their actions and lay down in their consciousness an understanding of what they each did that led to consequences they might have preferred to avoid.

There is safety in drama. Drama allows students to hide behind a symbolic mask and so venture into situations that could be dangerous in another class setting. Students can act out in symbolic form their real fears, hatreds, and desires without having to actually "own" them: They can hide by saying it was only the character they were playing who felt that way. Participants in drama feel they can risk failure because they are creating a fiction, not acting in the real world.

Improvisational drama can be a heady experience for students who are denied a wide range of social experience (and all young people, because of their relatively powerless status, are limited in experience, especially the experience of having real power to make a difference in a situation). In drama, participants have an opportunity to affect events in ways otherwise possible only in their private fantasies. Even those with limited verbal skills can move expressively, using gesture to play their part. Whenever a person goes a step beyond what he might do under ordinary circumstances in his or her real life, there is an excitement that comes from adventure, moving beyond and exploring new perspectives.

The aim of drama teaching is to help students understand themselves and the world in which they live. The teacher tries to set up situations upon which students can discover why people behave as they do, so that they can be helped to reflect on their own behavior. All too often in their real lives, young people act without even imagining the consequences, and the results can be disastrous—not only for them but for their communities as well.

Drama provides pressure for physical, emotional, and intellectual identification with a fictitious situation. This active identification is what characterizes all drama, regardless of the differences in the aims and structures of individual improvisations; it is this active involvement and identification with a fictitious character that is unique to drama. Through this involvement and identification, moral consciousness can emerge.

REFERENCES

Carroll, J. (1996). Escaping the information abattoir: Critical and transformative research in drama classrooms. In P. Taylor (Ed.), *Researching drama and arts education: Paradigms and possibilities* (pp. 72–84). London: Falmer Press.

Davis, J. H., & Behm, T. (1978). Terminology of drama/theatre with and for children: A redefinition. *Children's Theatre Review, 27*(1), 10–11.

Garcia, L. (1996). Images of teaching and classroom drama. *Youth Theatre Journal, 10*, 1–15.

Hartfield, G. (1982). *Workbook of sociology.* Stuttgart, Germany: Kroener.

Heim, M. (1993). *The metaphysics of virtual reality: Simulations use of computers*. New York: Oxford University Press.

O'Neill, C. (1985). Imagined worlds in theater and drama. *Theory into Practice, 4*(3), 158–165.

O'Neill, C. (1994). Drama in education. In A. Purvis (Ed.), *The encyclopedia of English studies and language arts* (Vol. 1, pp. 405–409). New York: National Council of Teachers of English and Scholastic.

Rice, D. R., & Sisk, P. F. (1980). Teaching elementary science through creative drama. *School Science and Mathematics, 80*, 61–64.

Saldaña, J. (with Wright, L.). (1996). An overview of experimental research principles for studies in drama and theatre for youth. In P. Taylor (Ed.), *Researching drama and arts education: Paradigms and possibilities* (pp. 115–131). London: Falmer Press.

Way, B. (1972). *Development through drama*. New York: Humanities.

ANOTHER RESOURCE

O'Neill, C. (1995). *Drama worlds: A framework for process drama*. Portsmouth, NH: Heinemann.

part I

Response to Moral Dilemmas in Literature and History

A lthough many theorists, such as James Britton, have emphasized the moral and evaluative nature of response to literature, we have only recently begun to look closely at the ways response to literature through drama can evoke moral reasoning. The studies reported in the next three chapters present intellectually stimulating and effective theoretical frameworks for analyzing responses to literature and historical events that evoke moral and emotional understandings. Peter Smagorinsky embeds his analysis in response-to-literature theory, and Paula Salvio embeds hers in Bertolt Brecht's dramaturgy. She shows how drama can conquer the inarticulateness of reader response in the face of confessional literature that evokes overwhelming feelings.

Wolf and Enciso (1994) observed that drama in response to literature helps readers imaginatively create a story world, including the multiple perspectives of various characters who have their own reasons for acting in ways that create problems for a protagonist. "The continual cognitive activity involved in drama—the engagement, the personal and negotiated interpretations of story, the shifts in perspective, the extensive problem solving, and the use of multiple symbolic systems—aligns well with current theory which regards literacy as active, strategic, and social in nature (p. 359). Karen Hume and Gordon Wells show how classroom dramas of historical events can create this same recognition of the complexity of human interactions and the multiple, shifting perspectives of the agents of historical events.

In Chapter 1, Smagorinsky shows how two groups of teenagers in a residential drug and alcohol rehabilitation facility use dance and drama to transmediate William Carlos Williams' short story, "The Use of Force." He shows how the interpretive process involves reliving and regulating their emotional experiences in their own lives, representing characters through physical relationships, reconstructing and extending the narrative rather than just reiterating it, and situating their dramatic text in an intertext. This process leads them to mediate their understanding of themselves and of the story.

Smagorinsky's examples show that students often have a grasp of the underlying tensions of a story that they can present most powerfully in a dance or drama, even before they can articulate their response verbally. Vygotsky rejected the view that what a child can talk about represents what he or she can understand. To prove his point, he asked children to act out what was in a picture instead of describing it. It turned out that in movement and gesture, children had a very fine grasp of relations; at the age of four or five, they dramatized the action in the picture, accompanying it with a narrative. Their reasoning capacity to express what they knew thus pointed to a level far above the level of their language.

In Chapter 2, Salvio shows how an artistic response to literature helps adult readers resonate to a collection of short stories, *Krik? Krak!*, by Hatian-American Edwidge Danticat. Because "the plot structure of this collection is recursive, fluid, and intertextual," as Salvio puts it, and the genre is documentary fiction, readers are responding not just to a text but to a real historical event. And because of the memory of an unspeakable massacre that boils in the blood of the survivors, readers are often too overwhelmed to respond. Salvio's goal was to use performance as a way to develop a sensibility that went beyond pure reason or intellect, as Henry James would put it.

Wells and Hume, in the third chapter, show how two teachers collaborated to bring a group of early adolescents from disaffection into inquiry. Their goal was to make history come alive through a process of community building and inquiry, but nothing jelled until the students role-played the building of a railroad. This dramatic and aesthetic challenge galvanized them into a recognition of the complexity of any historical event with its multiple perspectives and vested interests. What happened was experience as John Dewey (1959) would define it: resonant knowing.

REFERENCES

Dewey, J. (1959). *Art as experience.* New York: G. P. Putnam's Sons. (Original work published 1934)

Wolf, S. A., & Enciso, P. E. (1994). Multiple selves in literary interpretation: Engagement and the language of drama. In C. K. Kinzer & D. J. Leu (Eds.), *Multidimensional aspects of literacy research, theory, and practice* (pp. 351–360). Chicago: National Reading Conference.

OTHER RESOURCES

Britton, J. (1970). *Language and learning.* Baltimore: Penguin.

Holt, L. (1992). Many ways of knowing: Using drama, oral interactions, and the visual arts to enhance reading comprehension. *Reading Teacher, 45*(8), 580–584.

Siddall, J. L. (1998). *Fifth graders' social construction of meaning in response to literature: Case study research.* Unpublished doctoral dissertation, National-Louis University, Evanston, IL.

Taylor, P. (1998). *Redcoats and patriots: Reflective practice in drama and social studies.* Portsmouth, NH: Heinemann.

chapter I

The World is a Stage: Dramatic Enactment as Response to Literature

Peter Smagorinsky
University of Georgia

To most people, the word *drama* brings to mind the formal stage and those who act upon it. The theater, however, provides but one of drama's stages. Life itself is a drama, one that is played without the benefit of director, script, or second takes. Indeed, to some psychologists, the field of psychology itself consists of the study of the unfolding and developing drama of human consciousness as people negotiate the social and physical worlds they live in. Vygotsky, for instance, jotted the following notes in a manuscript in 1929: "Dynamics of the individual=drama... The individual as a participant in a drama. The drama of an individual... Psychology is humanized" (cited in Yaroshevsky, 1989, p. 217). From this observation Vygotsky assumed that the principle focus of psychology should be personality, "a character of the drama of life on the social stage" (p. 219). Vygotsky's notion of drama involves people in relation both to others and to themselves. His psychological theory, as Wertsch (1985) points out, emerges from a premise that the origins of consciousness are social. Thus, drama comes through transactions with other people. In addition, within the individual, dramatic tensions—such as the conflict between reason and emotion—are constant. The development of personality is therefore a consequence of the internal and external dramatic conflicts a person experiences in daily life.

Vygotsky saw a powerful relationship between these real, spontaneously enacted dramas and the world of art, in which formal drama plays a role. Art, according to Vygotsky, is a vehicle through which to regulate and understand emotions. Conceptions of art that make them peripheral to human development are, in Vygotsky's view, misguided:

[Vygotsky] belonged to a new generation of the Russian intelligentsia, which was inspired by the idea of an inner link between spiritual assimilation of the world and its practical transformation. Revealing the mechanism of art's impact on the real behavior of a concrete individual, without restricting oneself to determining its sociological roots and aesthetic specificity—that was Vygotsky's purpose. He endeavoured to prove that art is a means of transforming the individual, an instrument which calls to life the individual's "vast potential, so far suppressed and constrained." The view of art as ornamentation of life "fundamentally contradicts the laws of art discovered by psychological research. It shows that art is the highest concentration of all the biological and social processes in which the individual is involved in society, that it is a mode of finding a balance between man and the world in the most critical and responsible moments of life." (Yaroshevsky, 1989, pp. 148–149; Vygotsky qtd. in *Psikhologiy a iskusstra* [The Psychology of Art], pp. 320, 3330–3331).

Vygotsky thus asserts that two areas of consciousness typically regarded as separate—personality with its psychological foundation, and art with its dramatic inspiration—are in fact related and intertwined. His postulation that the development of personality is inherently dramatic and that art is inherently psychological suggests the powerful interdependence of the two and the necessity of both for the development of consciousness.

This view of the relationship between art's function of regulating and mediating emotions and personality's development through dramatic tension ought to have powerful implications for schooling. However, for the most part, the arts are primarily regarded as ornamental, as indicated by their peripheral status in school organization and budgets. That is, the arts are not regarded as essential to students' psychological transformations, but are seen as electives or extracurricular activities for students after they have experienced the "core" of the curriculum. Such a view is typical in schools that subscribe to the views of Hirsch (1987) and others who believe that schools exist primarily to transmit a specific body of essential content knowledge to students.

The perspective emerging from Vygotsky's developmental conception of psychology—one that complements Dewey's "progressive" vision of education—challenges this content-driven view of teaching and learning. Such educational approaches as the "British pedagogy of growth" (Applebee, 1974, p. 231) view schooling as an experience that leads to psychological transformation through activity and discovery. In this view, students' school experiences should involve engagement in processes that result in what Csikszentmihalyi and Larson (1984) have described as the "flow" of learning; that is, psychic growth through activities that involve equal levels of challenge and skill. Social transactions that lead students to new levels of complexity are essential to this conception of schooling. Yet, as many observers have noticed, schools rarely approach learning through its role in development, but rather follow a teacher-centered, transmission-oriented pedagogy that results in a "flat" (Goodlad, 1984) experience characterized by "mediocre sameness" (Sizer, 1984/1987, p. 6).

My goal in this chapter is to describe a classroom that is anything but flat or mediocre. Rather, the learning in this classroom is dynamic, growth-inducing, and multidisciplinary, avoiding the segmentation characteristic of most schools and uniting personality and artistic activity in ways consonant with Vygotsky's view of their essential relationship. Specifically, I describe students' dramatic responses to literature in two related media: acting and dance. The experiences of the students I describe support Vygotsky's contention that performance and personality are inseparable; that a dramatic interpretation of literature is also a dramatic performance of one's life. Furthermore, the description of the students and their interpretive acts should reveal the ways in which the students develop psychically through their dramatic enactments of the literary characters, as those characters embody aspects of their own emotional experiences.

THE SCHOOL

The research took place in a residential drug and alcohol rehabilitation facility that provided both therapy for recovery and public school educational classes. The students had committed themselves (sometimes reluctantly) to therapeutic, community-based treatment for 6 to 18 months. Because of federal and state laws related to confidentiality, no information that links data, location, and specific identities of individuals may be described or suggested. The names of the students focused on in this report are pseudonyms, and confidentiality agreements prevent us from reporting their specific academic records and personal histories prior to enrolling in the facility.

A general description of the school and classroom is possible, however. Among students in the facility, drug and alcohol addiction was a consequence and cause of personal turmoil, contributing to truancy, legal difficulties, personal instability, and a host of other problems that made academic learning problematic for them. The students I discuss were typical of the student body as a whole in the range of at-risk characteristics affecting them.

The fact that the school integrated the arts into the curriculum was an important factor in the students' recognition of the arts as an essential means of social, personal, and intellectual expression. The students lived at the school which was located in an isolated, rural community. Although the students could not leave the grounds without supervision, inside the facility they were entrusted with many responsibilities. Students were accountable for all aspects of daily maintenance, from cooking to cleaning. As part of recovery from addiction, they were engaged in daily formal therapy that extended to their social life both in the classroom and outside of it. To aid recovery, students needed to have a great deal of trust in one another and to support each other emotionally. Hugging, walking arm-in-arm, and otherwise displaying physical concern and support were common, regardless of gender. Students could only be accepted into the program by a vote of the other residents following a trial period.

THE TEACHER

The teacher had taught for a total of 15 years in public secondary schools, interrupted by a 7-year hiatus to manage a family-owned piano and organ business, which he continued to preside over when he resumed teaching. He was also a published poet, writing poetry for 30 years. Though not a formal performer of arts or music himself, his family had been extensively involved in the arts: His mother had been a painter and ceramic artist, his sister had trained as a concert pianist, and his brother had been a professional dancer and choreographer.

The teacher's graduate education had brought him into contact with the work of Howard Gardner (1983), whose theory of multiple intelligences stresses the potential for expression through spatial, musical, bodily/kinesthetic, interpersonal, and intrapersonal intelligences, in addition to the mathematical/logical and linguistic intelligences typically assessed in schools. Gardner's theory had helped the teacher account for his own experiences with creativity.

THE CLASSROOM

The facility employed only two teachers, each of whom taught a variety of subjects. This broad teaching assignment, following the elementary school model, enabled them to view learning as cross-disciplinary rather than as fragmented according to subject area, as is customary in mainstream high schools. Integrating the arts into content areas was a commonplace occurrence in the teachers' instruction and was accepted by students within a few months of their entering the school. Prior to the episodes I describe, for instance, students had written in response to slide projections of art, had interpreted literature through both writing and art forms of their choice, and had solved geometric problems through the physical representation of space.

THE STUDENTS AND THEIR WORK

Next, I describe an event that took place after the second month of school. The students were asked to read a short story, "The Use of Force," by William Carlos Williams. The story concerns a doctor who narrates an account of a house call he makes during a diphtheria epidemic. The doctor must extract a throat culture from a young girl who has displayed symptoms of the illness. The girl battles him savagely and hysterically to prevent him from examining her throat, and her parents try to help the doctor by holding her down and shaming her into complying. During the course of the struggle, the doctor develops contempt for the parents and passion toward the girl. Against his rational judgment, the doctor becomes lost in "a blind fury" to attack and subdue the girl. In "a final unreasoning assault," he overpowers her and discovers her "secret" of "tonsils covered with membrane." The story ends with a last act of fury in which the girl attacks the doctor "while tears of defeat blinded her eyes." Short and very intense, the story has consistently provoked strong responses from teachers and students in workshops and research, regardless of the age and experiences of the readers.

The students' task was to read the story and then produce some sort of "text" that represented their response to or understanding of the story. The teacher did not specify a medium for response; the students' only restriction was that they could either work alone or with a group of five or fewer. We had stocked the room with an abundance of resources, including paper, paints, markers, tinker toys, computer graphics software, and keyboard instruments. In addition, students could go to their campus rooms to get supplementary items such as guitars, dramatic props, and tape recorders with cassettes for soundtracks.

We videotaped the students as they read the story, decided whom (if anyone) to work with, and created interpretive texts. The videotape then served as a stimulus for interviews with groups of students about the interpretive processes experienced while reading the story, and working out a text to represent their understanding of it. In this chapter, I focus on two sets of students from the class: two young women who choreographed an interpretation of the relationship between the doctor and the girl, and four students who dramatized the actions of the four characters in the story.

The focus of my discussion is on the ways in which their performances served to regulate and represent their emotions, and on the ways in which their depiction of the characters represented their instantiation of critical emotional crises from their own lives. In this sense, the dramas that they performed were not simply interpretations of literary characters, but powerful emotional experiences in which they played out their own traumatic crises through their role portrayals. The experience of performing the drama and dance, therefore, allowed them to mediate the tensions in their lives in powerful and dramatic ways that enabled them to experience psychic growth.

THE STUDENTS

Jane and Martha were the dancers. Jane was a 16-year-old white female. She was a junior with average grades. Jane reported that she was an experienced dancer, having been involved with dance for four years. Martha was a 15-year-old Native American who was enrolled as a sophomore. Prior to arriving at the treatment center, she had limited experience with dance, all of which was recreational: "two step and…country dance, things like that." Martha did not consider herself to be a dancer: "See I am not really much of a dancer. I am more of a writer than a dancer. [When we were dancing] most of the time I just followed [Jane]." Martha's tendency to follow Jane was, according to their teacher, typical of their relationship. Jane was the older of the two, more outgoing, and somewhat dominant in their relationship. Their sharing of issues in the intensely therapeutic environment of the substance abuse treatment center helped to bring them together in friendship, a factor that influenced their decision to work together on their response to the short story.

The students who dramatized the story were Wes (age 18), Bart (age 18), Donnie (age 17), and Suzie (age 15). Wes was African American and Bart, Donnie, and Suzie were White. In general, their characteristics were similar to those of most of the students in the facility: All had been addicted to one or more drugs (including alcohol), most were behind in grade level, and many had erratic records of success in school and on standardized tests. Wes and Bart had been enrolled in the treatment program longer than any of the other 34 students at the school, and through their time together had become very close friends, a relationship (coupled with their age, seniority, and possibly gender) that led them to dominate decision making in the group. Donnie and Suzie tended to have less authority and often ran errands while Wes and Bart worked out the details of the performance.

INTERPRETIVE PROCESSES

In this chapter, I focus on the ways in which the students enacted their own knowledge and experiences through their portrayal of the characters from the story. I describe five types of processes: reliving and regulating emotional experiences, representing the characters through physical relationships, reconstructing the narrative, situating the interpretive text in an intertext, and mediating understanding of self and story. These processes illustrate the ways in which they engaged in "transmediation" (Suhor, 1984); that is, their translation of meaning from one textual medium to another. By doing so, they enabled growth of personality through a formal school experience that recognized the dramatic tensions that direct their development and legitimated the arts as an essential forum for learning.

Reliving and Regulating Emotional Experiences

Albert Einstein once said that "This is what the painter does, and the poet, the speculative philosopher, the natural scientist, each in his own way. Into this image and its formation, he places the center of gravity of his emotional life, in order to attain the peace and serenity that he cannot find within the narrow confines of swirling, personal experience" (qtd. in Holton, 1978, pp. 231–232). This emotional regulation figured strongly in the decision making of the students who interpreted "The Use of Force." Students' decisions to play particular characters were often based on connections they saw between their own experiences and those of the characters. Perhaps the most striking case of this sort of resonance came in Martha's decision to play the role of the girl. In their dance, Jane and Martha choreographed the relationship between the doctor and the girl. Martha saw the girl's reluctance to open up her mouth for the doctor as being much like her own fear of being "open" to other people. During her interview, she said that like the girl in the story, she felt "scared": "I felt like the little girl because we live in two different worlds.... I felt like the little girl because she was always trying to hide from the doctor and I was like hiding myself from the doctor." Martha's feeling that she needed to hide from the doctor stemmed from experiences similar to those of the girl in the story. She discusses those experiences in the following dialogue:

> Q: *When you dance a role, is there any real part of you that gets played out in the dancer?*
>
> Martha: It's tough for me. When I was hiding from [Jane in the dance] she was the doctor and I was the daughter, the little girl, and it was

just like me. I hate people trying to find out who I am so I was basically hiding the way I always hide but I was hiding to be somebody else. I felt like I was hiding in the little girl, but it was me that was hiding, because I do that all the time. I hide from everybody.

Q: *Did you feel for the character then?*

Martha: Oh yeah, I felt for the character. When I was dancing I was thinking about what I would do. I hated what the doctor did to her. I wanted to kill him.

Later in the interview, Martha returned to her feelings about her character:

Martha: My feelings for the kid started when I was reading the story because there have been many times when I have had some problems. I'm like I'm okay, get away. In a way I kind of knew how this girl was feeling whenever the doctor was trying to get into her mouth. I am like that with dentists. I hate dentists. I won't let them get into my mouth. I'm afraid they're going to pull out my teeth. It scares me. I try to keep my mouth shut too. I put myself in her position through the whole story knowing she was scared and very insecure because she knows she is going to die. She knows through the whole story she's going to die. She doesn't want her parents to know about it.

Q: *Is it just dentists? Earlier you were talking about how you don't like people in general getting inside you. So was it just a dentist or was it—*

Martha: Well, for people to know me, I don't like for anyone to know me; it is really scary for people to know me.

The students who acted out the story also appeared to have personal reasons for selecting the characters. Both Wes and Suzie, for instance, gave obvious reasons for playing their characters: Wes would play the doctor because he wore glasses, which went flying off his face at one point during the struggle; and Suzie would play the girl because of her gender. Yet other reasons appeared to influence their decisions. Wes, the oldest student with the greatest seniority in the program, was a very commanding and task-oriented person. Unlike many students who went through the recovery program, he was still "clean" several years after graduation, had passed a G.E.D. exam, and was considering going to college. The forceful doctor, then, suited his personality very well.

Suzie, too, had personal reasons for relating to the character of the girl, as revealed during the interview. One point of contention in the group's discussion of how to interpret the story concerned the age of the girl. Students had pictured her differently, based on their understanding of how children of different ages behave:

Donnie:	How old do you all picture? I picture about 8 years old.
Wes:	I picture about like 11 or 12.
Bart:	I didn't really think about the age.
Q:	*How about you, Suzie?*
Suzie:	I pictured her my age.
Q:	*How old are you?*
Suzie:	15.
Donnie:	So I didn't think a 15-year old would be sitting on her daddy's lap.
Bart:	Yeah, she was sitting on his lap.
Wes:	That's why I'm thinking of an 8-year-old.
Bart:	Now I didn't think a girl that old would be so defiant.
Wes:	Yeah.
Suzie:	I was that resistant.
Q:	*You were resistant when?*
Suzie:	When I went out to the dentist yesterday.

It is not clear why both Suzie and Martha used visits to the dentist to illustrate their resistance; although their interpretations took place at the same time, they did not discuss their responses to the story with one another. Regardless of the reason, Suzie's reference to her defiance at the dentist's office suggests that her recent experience of having resisted a doctor's attempt to look into her mouth might have affected her decision to choose the role of the girl, and might have influenced the way in which she interpreted and portrayed the character.

As Vygotsky would predict, the students' portrayal of the fictional characters was greatly informed by the tensions that had contributed to their own psychic development. The use of these dramatic media, consistent with growth models of schooling, was particularly conducive in facilitating students' personal development through artistic tools that they found valuable and useful.

Representing Characters Through Physical Relationships

According to John-Steiner, "In dance, the dramatization of human experience is enacted through movements, through a subjective and visual elaboration of the messages of the body" (1985, p. 158). For Jane and Martha, part of their attribution of meaning to the story came through their discussion of how physically to represent the relationship between characters, both in the movements of the individual dancers and in their motion in concert. As detailed in the previous section, each student brought to the story an emotional history that contributed to the students' character portrayals. How to depict that instantiation of personal experience became a key consideration in their enactments, particularly when each student's depiction of a character needed to come in relation to other students' portrayals of other characters. Often these relationships were represented through the physical positioning of the characters, particularly in the dance where movement, rather than speech, was the primary means of representation.

Jane and Martha's interpretation of the story provides a good illustration of how students can depict relationships physically. Jane explained at one point how they choreographed the relationship between the doctor and girl at the beginning of the story:

> You have to, it is like you are saying you have to put yourself in their position. When you read the story it tells, it is like in between the lines, it tells how the doctor feels about the girl, and it tells how the little girl feels. At the first of the dance we dragged, moved out, and we dragged out. It was like she was still closed out from the doctor, it was like he was feeling kind of depressed because he couldn't get into her and he knew she was dying. He had this idea in his head and he didn't want to believe it until he could prove it and he didn't want her to die because this would be the third kid that had died.

As the story progressed and the girl began to resist, Jane and Martha changed the spatial relations from the "dragged" choreography to oppositional movement: "When the doctor is trying to get her around to his way of thinking, we figuratively did it by going around in circles opposite each other," recounted Jane. The idea of placing the characters in diametrical opposition and circling one another represented both the doctor's attempt to persuade and the girl's effort to evade.

Later in the dance, the roles were reversed:

> *Martha:* The way that we set the dance up, we were kind of going in circles and she was chasing me or I was chasing her, but the way we set it up she was chasing me. I was getting real scared, kind of had up my own little wall.
>
> *Q:* *You talked about the dancers being opposite to each other in your dance. What part of the story were you showing when the girl was chasing the doctor? Do you remember when that was?*
>
> *Jane:* When she was enraged, she was trying to get back at me.
>
> *Martha:* That was the second time after we went down and came up again.

Jane and Martha reveal through their account of their planning process the ways in which they considered the relationship between the characters, the rhythms of the story, and possible ways they could repre-sent these considerations through the medium of the dance form they had selected. Without the benefit of language to explicate the relation-ship, they needed to develop codes that would represent their under-standing of the antagonistic relations between the two characters, informed, as reviewed previously, by their own involvement in situa-tions they viewed as similar.

Reconstructing the Narrative

Conventional schooling requires "faithful" attention to the language of literature, often reducing literary understanding to factual examina-tions (Applebee, 1993). The students interviewed for this research, how-ever, often revealed that their interpretations of the characters required them to rewrite the storyline to provide the emotional focus they sought. That is, in developing their own interpretive texts in response to the lit-erature they'd read, they found a subplot to the story that required an entirely different representation than that found in the original lan-guage of the story.

In the original story, for instance, the doctor becomes increasingly passionate in his efforts to extract the throat culture from the girl. At one point, the doctor narrates the following:

> I had already fallen in love with the savage brat, the parents were con-temptible to me. In the ensuing struggle they grew more and more abject, crushed, exhausted while she surely rose to magnificent heights of insane fury of effort bred of her terror of me.

The doctor relates in the passages that follow that "the worst of it was that I too had got beyond reason. I could have torn the child apart in my own fury and enjoyed it. It was a pleasure to attack her. My face was burning with it." The ending of the story is filled with passion and fury as the doctor overpowers the savagely resistant girl to examine her throat.

Jane and Martha's interpretation of this violent and combative denouement, however, was gentle and compassionate. Jane described their process of how to choreograph this scene:

> We did another dance at the very end and we were practicing on it and like she's sheltered like the little girl is hidden. She won't let anybody find out what her secret is and that's what she is doing. She is hiding and the doctor is trying to follow in her footsteps to try to figure out what is going on. And at the very end when it says that she did have [diphtheria], in the dance we made her die. She just fell and the doctor picked her up and

carried her. Because like we were going to have the doctor die with her because it was like the third patient he had died and he was dying inside, but [our teacher] didn't really like that. And after we started thinking you know how he gets underneath the skin real hard, it is like we started thinking about it too and he doesn't really die. He tries to help her and stuff. We went further than the story went.

Here, Jane and Martha attempted to represent the figurative death of the character by physically having her die. As they discussed how to dramatize it, their teacher dropped by and, through their discussion, they decided to try a different ending. They constructed another figurative representation of the story's ending, as described by Jane:

That is when they finally figured it out. It is like at the very end they walked together. It's like they walk two steps and when you do a little pause, the doctor shelters her and just looks at her because he's died with her. His whole life has just gone down the drain because it's another kid, he feels it's all his fault this time. And that is how I really felt when I was doing the dance.

Their representation of the story's ending is quite different from the literal action of the story, where the girl attacks the doctor in a rage. Jane and Martha chose to represent the feelings of the doctor in their dance, however, and therefore focused on his sense of loss. Their depiction of the relationship between doctor and patient involved the creation of a new storyline based on their understanding of the emotional state of the doctor. Their interpretation of the story required them to recreate the literal action of the original text in order to represent their view of the emotional storyline they developed through their infusion of the characters with personal meaning.

Situating their Dramatic Text in an Intertext

Intertextuality refers to the way in which thought is rooted in prior thought. The "text" that a person creates is derived from a previously encountered text, which in turn has been developed out of a prior network of other texts. Thought, therefore, has a social basis, with each thought emerging from previous thought and serving as the basis for subsequent thought.

The four students who created a dramatic text drew on a network of imagaic texts adopted from popular culture (film and television) in order to create their own interpretation. So as to get a sense for how to represent the characters, the students attempted to situate the story and their production historically. In doing so, the students discussed incidents from the story and how they fit in different time periods:

> Donnie: Me and Suzie started talking about when this probably took place. I said, well, doctors don't make house calls no more that I know of. I mean, I am sure there is a doctor that will.
> Suzie: I thought it was like, in the late 1800's or something.
> Donnie: Like *Little House on the Prairie*.

The decision of where to situate the story historically had an effect on how they would portray the characters. Among their considerations was the question of whether or not to have Suzie wear a costume for her depiction of the girl. A large part of the dispute centered on when and where they thought the story had taken place, and how they thought people had dressed during that period:

> Bart: [Donnie] said, because she wanted to put on Colonial dress or something like that, *Little House on the Prairie*. And I was saying, no, man, this ain't *Little House on the Prairie*.
> Q: *Why did you want to* [wear the dress], *Suzie?*
> Suzie: Because like I was talking to Donnie, and was asking him if it was in the old timer days, and he was going like, "yeah it was."

The question of whether the story had taken place in "old timer days" or not was an important question in the group's interpretation of the story. Drawing on their knowledge of historical periods (at least as they understood history through popular culture), the group debated how the characters would dress and what their roles and responsibilities would be (e.g., whether or not doctors made house calls). In discussing the setting of the story and how it would affect their production, the group negotiated an understanding of both the text they were interpreting and the text they were producing.

The students also made emotional connections between "The Use of Force" and films they had seen. The girl's increasing rage and resistance reminded some members of the group of the film *The Exorcist*:

> Wes: I tried to play the doctor. The story reminded me of *The Exorcist*, with the girl and the devil.... The way she was resisting him and not opening her mouth and stuff. The guy in *Exorcist*, I don't know, it has been so long since I have seen him.
> Bart: They were trying to help her.
> Wes: Yeah, they were trying to help her, and she was like spitting the green goop out and then when they said [in the story] the blood

was coming out her mouth, that made me think even more about [*The Exorcist*].

Donnie: *The Exorcist* was about Satan. What is that called when Satan supposedly takes over her body?

Bart: Possessed.

Donnie: Possessed. And this little girl—

Bart: Yeah, that little girl was possessed.

Donnie: She was just real crazy.

Q: *Did you think that the girl in the story was possessed?*

Bart: I didn't.

Q: *No? Wes?*

Wes: Not really possessed, it just reminded me of just a little girl, because the girl in *The Exorcist* was cute and all of a sudden she turns out to be real evil and stuff, and that is what this says, it says she was real attractive when she was little, and then she turns out to be where she didn't want to do anything and bit the stick off, you know, and the blood was coming out of her mouth, and then she still resisted. That just made me think, she has got a problem. She got real violent.

Q: *So how did the mask* [an angry mask that the players had considered earlier for Suzie to wear] *fit in with that thing with* The Exorcist?

Wes: Because at first the girl was all calm and stuff, and on the outside she looked real calm. Just from reading that story, you know, you could pick up on her attitude, how it changed once he tried to get something extracted and her cooperation from her. And then when she got all bothered, and stuff, that mask was crazy.

In addition to *The Exorcist*, the students discussed the film *Misery* and the emotional swings of the characters, and looked for ways to incorporate elements of both films into their production. Thus, the students were able to use their prior knowledge of stories and story representation to enhance their interpretation of "The Use of Force."

Mediating Understanding of Self and Story

So far I have focused on the ways in which the students' recreation of the story through dramatic means represented the ways in which their prior understandings and experiences enabled them to infuse the story with unique meaning. A pedagogy of growth, however, stresses the ways in which learning activities are *developmental*; that is, they enable growth through the processes of learning. The research I am reporting here confirms the way in which the students' composing of their dramatic texts can not only represent the understanding of themselves and the story, but change their understandings as well.

When discussing what sort of dress the girl would wear, for instance, the group that acted out the story considered how the dress fit in with the way in which they viewed the tone of the production:

> *Bart:* I don't know. That dress it would make it look like she was a lit-tle...it just wouldn't look right just to fit the whole atmosphere of the play.
>
> *Wes:* I didn't think it would either, because she said it was real pretty, and I didn't think that would get—
>
> *Donnie:* See, the reason we thought about this is because in the story it says a little fully dressed girl.
>
> *Suzie:* Not if you see the dress, then you would understand. It is like, it is real baggy, and it has flowers on it and stuff.
>
> *Wes:* I thought it would have one of them like penitentiary or work dresses or like a sweater or cardigan.
>
> *Q:* *You would think that would be a good dress to wear?*
>
> *Wes:* That is what I pictured in my mind, something drab, not some-thing fancy.

Their production of the text helped them think through the charac-ters and what they represented in the story. Similarly, in discussing how *The Exorcist* had influenced their interpretation of the story, Wes realized that he viewed the girl as "possessed," which enabled him to envision her in a particular way and interpret the story according to that vision.

Bart, too, developed his thinking about the story by situating it in prior classroom activities. He said that during the production of the play

> I was thinking about the extended definition of what abuse is, because they were talking about if you are a child abuser. Is it really abuse if someone cuts their hand and you give them a shot? That is hurting them, but it is to help them out later. I was thinking about that. How ambiguous abuse can be. What abuse means.

Through his participation in the play, Bart continued his prior delib-eration of the definition of abuse. Bart also opened his mind to more imaginative interpretations of the story through his engagement in group decision making. Originally he "wanted everything to stay as close to the story line as possible," disputing the suggestion that Suzie should wear a frightening mask to denote her anger. Eventually, though, he said that "then I thought about it, I was just being closed-minded." Through the process of producing the play, Bart began to see interpre-tive possibilities that he had previously not realized.

Jane and Martha similarly developed greater understandings through their choreography of the dance. As related previously, they tried several different endings to their interpretive dance. Through the teacher's intervention, they rejected one as insufficient in accounting for the characters' state of mind; through the process of reconsidering how to choreograph the final scene, they came to a more fully developed interpretation of the characters and their relationship. Their understanding of the story thus changed through the process of choreographing the dance.

Jane reported that she also experienced a change in her understanding of the doctor's perspective through her portrayal of him. When asked if she had learned anything new in the process of creating the dance, Jane replied,

> *Jane*: I finally figured out what it is like to be in that position of the doctor. That is why I didn't hate the doctor so much because I knew how he felt and I also knew how the little kid felt and I felt sorry for the kid.
>
> *Q:* *Are those things you learned while doing the dance?*
>
> *Jane:* How the doctor felt. I knew his feelings, but knowing it and feeling it is totally different things.

Later in the interview, she added, "[I learned] about myself, that I can feel their feelings. I see how they feel." In addition to experiencing the rational change in thought expected in school, Jane revealed that she also went through an emotional change as a result of her portrayal of the doctor.

These remarks reveal the ways in which the students engaged in, to twist an old phrase, "acting to learn." Just as writers are often seen as "writing to learn," the students used a different set of tools to engage in a process of mediation. The opportunity to act out emotional tensions appears to have a unique potential for enabling students to grasp their own developmental conflicts. Structured by the signs offered by the literary text, the interpretations reveal understandings that took on different forms and meanings through the dramatic medium of response.

FINAL THOUGHTS: DRAMA AND THE CORE CURRICULUM

There is the possibility that in our desire to acknowledge different intelligences, we may develop a deterministic attitude toward them. Although most people don't think about it that way, the school curriculum is fundamentally a mind-altering device. It's a device for changing minds, changing the way people think. Moreover, schools are not just for changing the way people think, but for improving the way people think. We need therefore

to exploit the power of the curriculum to optimize whatever potential intelligences individuals possess. Further, we must remember that there is at
least one important lesson that the study of culture teaches—different cultures prize and develop different cognitive abilities. The environment
shapes the curriculum. (Eisner, 1990, pp. 41–42)

At the beginning of this chapter, I reviewed Vygotsky's view of the role
of the arts in regulating emotion, and the role of arts in formal education. Dramatic tension is an essential part of personality development,
while dramatic arts are typically peripheral to the goals of conventional
schooling. The research I have reviewed substantiates Vygotsky's view of
the importance of dramatic art in understanding emotional experiences.
The research also reinvigorates Vygotsky's questions about the role of
the arts in schools, suggesting that treating the arts as ornamental
ignores their basic role in human development. Eisner's observations
about the role of multiple intelligences (Gardner, 1983) in the curriculum are compatible with Vygotsky's perspective on what is "basic" in
education.

The study of literature, in particular, seems amenable to a closer relationship with the arts. Literature *is* an art in the conception of many,
serving the same purposes of emotional regulation, symbolic representation, social commentary, and other functions as sculpture, opera, and
other art forms. Why, then, should it be treated as a subject to be studied rather than as a process to be experienced? The students I have discussed in this chapter reveal the ways in which the short story "The Use
of Force" provided them with a structure through which to understand
their prior experiences better and bring order to previously inchoate
emotions. Their dramatic enactments enabled them to play out their
personal histories in ways that revealed an understanding of the story
(even when departing from the literal storyline) and infused the characters with enormous vitality. Such experiences, according to Applebee
(1993) and other observers of school, are rare for most students.

I should stress that simply requiring students to engage in drama is
not a guarantee of meaningful experiences. Indeed, all did not flow
smoothly for all students in the research I have discussed. Jane and Martha, who were close friends, operated with remarkable cooperation and
common purpose in the choreography of their dance, perhaps aided by
their mutual acceptance of Jane as director of the production and dominant figure in their personal relationship. The other group, however, at
times functioned with a great imbalance in authority. Wes and Bart, the
two oldest students and the two closest friends, clearly dominated the
group's decision making when they had trouble resolving a conflict or
when they needed someone to perform a menial task such as getting a

prop from a dormitory room. When Bart dismissed Suzie's ideas regarding the appropriateness of her dress, she said, "I felt like my opinion didn't count. It was like, 'No, man, we ain't going to have that.'" Suzie seemed disempowered at critical points of decision making, possibly due to her youth, her lack of seniority in the treatment program, her gender, or a combination of reasons. Wes and Bart treated Donnie in much the same way, sending him on errands to get their props:

> *Bart*   We sent Donnie, because me and Wes was doing most of the figuring out and so we sent Donnie to go get the tongue depressor and he knew about where they were.
>
> *Donnie:*   Yeah, they are getting ready to send me off again [on the videotape]. I feel like a go-fer, you know, having me go get everything.

Yet their treatment of Suzie was more severe than their treatment of Donnie, at times bordering on cruelty. When she said that she could not act mad, they tried to anger her through taunts and even physical harassment. The interactions within the group suggest that collaborative learning is not always the harmonious interaction that it is often portrayed to be. Suzie, being both young and female, often got ganged up on and was either overpowered into silence or frustrated into cooperating; Donnie, as a younger and less assertive group member, was often treated as a "go-fer." The group dynamics, while apparently productive in helping the group produce their play, seemed to reinforce the power roles within the group and limit the contributions of the younger members. I would recommend caution, therefore, in considering drama to be a panacea for educational problems.

Yet dramatic performance has great *potential* for helping to achieve the goals of a growth-centered pedagogy. If students, teachers, and community members agree that the development of a healthy personality is a central aim of schooling, then drama can be an important part of education in any subject area in which emotional growth is important. The main problem seems to be a question of consensus: What is the purpose of education? The answer to this fundamental question is not likely to be uniform across all school systems, or even within particular communities. From a psychological perspective, however, I would say that if we are concerned with the emotional health of students, then we need to make issues of personality development central to schooling; and if we are concerned with the psychic well-being of our students, then they should have access to the tools that enable them to explore and regulate their emotional experiences. With that as a premise, I can say that, based on the research I have reviewed, the inclusion of dramatic opportunities for students in their transactions with subject matter has the potential to help them both read literature resonantly, as Wolfe (1988) has elegantly recommended, and read their own histories with insight and understanding.

NOTES

[1] See Smagorinsky, 1995; Smagorinsky & Coppock, 1994a, 1994b, 1994c, 1995a, and 1995b, for more detailed reports on specific case studies.

REFERENCES

Applebee, A. N. (1974). *Tradition and reform in the teaching of English: A history.* Urbana, IL: National Council of Teachers of English.

Applebee, A. N. (1993). *Literature in the secondary school: Studies of curriculum and instruction in the United States* (NCTE Research Report No. 25). Urbana, IL: National Council of Teachers of English.

Csikszentmihalyi, M., & Larson, R. (1984). *Being adolescent: Growth and conflict in the teenage years.* New York: Basic Books.

Dewey, J. (1916). *Democracy and education: An introduction to the philosophy of education.* New York: Free Press.

Eisner, E. W. (1990). Implications of artistic intelligences for education. In W. J. Moody (Ed.), *Artistic intelligences: Implications for education* (pp. 31–42). New York: Teachers College Press.

Gardner, H. (1983). *Frames of mind: The theory of multiple intelligences.* New York: Basic Books.

Goodlad, J. (1984). *A place called school: Prospects for the future.* New York: McGraw-Hill.

Hirsch, E. D., Jr. (1987). *Cultural literacy: What every American needs to know.* Boston: Houghton Mifflin.

Holton, G. (1978). *The scientific imagination: Case studies.* Cambridge: Cambridge University Press.

John-Steiner, V. (1985). *Notebooks of the mind: Explorations of thinking.* New York: Harper & Row.

Sizer, T. R. (1987). *Horace's compromise: The dilemma of the American high school.* Boston: Houghton Mifflin. (Original work published 1984)

Smagorinsky, P., & Coppock, J. (1994a, Fall). Exploring an evocation of the literary work: Processes and possibilities of an artistic response to literature. *Reader,* 62–74.

Smagorinsky, P., & Coppock, J. (1994b). Exploring artistic response to literature. In C. K. Kinzer & D. J. Leu (Eds.), *Multidimensional aspects of literacy research, theory, and practice* (pp. 335–341). Chicago: National Reading Conference.

Smagorinsky, P., & Coppock, J. (1994c). Cultural tools and the classroom context: An exploration of an alternative response to literature. *Written Communication, 11*(3), 283–310.

Smagorinsky, P., & Coppock, J. (1995a). Reading through the lines: An exploration of a dramatic response to literature. *Reading and Writing Quarterly: Overcoming Learning Difficulties, 11*, 369–391.

Smagorinsky, P., & Coppock, J. (1995b). The reader, the text, the context: An exploration of a choreographed response to literature. *JRB: A Journal of Literacy, 27*, 271–298.

Suhor, C. (1984). Towards a semiotics-based curriculum. *Journal of Curriculum Studies, 16*(3), 247–257.

Wertsch, J. V. (1985). *Vygotsky and the social formation of the mind*. Cambridge, MA: Harvard University Press.

Wolfe, D. P. (1988). *Reading reconsidered: Literature and literacy in high school*. New York: College Entrance Examination Board.

Yaroshevsky, M. (1989). *Lev Vygotsky* (S. Syrovatkin, Trans.). Moscow: Progress Publishers.

chapter 2

Reading in the Age of Testimony

Paula M. Salvio
University of New Hampshire

INTRODUCTION

I n *Krik? Krak!*, a collection of short stories, the Haitian-American writer, Edwidge Danticat, uses lyric language to usher her readers into a history that is rarely discussed in social studies or English classes in the United States: It is the 1937 massacre of Haitian women at the hands of Dios Trujillos' soldiers along the Dominican border, the terrorism of the Tonton Macoutes, and the linkage of generations of women through a tradition of story telling.

Initially, it seems each story in this collection stands alone. The reader soon recognizes, however, that the plot structure of this collection is recursive, fluid, and intertextual. As a writer, Danticat does not submit to a humanist ideology of the literary (Hedrick, 1996); rather, she mixes and mingles fiction with autobiography and diary devices with poetry to create what Maureen Shea (1994, p. 150) describes as "documentary fiction," a form of literature in which the "reality represented is openly partial,...a 'huello de lo real [trace of the real].'" This trace of the real is akin to the literary style of magic-realism, fantastic literature, or the real-marvelous—literary forms and cultural practices which include strategies for exploring, and sometimes transgressing, political, geo-graphical, and ontological boundaries. Magic-realism calls into ques-tion the structures of rationalism and reality that are used by dominant cultures to craft history. B. K. Marshall writes that the mystique of

*I would like to thank my colleagues Cinthia Gannett and Richard Blot for reading ear-lier versions of this chapter. Additional thanks also go to Pat Wilson and Diane Freedman for their generous and insightful comments.

magic-realism is that it "works to replace what is missing" (qtd. in Ellsworth, 1997, pp. 180–181). The secrets of history surface in magic-realism, at times posing unsettling questions about power and owner-ship, and most often using magic as a tactic for survival. "More than anything," notes Marjorie Agosin (1992), "fantastic literature offers ter-ritories and spaces for subversion, disorder and illegality by using the only code possible: the imaginary.... Whatever genre it occupies, it has the option, or better said, the desire to act through what has been cul-turally defined as forbidden and marginal" (p. 13). In the context of teacher education, this literature can provoke important questions about history, the constitution of truth, and social justice. Elizabeth Ellsworth notes that magic-realism continually poses the questions: What's count-ing as "real" here? What's counting as unreal, excessive, distorted? Who's counting it as real and why? (1997, p. 179).

Krik? Krak! uses magic and the power of dreams as cultural correctives to urge readers to scrutinize the "rhetoric of realism" employed by tradi-tional social studies textbooks, literature, and news accounts to position the Haitian people in history. Danticat draws on geographic locations, historical inheritances, and family lineages to join together women who stand apart in time, but who share the consequences of unspeakable his-torical circumstances. Her written portraitures are testimony to the way the "nine-hundred and ninety-nine women who boiled in her [my mother's] blood lived and died and lived again." Writes Danticat, "The spirit of these women lives in my blood" (1991, p. 224).

Danticat's use of magic-realism takes on the status of testimony because it imparts what Shoshanna Felman (Felman & Laub, 1992) describes as a "first hand carnal knowledge of a historical passage through death, and of the way life that will forever be inhabited by that passage and by that death; a knowledge of the way in which 'this history concerns us all,' and how history is the body's business," (p. 111). Testi-monial literature documents human suffering and human triumphs; it shows raw historical accounts that have gone unnoticed, that have been fragmented or shattered. In legal contexts, testimony is given when the truth needs to be uncovered.

In this chapter, I examine how particular dramatic conventions can be used to read testimonial literature in the classroom. Because testimony can call upon readers and students to bear witness to "the consequences of unspeakable historical circumstances," it often moves us toward inar-ticulateness. This inarticulateness is a signature of bearing witness. It marks the moment at which we are confronted with the unknown, with information that is detached from all we have known beforehand. Testi-monial literature, writes Felman (Felman & Laub, 1992), "cannot be subsumed by familiar notions; it does not simply *report the facts*, but, in different ways...makes us encounter strangeness...the more we look closely at texts, the more they show us that, unwittingly, we do not even know what testimony is and that, in any case, it is not simply what we thought we knew it was" (p. 7).

My focus is on the place of inarticulateness in reader response. I explore my attempts to use dramatic conventions with my students, not necessarily to make this experience of inarticulateness apprehensible to ourselves and to one another, but rather to consider the ways in which these moments of lost speech and bewilderment provoke discontinuities in our own emotional capacities and knowledge. What discontinuities in our knowledge surface as the cultural secrets of Haitian history are laid before us? How can performance be used to draw us, in the words of Ellsworth (1997), "in and through the discontinuities and ongoing cultural and personal silences that personal and social histories introduce into our very beings as educators"? Continues Ellsworth, "How might we do this without denying those silences and histories, and without canonizing them through irresponsible...assertions of understanding and continuity?" (p. 116).

I also consider the extent to which the silent gaps in the curriculum, those interval spaces that elude expression, might contain potential for developing a particular form of virtue which is akin to the Jamesian ideal of perceptual sensitivity to the nuances of one's immediate situation. This ideal also resonates to the Aristotelian conception of the virtuous agent as someone who, in some sense, sees the *particular* ethical requirements a situation presents. This consists of, notes Martha Nussbaum (1990), a perceptual capacity for sensing what must be done without having to mechanically appeal to and then apply an abstract or authoritative set of principles which disregard the historical, emotional, or personal attachments and desires that are fused through a given situation. Can reading testimony offer educators opportunities to develop a sensibility that, Henry James argued, must go beyond pure reason or intellect? The form of virtue I have in mind is akin to what James characterizes as not simply an intellectual grasp of propositions, or particular facts—it is perception. It is "seeing and feeling through a complex, concrete reality in a highly lucid and richly responsive way; it is taking what is there, with imagination and feeling" (see Eckstrom, 1995, p. 100). Attending to detail in a work of literature, particularly a work that challenges our focus, is amidst the kind of work we must practice if, according to Nussbaum, we are to develop a capacity for moral judgment. I do not argue that my students and I exhibit high standards for moral judgment in the project I am about to discuss. Rather, I suggest that using dramatic conventions to respond to testimonial literature holds some important possibilities for developing these capacities.

I also consider the ways in which performance can be used to address, in action, a crisis or a trauma that exceeds any conceptual framework or any one person's capacity for understanding. In this performative address, we seek to remember the losses and the triumphs of the people for which Danticat writes, so they may be reborn into historical memory and not die once and for all (Behar, 1996).

Finally, I explore the extent to which dramatic conventions can serve to complicate the meaning of a testimony such as that of Danticat. The testimony of Danticat comes to us from a culture completely different from our own, a culture that I, as a teacher, knew very little about. Thus the questions: What value is embodied in this literature? What educative import does testimony hold for my female students' lives, all of whom are or hope to be teachers themselves, all of whom are White and live in rural communities throughout southern New Hampshire?[1] What value does reading a text such as *Krik? Krak!* hold for my students? And so, I intend to define what it means for students in teacher education to read testimony, a form of literature often resistant to the norms of a typical English classroom. Testimonial literature, particularly when it takes the form of magic-realism, resists being categorized as a pure genre; it is, at once, fiction and non-fiction, poetry and prose, autobiography and social documentary. Testimonial literature lacks a traditional, Aristotelian plot structure, often disrupting possible identifications between a reader and the key characters through overt horror or the use of shock. The alienating features in testimonial literature undermine possibilities for a consumptive or passive form of empathic identification. These disruptions wrench the reader from her normal world view and challenge learned habits of reading. What we thought we knew well is altered or called into question, thereby asking us, as readers, to scrutinize what we take to be "real."

Given these features, I suspected early on, in reading *Krik? Krak!* in my course, Foundations of Reading Instruction, that it would be far too jarring and hence, far too easy, to dismiss it or keep it at a distance because it embodied a matrix of cultural practices, beliefs, and geographic locations that profoundly challenge our historical perspectives and our conceptions of what constitutes literature, as well as our emotional capacities. When asked how she experienced reading *Krik? Krak!* in the solitude of her home, Wendy Skolds, one of the ten women in the class, wrote:

> I had a very difficult time reading this book in private. I could not even finish reading the first short story alone.... When I did not have anyone to share the book with I found myself reading quickly. I wanted to get away from the pain as quickly as possible. I think one of the reasons I did not

understand what I had actually read when I finished the book the first time is that I did not allow myself to get close to it. I kept my distance so that I would not have to feel the pain or admit that such terrible things actually happened.

Like Wendy, I learned that this book could not be read by oneself. When I began to read *Krik? Krak!* during the summer of 1995, I too found myself reading it aloud to friends, family, and neighbors. As I read aloud, I entered the presence of others who fell silent in the face of accounts of women and men raped by soldiers, and the weekly journeys to prison to visit mothers who had been arrested for being accused of "having wings of flame" (Danticat, 1991, p. 35). Danticat writes:

> My mother had grown even thinner since the last time I had seen her. Her face looked like the gray of a late evening sky. These days, her skin barely clung to her bones, falling in layers, flaps, on her face and neck. The prison guards watched her more closely because they thought that the wrinkles resulted from her taking off her skin at night and then putting it back on in a hurry before sunrise. This was why Manman's sentence had been extended to life. And when she died, her remains were to be burnt in the prison yard, to prevent her spirit from wandering into any young innocent bodies. (p. 36)

Manman is held under suspicion because her body—hungry, beaten, and condemned to death—transforms into a ghost-like figure. Her skin is used as evidence against her, for the prison guards are certain that Manman escapes the confines of her body and slips out of her skin at night. Danticat's ancestral history is not a fictive rendering, rather it is all too "real," rooted in documentary fact, and speaks to us of the persistent subjugation of Haitian people at the hands of Dios Trujillos. Moreover, this history provokes associations of other moments in history when women were condemned to death for believing to possess supernatural, malevolent powers. This rendering bespeaks a vow not only to retell of this subjugation, but to remember it.

As I read *Krik? Krak!*, I continually felt as if I were walking along the streets of a foreign city where my customs of responding to literature through conversations and writing held little significance. Danticat's writing, itself a work of art, challenges the realities that we claim, and in so doing, it challenges the *I* that we believe ourselves to be. Testimonial literature such as that of Danticat calls for new habits of reading.

Testimonial literature often brings about a crisis of language. Consequently, a reader may be moved to feel bewildered and speechless. At the same time, however, testimonial literature asks the reader to tell and to remember the historical events inscribed on the pages before her. It was this state of inarticulateness that most compelled me as a teacher, for I realized that this was a vulnerable state. It marks the moment at which a reader might, for fear of being made vulnerable, push the text aside and discount it as too foreign, too interfering, too irrelevant, or too odd.

Because Danticat's writing ushered us to a place where ordinary speech felt irreverent, I found myself turning to the dramaturgy of Bertolt Brecht. Brecht recognized both the limits and the injuries of discourse. He was suspicious of a dramaturgy that privileged spoken language; consequently, his dramaturgy draws on the highly stylized gestures of the body, as well as on cultural artifacts and objects to represent the skills, beliefs, emotions, social attitudes, and socioeconomic class of a people. In Brecht's theater, the actor's body is itself a register for social relations and values. He believed that the social actions of the body conveyed social values and emotions that work across language and cultural barriers and frequently reveal unexpected contradictions between what people verbally claim they believe and value and what is revealed through their physical gestures. The theatrical conventions Brecht is most noted for—the social *geste,* montage, and use of details (which are cultural objects or artifacts that come into the hands of the actors)—provoke the audience to critically appraise their emotional investments and unsettledness.[2]

KRIK? KRAK! TESTIMONIAL LITERATURE AND THE QUESTION OF BELONGING

"In the era of the Holocaust, of Hiroshima, of Vietnam—in the age of testimony," writes Felman, "teaching, I would venture to suggest, must in turn testify, make something happen, and not just transmit a passive knowledge, pass on information, that is preconceived, substantiated, believed to be known in advance" (Felman & Laub, 1992, p. 53).

As I read *Krik? Krak!* over the summer months and began preparations to teach this material in the fall, I found myself spending time in the periodical section of the library, tracking down the portrayal of the 1937 massacres in the United States newspapers. I wanted to match the testimony of Danticat to the reports of American journalists, and to explore the gaps in these representations, asking myself: What would be omitted? Which perspectives would be privileged and accepted?

On November 6, 1937, *The New York Times* printed a report of what they referred to as the "wholesale killings of Haitian emigrants to the Dominican Republic." The *Times* reported that although fragmentary reports of these killings had been filtering into the State Department for some time, "official cognizance of these killings was taken only today." These large-scale massacres had been taking place since early October. The current reports of these incidents were based on stories from what the *Times* refered to as "alleged survivors" who had reached Santiago de Cuba, and on letters received by relatives in the western part of Haiti. One of the most disturbing documents was a letter printed in the *Times* that was written by Andres Pastoriza, the Dominican Minister:

> November 6, 1937: I have been authorized by my government to make the following statement: The Dominican government has not mobilized troops nor has had any reason to do so because the incident at the border is considered as closed with the exception of the investigation which is customary in incidents of such a nature where guilt is presumed in order to establish responsibilities and to determine judicial sanction against guilty parties. This incident is not of a different nature from many which have occurred since the year 1844 between Dominican and Haitian farmers, and the number of victims which is claimed is absolutely ridiculous.

Pastoriza's letter casts the massacre as an unremarkable "incident." The testimony of survivors is held under suspicion and, finally, undermined by official reports that refer to the "alleged" victims as "squatters who for many years have been in the habit of taking up unauthorized land in the border territory." Cast as squatters, the victims of the massacre are officially stripped of any national, local, or familial identity. Like so many persons who are relegated to locations that span beyond the borders of the English and social studies curricula, the questioning of Haitian testimony signifies a pervasive cultural practice to cast as deviant, excessive, or questionable the testimony of persons who challenge the vested interests of colonial policy (Donnell & Welsh, 1996).

Just as testimony is used in the United States court system to corroborate evidence, to re-establish the facts, and to determine truth, so literary testimony functions as a means through which to remap the territory of history. Danticat's work remade the narratives and allegories of nationhood, joining Caribbean writers such as Claude McKay, Thomas MacDermot, Jamaica Kincaid, and Paule Marshall—all of whom contribute and share a desire to, in the words of Donnell and Welsh (1996), "decolonize and indigenize imaginatively and to claim a voice for history, a geography and a people which had been dominated" (p. 4).

Danticat rewrites the official documents I quote above by transforming them into narratives of allegiance, struggle, and hope. She undermines a monolithic discourse of victimization by recasting the women in her stories as full-bodied, complex persons who not only fear, but both resist and comfort one another in the face of unspeakable destructiveness. In the following passage, Danticat draws on the words passed down through persons who survived the bloodshed in the Massacre River, the very river that binds the women of *Krik? Krak!* together.

"Sister, I do not want to be the one to tell you," she said, "but your mother is dead. If she is not dead now, then she will be when we get to Port au Prince. Her blood calls to me from the ground. Will you go with me to see her? Let us go to see her.... She will be ready for burning this afternoon."

My blood froze inside me. I lowered my head as the news sank in. ...

"Sister," she said, "life is never lost, another one always comes up to replace the last."

"Why did you not ask your mother, Jacqueline, if she knew how to fly?"

Then the story came back to me as my mother had often told it. On that day so long ago, in the year nineteen hundred and thirty-seven, in the Massacre River, my mother did fly. Weighted down by my body inside hers, she leaped from Dominican soil into the water, and out again on the Haitian side of the river. She glowed red when she came out, blood clinging to her skin, which at that moment looked as though it were in flames.

No matter how much distance death had tried to put between us, my mother would often come to visit me. Sometimes in the short sighs and whispers of somebody else's voice. Sometimes in somebody else's face. Other times in brief moments in my dreams. "There is that old Marie," my mother would say. "She is now the last one of us left." Mama had introduced me to them, because they had all died before I was born. There was my great grandmother Eveline who was killed by Dominican soldiers at the Massacre River,...and...my grandmother Defile who died with a bald head in a prison, because God had given her wings. (Danticat, 1991, p. 49)

The first night we discussed this book in class, the women felt that the experience of reading this collection of stories was "beyond language." We couldn't seem to articulate the meaning these stories held for us. It was as if this collection of stories had metamorphasized into literary testimony, and we, as readers, were asked to bear witness to secreted moments in history. "To bear witness," said the poet Paul Celan in a 1948 speech, "is to bear the solitude of a responsibility, and to bear the responsibility, precisely of that solitude" (see Felstiner, 1982). And yet, as Felman (Felman & Laub, 1992) points out, "the paradox is that to bear witness is also to transgress the confines of that isolated stance, to speak for others and to others" (p. 3).

How is one to speak when words are not available, even though one is obligated to say something? Writes Ray P. McDermott:

Occasions in which people are left without words are systematic outcomes
of a set of relations among a group of persons bound in a social structure.
The claim is that inarticulateness is not well understood as an individual
disability, but better understood as a well orchestrated moment in which
inarticulateness is invited, encouraged, duly noted and remembered, no
matter how much lamented.... Every utterance has its biography and cuts
its own figure, and, if we are careful enough to describe its points of contact with ongoing events, we can learn a great deal about the powers of the
talk that constructs, maintains, and resists the order of those events. (1988,
p. 18)

The social structure of testimony resists the order of easy or conventional forms of response, in part, because it thrusts us into a state of dissonance between what we believe we know and what we are presented
with. This dissonance intersects and cuts through the shape and semantic layerings of our daily use of language, thereby making even more
complicated the project of expression (see Bakhtin, 1934, p. 39, as cited
in McDermott, 1988). What inarticulateness offers us, suggests McDermott, is "an invitation to listen in a new way." Continues McDermott, "If
you cannot understand your spouse or your neighbors,...work hard to
alter the conditions that keep you unable to discover what you need to
be talking about, with whom, and to what end.... If this procedure of
finding a new phenomenon...helps to make our lives better by having us
appreciate people where previously we could only find disability, we can
call it a blessing and a call to organize a better world." (p. 40). What is
perhaps most difficult to address about inarticulateness, notes McDermott, is that most often, when we are in the presence of people who are
indeed inarticulate, whether they be our students, a people different
from us, or a history we cannot apprehend, we eventually realize that
the conditions that foster their apparent inarticulateness—the seemingly
fragmented text of Danticat, "so hard to follow," as one student initially
complained—are the same conditions that render us articulate—"we did
not know how to listen" (p. 43).

After sitting quietly for perhaps the first 15 minutes of class, and in an
effort to "transgress the confines of our isolated stance" (Felman &
Laub, 1992, p. 7), we began to take an inventory of the figures, fictional characters, and historical incidents that we admitted to knowing
little about. Who is the Generalisimo, Dios Trujillo? Who were the
troops sent to massacre the Haitian women in 1937? How are the
women in this book related to one another? We drew a genealogy of the
characters, which provoked other questions: How does a people construct a memory when there is a history of massacres, when a people are
dispersed, when writing is forbidden? Rita, a member of the class, asks
us to imagine the horror of leaving your home in the dark of night.

Another class member, Jean, speaks of the loss of heritage, and another, Laura, notices that Danticat's fragmented poetic structure mimes the fragmentation of lives and the dismemberment of bodies.

After our initial discussion, many of us once again sat still and in silence. Jean broke our silence by pointing out the ways in which Danticat provoked her to recognize the hollow stereotypes she held of the Haitian people. "I am stunned at my own ignorance," Wendy, a student in the class, said to us, "...of the brutal murder of women who had died at the hands of Dios Trujillo's soldiers in the Massacre River in 1937." Writes Danticat, "This river separated Haiti from the Spanish speaking country that my mother had never allowed me to name because I had been born on the night that El Generalisimo, Dios Trujillo, the honorable chief of state, had ordered the massacre of all Haitians living there" (1991, p. 33). Carol, another one of the participants in the class, writes the following entry in her process notes:

> I began reading *Krik? Krak!* over lunch one day and literally could not stomach the suffering and despair. I am impressed by the emotion that simple objects signify in Danticat's stories and how we as women or interpreters of the text began to react. We placed great value in a baby's bib, a quilt or a passport.... It frightens me to think that in Haiti women writers are killed. Perhaps there was a compulsion for Danticat's tales to be told as she is the voice of "a thousand women before." She speaks for them via "the blunt tip of her pencil."

The suffering Carol writes about in her notebook is registered in the objects that appear throughout Danticat's stories, objects that are inscribed with the social values and beliefs of the women for which she writes, for example, marrow bones for bone soup, a weeping Madonna, the razor blade Celiane uses to make her face unrecognizable to herself and her family after she is raped by soldiers. As the class read through this collection of stories, I continually asked them to track objects that appeared throughout the story and to study whose hands these objects passed through. Thus the questions: Who is permitted to take possession of these objects? What symbolism is lodged in their structures?

Together, we began to learn that to take on the role of a belated witness to another's suffering is to lose speech in order to break through our own limitations in knowledge and challenge our own world views, not necessarily through discursive language, but through the emotional life felt in our bodies, delivered to us through felt perception (Felman & Laub, 1992). Although we feel the inadequacy of our own spoken language, we can begin to perceive the sensory feelings provoked by the disorderly images which Danticat spins with her own hands, herself a

"Kitchen Poet" who "places her fingers around the contours of a pen" (1991, p. 220) to write of the generations of women in her family. "Writing," Danticat tells us, "was as forbidden as dark rouge on the cheeks or a first date before the age of eighteen. It was an act of indolence, something to be done in a corner when you could have been learning to cook" (p. 219). She continues:

> You hear this scraping from her. Krik? Krak! Pencil, paper. It sounds like someone crying. Someone was crying. You and the writing demons in your head. You have nobody, nothing but this piece of paper, they told you. Only a notebook made out of discarded fish wrappers, panty-hose cardboard. They were the best confidantes for a lonely little girl. When you write, it's like braiding your hair. Taking a handful of coarse unruly strands and attempting to bring them unity.

Woven into Danticat's phrases are images the teachers will use to engage their bodies in the act of literary interpretation. In the following section, I document the process the students engaged in as they moved from locating images to composing a memorial for the women of Haiti, a memorial that we would collectively transform into "a promissory note."

A SEA CHEST OF ARTIFACTS

> The *literature of testimony* is thus not an act of leisure but an art of urgency: it exists in time not just as a memorial but as an artist's promissory note, as an attempt to bring the *backwardness* of consciousness to the level of precipitant events. (Felman & Laub, 1992, p. 114)

During the second week of our discussion of *Krik? Krak!*, I asked students to choose from among three different theatrical conventions to respond to this text.[3] These theatrical conventions, adopted from the theater of Brecht and the work of Jonathan Neelands, were used to develop responses to particular questions the teachers in the class developed about this book. The teachers chose from among three conventions to pursue their questions: *montage, context building,* and *reflective action.* Each of these theatrical conventions are forms of poetic action that function to bring a fresh perspective to a work of art by opening up alternative channels of communication. Additionally, they work at the level of symbolic interpretation and often heighten a reader's emotional involvement with a literary work of art (Neelands, 1990).

BUILDING UP A CONTEXT

To get started on building a context, I asked students to begin collecting actual props that appear in the text and to pay careful attention to who handles those props. Props are important objects that come into the hands of the actors and are imbued with meaning. The attitudes an actor expresses as she handles her props are what Brecht referred to as "details" (1972, pp. 346–347). According to Brecht, the gestures and objects used by an actor converge to convey social values, intentions, and beliefs. For example, in his notes and variants for his play *Mother Courage and Her Children*, Brecht writes:

> Even minute details are very revealing, e.g., the fact that when the recruiters step up to her sons and feel their muscles as if they were horses, Mother Courage displays maternal pride for a moment, until the sergeant's question ("Why aren't they in the army?") shows her the danger their qualities put them in: then, she rushes between her sons and the recruiters. The pace at rehearsals should be slow, if only to make it possible to work out details; determining the pace of the performance is another matter and it comes later.
>
> A *detail*
> In pulling a knife, Mother Courage shows no savagery. She is merely showing how far she will go in defending her children. The performer must show that Mother Courage is familiar with such situations and knows how to handle them. (1972, pp. 346–347)

These examples illustrate the important liaison that an actor has with the objects that come into her hands. The attitudes that are expressed as an actor handles a prop are not arbitrary; rather, they must convey emotional allegiances, social attitudes, and beliefs.

The students in the context building group decided to create a sense of place by designing a collective *image* that would represent one of the places or people in the drama *Krik? Krak!* The image would then become a concrete reference for "an idea half-perceived."[4] In this case, the students wanted to more fully understand the historical events that tied the women in *Krik? Krak!* together. The questions that the women asked at the outset of our discussions, and hence, returned to for this project were: How are the women in this collection of stories related? What cultural threads mark their relationships? What cultural conversations are lodged in the images Danticat renders?[5] I suggested to the class that they might use illustrations from historical documents. They might, for example, create a facsimile of Grace's United States passport, or use media imagery of Port au Prince. Other suggestions included collecting portraits of the politicians rendered in the book , or cartoons, comics, or posters that might refer to the historical time period about which Danticat writes.

This context building activity calls for a representation of an image that refers to an idea or concept that they felt warranted further exploration. It does not call for the live, physical enactment that the women of this class went on to perform. I expected that this image would be inscribed on a large poster board, a flat image, so to speak, projected on a screen, rather than performed through the reverent gestures of the students' bodies. Although the students had used Brecht's social *geste* to interpret particularly troubling images in this text earlier in the course, they were not explicitly asked to draw on these methods for this project. Yet, "as readers," writes Jean:

> We all agreed that we simply could not read this book as bystanders. We could not remain on the outside and look in. This sad story found its way inside all of us and created a haunting effect. As classmates and fellow readers of this story, we needed each other—to be able to talk and express our feelings. As it is turning out, this project is becoming a means of great expression for our group.

Jean and her colleagues began to compose a series of responses to one of the stories, entitled "The Missing Peace," by literally creating a quilt "similar to the quilt sewn by the character Emile, the difference being," as Jean points out, "that the items sewn on the quilt would reflect images or memories from all of the life stories in the book." It was to be a quilt of "personal diaries passed on from generation to generation." Although the stories written by Danticat appear to be separate, they are in fact interrelated. Throughout this collection of short stories, the facial features of one character are reproduced in another, thus inscribing a sense of continuity among generations. The experience of massacres, hunger, loss, and exile is inscribed into the face of each woman Danticat renders in her work. "You remember thinking while braiding your hair," writes Danticat, "that you look a lot like your mother. Your mother who looked like your grandmother and her grandmother before her" (1991, p. 222).

The class begins to understand how Danticat links her characters together by family lineage, geography, religious affiliations, and cultural practices. The images Jean and and the rest of the group planned to inscribe into the quilt patches would come from the seemingly disparate stories written by Danticat. Over the course of several weeks, as the group worked on using theatrical conventions that pertain to context building to compose their response, they found themselves expanding on their quilt. Jean writes:

> First, we decided to display the quilt in a bureau drawer adding an even more personal theme. Then, the bureau was replaced with an old trunk—one that had traveled far and had carried the memories and the mementos of many lifetimes. We wanted to show the strong connections of the women in the book to each other. Although they were separate, they are one and so all of the tangible pieces of their lives are kept in one safe place. We then decided to look through the book for specific ideas and colors that were represented throughout the stories. We changed our plan of sewing a quilt to one of draping a purple cloth in the trunk and then placing the items on top of the cloth. While skimming through the stories, we began to recite small excerpts that meant something to us. In our excitement, we decided to add these to our presentation, therefore turning it into a creative dramatic presentation.
>
> Finally, we decided to dim the lights—leading to the idea of candle-light—and add music. We realized that what we had created was a funeral of sorts—a eulogy to those women who, by reading their story, have become part of us too.

As I listened in on the students' planning sessions, I noticed that they began to move away from the representation of an image to the staging of events. One of the first indications of their movement toward creating a eulogy was the approach they took to gathering props for this event. Generally, in the theater, the prop mistress is not interested in whether or not the props have personal importance to the actors; she does not ask the cast to bring in props that are imbued with meaning for them. Here, however, in this small group of ten women, each person brought in objects that held emotional significance for them and, at the same time, represented the values and identities of the characters in the book. Each object tied them to the women of Port au Prince, linking their lives so that they, as readers, could establish a relationship with a social world that extended beyond their own.

The participants chose their objects for their dialogic capabilities—that is, the capacity the objects had to generate a dialogue in symbols between the women of Port au Prince and the women of southern New Hampshire. Bakhtin uses the term *dialogism* to refer to the characteristic ways in which meanings, as they are expressed in discursive as well as gestural, symbolic, and iconic forms, interact and condition each other. How meanings will affect each other and the extent to which they will do so is determined at the point of utterance (Bakhtin, 1981). The moment of utterance is a moment of social, historical, political, and emotional significance; it is a moment in which the psyche is engaged with the outer world and has the potential to exert agency. As readers who were moved to *inarticulateness*, each woman used her select objects as a medium through which she could begin to negotiate her will and desire for expression with the ensemble of readers of which she was a part. Through this process, the objects themselves accrued dialogic properties and became a medium through which to mediate expression when the readers fell into a state of bewilderment and felt at a loss for words.

If, as readers, we moved too quickly to articulateness or fluency, I am afraid that we would have become more vulnerable to what McDermott (1988) refers to as total conformity, reproducing old ways of understanding and living. McDermott notes that the objects marking Danticat's text, and which find their "equivalent" in the objects the women use in their own work, also function to produce breakthroughs by which their world is temporarily, albeit imaginatively, altered.

The objects marking the narrative landscapes of *Krik? Krak!* are also inscribed with cultural conversations that evoke the emotional lives of the readers. These conversations are registered in icons and symbols rather than simply words. The bib of the dead infant, baby Rose, provokes emotions which, although unspeakable, are not inapprehensible. The ocean-drenched journal and the prized United States passport symbolize the painful and contradictory feelings of loyalty and betrayal many of the characters felt toward their country. Objects like the Madonna contain social, folk, and religious narratives that shape the social life of Haiti and do not exist as referents to themselves.

As the women in this group prepared to compose a literary response to a series of scenes in *Krik? Krak!*, they in effect prepared to bring the women of Haiti before us, in our seminar room. Their initial intentions did not include the staging of such an event, but several of the women agreed with Lisa, another member of the class, who said after their presentation:

> The act of composing a collage or visual image was not enough. We started out thinking about a collage, or drawing a picture. We planned to get out the glue gun and paste away. But then we realized this wasn't enough. It didn't get our feelings through. We wanted to explain why we put the things in the trunk. We wanted people to understand why each object was placed in the trunk.

READER RESPONSE AS TESTIMONIAL

"Testimonies," writes Dori Laub (Felman & Laub, 1992), "are not monologues; they cannot take place in solitude. The witnesses are talking to *somebody*: to somebody they have been waiting for a long time" (pp. 70–71). As the women in this class prepared to give testimony to the political struggles they bore witness to in *Krik? Krak!*, they in turn asked each of us to bear witness, not to their performance, but to the events their performance represented. They hoped to evoke our intimate and total presence. "For the testimonial process to take place," writes Laub, "there needs to be a bonding, the intimate and total presence of an *other*--the position of one who hears" (p. 70).

The women begin their eulogy by dimming the lights. They stand in a half circle around an old, green, wooden sea chest that they have brought in. As Carol prepares to read, Rita lights a candle for her to read by.

> *Carol*: Krik? Krak! Somewhere by the seacoast I feel a breath of warm sea air and hear the laughter of children. An old granny smokes her pipe, surrounded by the village children.... We tell stories so that the young ones will know what came before them. They ask Krik? We say Krak! Our stories are kept in our hearts. (qtd. from Dantcat, 1991, opening page)

This pattern is repeated. Each time someone takes her turn to read, the woman who stands beside her lights a candle for her to read by. During the reading, another woman places the objects that are symbolized in the passage inside the wooden sea chest: an ocean-soaked journal, marrow bones for soup, a paintbrush, a passport, black butterflies, an infant's bib, a purple cloth, and a dried red rose.

> Perhaps I was chosen from the beginning of time to live here with Agwe at the bottom of the sea. Maybe this is why I dreamed of the starfish and the mermaids having the Catholic Mass under the sea. Maybe this was my invitation to go. In any case, I know that my memory of you will live even there as I too become a child of the sea. (Danticat, 1991, pp. 27–28)
>
> "Caroline called," Ma said. She was standing over the stove making some bone soup when I got home from the cemetery. "I told her that we would still keep her bed here for her, if she ever wants to use it. She will come and visit us soon. I knew she would miss us."
>
> "Can I drop one bone in your soup?" I asked Ma.
>
> "It is your soup too," she said. She let me drop one bone into the boiling water. The water splashed my hand leaving a red mark.
>
> "Ma, if we were painters which landscapes would we paint?" I asked her.
>
> "I see. You want to play the game of questions?"
>
> "When I become a mother, how will I name my daughter?"
>
> "If you want to play then I should ask the first question," she said.

"What kinds of lullabies will I sing at night? What kinds of legends will my daughter be told? What kinds of charms will I give her to ward off evil?"

"I have come a few years further than you," she insisted. "I have tasted a lot more salt. I am to ask the first question, if we are to play the game."

She thought about it for a long time while stirring the bones in our soup. (pp. 215–216)

A thick red ribbon runs through the objects placed in the sea chest. This red ribbon symbolizes the Massacre River that binds the women of these stories together. It is the thread that Jean feels now binds them. "The thread that ties us is like the red river that connects the women of Haiti. The thread for the book was the river itself and here it is, the thread. It is the river and its memories that links and binds the women Danticat writes for. It is going through us now."

Here, the class not only begins to locate the social and historical relationships that tie the women of Haiti together, but they also develop a symbolic representation for these relationships, thereby asking their audience—also members of the class—to respond both to the "aesthetic objects" as well as to the social reality reflected in them. In this sense, the participants create a form of art that seeks to link the lived reality of the Haitian people to our developing perceptions of Haitian history (Ybarra-Frausto, 1991).

After their performance, there was, once again, silence. Then I said, interrupting the silence, "Remember the assignment. You were to create one image that would represent an idea half perceived. What happened? Instead of an image, you performed an event. Do you want to talk about the process of composing this event?"

Amy, a student in the class, begins by talking about how it initially felt strange to create a ritual remembrance for characters who are not real, although they represented real people. Carol continues:

Carol: I said that we had a memorial service, a Mass. Here, we put things into a box. Somehow the memory of this book has stayed with us; the memories of this book have become a part of us. The religious threads kept surfacing during our work together. Like culture, like the practice of voodoo, it becomes a piece of us as readers...essentially, what we did was to create a memorial service for the people in this book, a memorial for the stories.

Laura: I felt like I was watching a memorial service, not a class project. Did you plan this or did it just happen?

Jean: We started out thinking of a picture. We thought we would use items that were symbolic in the book, you know, take out the glue gun and make an image. But the project just kept progressing because we felt that an image alone wouldn't be enough.

Lisa: And we wanted the audience to understand why we placed each object in the trunk; we felt that was very important. This is, in part, why we read as we placed objects in the trunk.

Wendy: From my own experiences with memorial services you go to the service and remember the person. You recount what was special, what you loved, and what was significant about them, and then you leave these memories and the person in the church or in the hall. This was a memorial in the truest sense of the word because it contained memories...memories should keep people alive. So often in memorial services it's death and it is not alive and it is death and it is finished and it is over. I wrote this:

> *As I was reading about the pain and love the shame and the fear felt among these women, I know that I could not survive such intense emotions. How do these women endure? Where do they find their strength? Does only tragedy breed such strength? Do I ever want to be so strong? And yet they remain; they are here before us in the chest. The women who cook bone soup and see their husbands meet tragic ends.*

For me they are still here, stronger than ever. For me, this memorial service...contains memories of the women of Haiti that we can take with us tonight.

DISCUSSION

In the context of curriculum studies and teacher education, I would venture to say that the act of reading testimonial literature should move each of us toward a state of obligation and commitment to educate ourselves and our students about the histories and achievements of people whom we have failed to recognize in our classrooms. If we hope to respectfully engage one another in the history of diverse people, rather than solely in the dominant, elite versions registered in so many English and social studies curricula, then we must not only turn to the literary testimony of writers such as Edwidge Danticat, but we must seek out performative ways of responding to this work, ways that move us beyond our current capacities for understanding history and literature. This move means that the reader locates ways to mediate the dissonance between the discursive, daily language she uses and the events in history that are unimaginable and heretofore unspeakable. To mediate this dissonance requires that readers work with symbolic systems other than words that have the potential to engage the emotional life of the reader and, in turn, strengthen the capacity to perceive and to hold the particular ethical requirements that are called for in reading and responding to testimonial literature.

How, you might ask, does the gestural life of the body extend our habituated ways of reading this testimonial piece of literature? Recall that the class finds the act of writing and talking about this collection of stories limiting. Jean writes in her process notes that they cannot just read this book as "bystanders." While a bystander is present at an event and may see it, she does not take part in the event. The position one takes as a bystander is distinct from the act of bearing witness. To be a bystander implies a detached, disinterested attitude; an attitude that feels no moral obligation to report to others what one has seen. To bear witness, however, is to actively perceive what has happened to others in one's own body, with the sight (insight) usually afforded only by one's own immediate physical involvement (Felman & Laub, 1992). "In a civilization where murder and violence are already doctrines in the process of becoming institutions," wrote Albert Camus in 1948, "and where the executioners have gained the right to become administrative managers, the artist must testify not to the law, but to the *body*" (emphasis added; cited in Felman & Laub, 1992, p. 108).

The teachers in this class take the body as a point of departure by recognizing their immediate physical involvement with these stories—physical responses that included shame, loss, regret, confusion, bewilderment, ignorance, and reverence—as sources of potential insight into a world for which we previously had little feeling.

Throughout the process notes kept by the students, there was a desire to use a theatrical convention that would enable them to craft speech and action in ways that conveyed the increased emotional involvement they experienced as readers. Their emotional responses demanded forms that would make their literary experience apprehensible to themselves and to others. Moreover, these responses asked that they, as readers, attend to and hold the details embedded in the text, and that they interpret the complex knots of images and actions without reducing them to easy formulas for understanding. The use of poetic action, rather than linear analysis or argumentation, summoned each reader to use symbolic action as a medium for interpretation. The objects each person collected functioned as symbols for the values and beliefs held by the women Danticat commemorates in her writing. Like the symbolic meaning lodged in a crucifix, a Menorah, or a pair of rosary beads, objects like marrow bones, salt, and a statue of the Madonna took on symbolic weight and in turn functioned to mediate the dissonance between states of bewilderment and inarticulateness. The objects composed a memorial for the women in *Krik? Krak!*

The eulogy performed by the women in this class not only commemorates the struggles and achievements of the Haitian people, but it functions as a promissory note that bespeaks an ethical obligation to, in Jean's words, "seek more." At the end of their eulogy, I asked each student what they believe this book asks of us. I pointed out the importance of being moved emotionally, so that we can move toward social action. There is, once again, silence. Then, Jean responds, "We must seek more. I want to continue to find out more, not just about Haiti, but about other places in the world, local places, the places in our midst. By getting involved in this material, we have altered our perspectives, our point of view." Our points of view begin to shift by virtue of the physical sensations and actions that are expressed through embodied action. In effect, the eulogy functioned as a form of testimony which, by definition, cannot offer a completed statement, a totalizable account of the events they bore witness to as readers of *Krik? Krak!* (Felman & Laub, 1992). "In the testimony," writes Felman and Laub, "language is in process and on trial, it does not possess itself as a conclusion.... Testimony is, in other words, a discursive practice, as opposed to a pure theory. To testify—to vow to tell, to promise and produce one's own speech as material evidence for truth—is to accomplish a speech act, rather than to simply formulate a statement. As a peformative speech act, testimony is, in effect, *action*" (p. 5). The teachers do not speak *about* commemorating the women of Haiti; they physically enact a commemoration, and by doing so, they physically articulate and explore meanings, values, and cultural practices that expand the limited understanding we previously possessed about the Haitian people. By keying pedagogy as a performative event, the readers of *Krik? Krak!* drew on the gestural life of their bodies to rearticulate, resignify, and amplify the discursive possibilities available to them.

The eulogy is itself a "performative deed," which requires that readers do more than conceptualize reading as an isolated act of individual response to distant others. Testimonial reading, writes Megan Boler (1997), emphasizes a collective educational responsibility to take up particular tasks. This task is at minimum, notes Boler, "an active reading practice that involves challenging my own assumptions and world views" (pp. 261–262), as well as a persistant effort not to confuse the work accomplished by the women Danticat writes about with the work we ourselves have yet to do. Our moments of inarticulateness in the face of many of Danticat's stories—as well as the silence of the dead for whom Danticat writes, and the silence in the landscapes of Haiti—demands a different form of attention. *Krik? Krak!* demands that as readers we learn to listen to testimonial literature differently, and that we make a commitment to interrogate our responses to the experiences of those we read about. Performance offers one means through which to begin this interrogation and places in relief the incommensurability of our different cognitive, emotional, and historical positions, without fore-closing on the possibilities for learning from these incommensurabilities (Boler, 1997). Moreover, performance differentiates each of us not by what we see in the work of Danticat, but what we fail to see and what we as a nation have failed to witness.

NOTES

[1] The composition of students in this course represents the demographics throughout the predominantly White campus at the University of New Hampshire. Out of a student population of 12,500 students (including both undergraduate and graduate students), there are 183 persons identified as Asian American; 117 persons identified as Hispanic; 90 persons identified a African American; and 12 students identified as Native American. The presence of students from diverse ethnic backgrounds in the Education department in which I teach is limited to five African Americans, and two Asian Americans out of a group of 405 masters' students in education.

[2] Brecht used theatrical devices, such as montage, reading against the text, and the social *geste* (which is a frozen slice of action), not to do away with emotion or to discourage the actor to give up all attempts to get the audience to empathize, but to engage the audience in distinctly different ways. "The Brechtian actor" writes Elizabeth Wright, "does not gain sympathy for himself by provoking a personal act of empathic identification, but gains it for another by demonstrating that person's plight in his relation *to* others. A work task, for instance, is not a social *gestus*, if it does not imply a social relation, such as exploitation or co-operation" (1989, p. 27).

[3] Once the women had formed groups according to the conventions they would use to interpret their literary material, I asked them to keep a process journal that documented the methods of interpretation they used to read and re-read *Krik? Krak!*. The following section of this paper reports on the group of teachers who used *context building* as a medium for interpretation, thus this data represents a subset of the larger group's project. I intentionally situate this research project in my own classroom so that the pedagogical event can at once function as a process of research which continually involves teachers and teacher candidates in the construction and validation of the meaning that I ascribe to this work (Lather, 1991). The data consists of process notes the teachers kept throughout the project, videotaped recordings of the performances, and my own descriptive field notes of the work of smalll groups, as well as larger group discussions. Additionally, I conducted exit interviews with the women immediately after the course was over in December, 1995, as well as five months later in May, 1996. My intention during these interviews was to ascertain the extent to which this experience has influenced their own pedagogical practices, particularly with respect to their selections of and engagement with reading materials

that represent diverse cultural practices and histories. Domain analysis was the key method of interpretation I used for the data sets discussed throughout this paper (Spradley, 1980).

[4] Philosopher of education, Harry Broudy (1988) argues that the cultivation of a student's intellect is contingent upon his or her ability to decode aesthetic clues, especially during a historical period in which "reality" is thoroughly imagistic. Broudy maintains that the image is used for political purpose and believes that students must learn to decode and be critical of such usage. Educators such as Maxine Greene (1991), Elliot Eisner (1991) and Elizabeth Vallance (1977) maintain that curriculum, like art, is a human construction that represents the transformation of knowledge, perception, and understanding inexpressible through other orders of representation.

[5] Before exploring the cultural concepts rendered in *Krik? Krak!*, concepts such as matrilineal heritage, intimacy, and memory, the women in the class spent time reading and discussing Elizabeth Vallance's "The Public Curriculum of Orderly Images" (1995). Vallance distinguishes between a curriculum or orderly and disorderly images, in part by suggesting that the orderly image is often designed to reach us in some familiar, recognizable way. Also, very visible public structures, such as public sculpture, billboards, and other elements of the manmade environment, offer images that can remind us of what we think we know; the statue of a local hero, usually a soldier, in a city park is a common example. It doesn't challenge our assumptions at all. Its very purpose is to reinforce our shared image bank of what soldiering is like. The purpose of this kind of public image is usually distinctively narrative. It tells or reminds us of a story, or, in the case of billboards, makes a statement or suggests a story that we are able to be enticed to join. Vallance explores why the public resists what she refers to as "difficult art." Her work is especially useful for working with "difficult literature" that possesses disorderly images which challenge our everyday perceptions and beliefs. She encourages educators to work with students to develop a capacity to interpret the disorderly images in art that challenge the social values and beliefs we take for granted and to "propose new worlds, different from the ones we know" (Varnedoe, 1992).

REFERENCES

Agosin, M. (1992). *Secret weavers: Stories of the fantastic by women writers of Argentina and Chile*. Fredonia, NY: White Pine Press.

Bakhtin, M. M. (1981). *The dialogic imagination* (M. Holquist, Ed.; C. Emerson & M. Holquist, Trans.). Austin, TX: University of Texas Press.

Behar, R. (1996). *The vulnerable observer: Anthropology that breaks your heart*. Boston: Beacon Press.

Boler, M. (1997). The Risks of empathy: Interrogating multiculturalism's gaze. *Cultural Studies, 11*(2), 253–273.

Brecht, B. (1972). *Collected plays, vol. 5*. New York: Vintage Books.

Broudy, H. (1988). Aesthetics and the curriculum. In W. Pinar (Ed.), *Contemporary curriculum discourses* (pp. 332–342). Scottsdale, AZ: Gorsuch Scarisbrick.

Camus, A. (1966). *Resistance, rebellion, and death* (J. O'Brien, Trans.). New York: Knopf. (Original work published 1948)

Danticat, E. (1991). *Krik? Krak!* New York: Soho Press.

Donnell, A., & Welsh, S. (1996). *The Routledge reader in Caribbean literature*. New York: Routledge Press.

Eckstrom, L. (1995). Moral perception and the chronotope: The case of Henry James. In A. Mandelker (Ed.), *Bakhtin in contexts: Across the disciplines* (pp. 99–116). Evanston, IL: Northwestern University Press.

Eisner, E. W. (1991). *The enlightened eye: Qualitative inquiry and the enhancement of educational practice*. New York: Macmillan.

Ellsworth, E. (1997). *Teaching positions: Difference, pedagogy and the power of address*. New York: Teachers College Press.

Felman, S., & Laub, D. (1992). *Testimony: Crises of witnessing in literature, psycho-analysis, and history*. New York: Routledge Press.

Felstiner, J. (1982, July/August). Translating Celan's last poem. *American Poetry Review, 23*, 59.

Greene, M. (1991). Forward. In C. Witherall and N. Noddings (Eds.), *Stories lives tell: Narrative and dialogue in education* (pp. ix–xi). New York: Teachers College Press.

Hedrick, T. (1996). Rigoberta's earrings: The limits of teaching testimonio. In A. Carey-Webb & S. Benz (Eds.), *Teaching and testimony: Rigoerta Menchu and the North American classroom* (pp. 223–235). Albany, NY: State University of New York Press.

Lather, P. (1991). *Getting smart: Feminist research and pedagogy within the postmodern*. New York: Routledge.

McDermott, R. P. (1988). Inarticulateness. In D. Tannen (Ed.), *Linguistics in context* (pp. 37–68). Norwood, NJ: Ablex.

Neelands, J. (1990). *Structuring drama work*. Cambridge, England: Cambridge University Press.

Nussbaum, M. (1990). *Love's knowledge: Essays on philosophy and literature*. New York: Oxford University Press.

Shea, M. (1994). *Women as outsiders: Undercurrents of oppression in Latin American women's novels*. Bethesda, MD: Austin & Winfield.

Spradley, J. P. (1980). *Participant observation*. New York: Holt, Rinehart & Winston.

Vallance, E. (1977). The landscape of the Great Plains experience: An application of curriculum criticism. *Curriculum Inquiry, 7*(2), 87–105.

Vallance, E. (1995). The public curriculum of orderly images. *Educational Researcher, 24*(2), 4–13.

Varnedoe, K. (1992, June 14). *Untitled commencement address, Stanford University*. Stanford, CA: Stanford University News Service.

Wright, E. (1989). *Postmodern Brecht: A re-presentation*. New York: Routledge Press.

Ybarra-Frausto, T. (1991). The Chicano movement/The movement of Chicago art. In E. Karp & S. D. Lavine (Eds.), *Exhibiting cultures: The poetic and politics of museum display* (pp. 128–150). Washington, DC, and London: Smithsonian Institute Press.

OTHER RESOURCES

Anzaldua, G. (Ed.). (1990). *Making face, making soul: Haciendo Caras: Creative and critical perspectives by feminists of color.* San Francisco: Aunt Lute Books.

Austin, J. L. (1962). *How to do things with words.* Cambridge, MA: Harvard University Press.

Bachelard, G. (1958). *The poetics of space.* Toronto: Orion Press.

Bauman, R. (1977). *Verbal art as performance.* Prospect Heights, IL: Waveland Press.

Bogdan, D. (1992). *Re-educating the imagination: Towards a poetics, politics, and pedagogy of literary engagement.* Portsmouth, NH: Boynton/Cook.

Bordo, S. (1993). *Unbearable weight: Feminism, Western culture, and the body.* Berkeley, CA: University of California Press.

Brecht, B. (1957). *Brecht on theatre: The development of an aesthetic* (J. Willett, Ed.). New York: Hill and Wang.

Hooks, B. (1994). *Teaching to transgress.* New York: Routledge Press.

Karp, I., & Lavine, S. D. (1991). *Exhibiting cultures: The poetics and politics of museum display.* Washington, DC: Smithsonian Institute.

Langer, S. (1957). *Problems of art.* New York: Charles Scribner's Sons.

Lutz, C. (1988). *Unnatural emotions: Everyday sentiments on a Micronesian atoll and their challenge to Western theory.* Chicago: University of Chicago Press.

Martin, B., & Mohanty, S. T. (1986). Feminist politics: What's home got to do with it? In T. de Lauretis (Ed.), *Feminist studies/Critical studies* (pp. 191–212). Bloomington, IN: Indiana University Press.

Moraga, C. (1983). *Loving in the war years.* Boston, MA: South End.

Rosenberg, P. (1996). Underground discourse: Exploring whiteness in teacher education. In M. Fine (Ed.), *Offwhite: Essays on race, culture and society* (pp. 35–46). New York: Routledge.

Salvio, P. (1966, Spring). On the forbidden pleasures and hidden dangers of covert reading. *English Quarterly, 27*(3), pp. 8–15.

Spellman, E. (1991). The virtue of feeling and the feeling of virtue. In C. Card (Ed.), *Feminist ethics* (pp. 213–232). Lawrence, KS: The University of Kansas Press.

Turner, V. (1969). *The ritual process: Structure and anti-structure.* Ithaca, NY: Cornell University Press.

chapter 3

Making Lives Meaningful: Extending Perspectives Through Role-Play

Karen Hume
Durham Board of Education, Ontario, Canada

Gordon Wells
Ontario Institute for Studies in Education

> When focusing on the means to make the lives of others meaningful to students, on humanizing knowledge, on imaginatively engaging with people's hopes, fears, and intentions, and so on, we are focusing on matters that are intricately bound up with morality.
> Kieran Egan (1992)

History, as presented in school textbooks, is often a cool, impersonal subject. There is little about the experiences of "ordinary" people; little consideration of how their lives were affected by the economic issues and political decisions that constitute the main subject matter of many of the texts. Consider the following, taken from a text for intermediate grades, which is described as "Canada's Story from 1867 to 1986." In Chapter 3, "The Expansion of Canada, 1867–1878," there is a one-page section on opening up the West:

Under Prime Minister John A. Macdonald, Canada had won the race with the United States for the vast lands in the West. But Macdonald knew that Canada had to work hard to hold the West.

To open up these lands to settlers, the federal government did four things....

Fourth, a railway had to be built from eastern Canada to British Columbia. The railway was necessary to carry settlers to the West and to tie the country together. Who would build the railway to the Pacific?

The answer to this question is provided in Chapter 4, "Macdonald's National Policy," where the building of the railway is given another full page. Here is the second paragraph of that section:

Building the railway was a real challenge. The tracks had to be laid across the rock and swamps of northern Ontario, over the southern prairies, and through the steep mountain passes and deep river gorges of the Rocky Mountains. The rock had to be blasted. The C.P.R. spent more than $7,000,000 on dynamite, nitroglycerin, and black powder. Tunnels were dug, swamps were filled, and bridges were built.[1]

There are many features of this sort of text that are difficult for young adolescents. Note, for example, the anthropomorphic image of the railway tying the country together and, by contrast, the absence of human subjects, particularly in the last sentence, where the verbs that name the difficult tasks are presented as agentless passives. But, at a more fundamental level, what makes the text difficult is the overall impersonality that is the result of seeing the events of the past in terms of a synoptic pattern of unfolding events, viewed from the perspective of the present.[2] Clearly, for the textbook writer, presenting this pattern takes precedence over "imaginatively engaging with people's hopes, fears, and intentions" in the way that Egan (1992) describes.[3] Not surprisingly, therefore, history is not a particularly popular subject in the intermediate grades, for both students and teachers.

Aware of the problems, Karen Hume decided to adopt a different approach to her unit on Canadian history, which occurred fairly late in the year. In keeping with her overall aims for the class, she wanted her students to work on topics that really interested them, do their own research, and make a representation of what they had come to understand that would be interesting and informative for their peers. In other words, she planned to invite them to become makers of history rather than simply passive consumers of texts written by others. However, this was no easy task—as we shall now explain.

THE PARTICIPANTS

From the beginning of the school year, Karen had been trying to develop the ethos of a community of inquiry in her classroom. In so

doing, she was asking her students to engage in a process of active construction of knowledge that was, in many respects, similar to the one she
used as a teacher-researcher.

Several years before, Karen had enrolled in a part-time graduate
degree program in education, where she met Gordon Wells, a professor
of education and an advocate of action research, which he sees as a way
of making theory and practice mutually reinforcing and an opportunity
for personal as well as professional development. We have now been
working together for a number of years, Karen participating in courses
with Gordon at the Ontario Institute for Studies in Education in the
University of Toronto, Gordon participating in Karen's elementary
school classroom (grades 6, 7, and 8), and together making conference
presentations about what we are learning in the process.

True collaboration between classroom teachers and university profes-
sors is still, unfortunately, relatively rare. But when it is successful, as in
our case, it can be extremely beneficial for both parties—and also for
the students involved (Hume, 1998). In fact, we are both members of a
larger group, the Developing Inquiring Communities in Education
Project (DICEP)[4] which, as its name suggests, is committed to extending
this form of collaborative inquiry as a means both of improving the
quality of education and of increasing understanding of the conditions
that make this possible (Wells, in press-a; Wells, et al., 1994). Having a
group of colleagues with whom to discuss the work that is reported here
certainly helped us to understand its significance.

In an attempt to establish inquiry as the mode of learning and teaching in her classroom, Karen had used a number of non-standard topics
and a wide variety of approaches that, she hoped, would encourage student negotiation of the curriculum and student-developed questions that
would form the basis for both practical and theoretical investigations. In
order to stimulate her students' imaginations by connecting knowledge
with emotion through story (Egan, 1992), Karen provided students with
numerous "real life" examples of communities dedicated to knowledge
development, speaking of the focused efforts and intellectual challenges
of a team of researchers in a science lab, or the pleasures and the creativity of a group of writers developing a movie script. Much activity,
time, and effort was expended in encouraging students in the co-con-
struction of a unique and positive class identity, both intellectual and
affective.

Nevertheless, that spring, as Karen looked ahead to having many of
these students in her class the following year, her feeling was generally
one of having failed to engage them, either intellectually or affectively,
in anything like the community she had envisioned. Where she imagined
students and teacher collaboratively exploring a topic of fascination to

them, asking questions, building on each other's contributions in rich class discussions, arguing points with passion and conviction, yet with an ongoing awareness of and respect for the group as a whole, the majority of students routinely responded to anything they saw as related to school with resistance, suspicion, or—worst of all—shrugs of indifference.

Perhaps this negative emotion might have provided a place from which to start building a more positive class identity. But even here there were difficulties, as students seemed quite unable to see that there could be multiple points of view. From their perspective, the people they knew were clustered into three groups. One group consisted of the adults, doing their best to prevent you from doing as you wished. The second group, and at this age understandably the most important, was "friends." Your friends were always right, no matter what they said or did, as long as they didn't "dis" (disrespect) you. The third group consisted of "others"—your classmates, students in other classes, people who generally didn't affect you one way or the other. Between these three groups, there was no possibility of dialogue; there was only "them" and "us."

Some of Karen's students must have been exceptions to this overwhelmingly negative portrait and, indeed, a handful were. However, the overall tone of the classroom was created and maintained by those who, in a myriad of subtle and not-so-subtle ways, expressed the view, "School is work and work, by definition, cannot be fun. That which is not fun cannot be interesting."

In a continuing effort to find a way out of this dilemma, Karen looked back to the short term successes and enthusiasms expressed during a study of light and a media unit about animation. Hoping to build on these, she started the study of Canadian history with a project in which the processes of inquiry were linked with the hands-on product development that was the preferred mode of activity in the classroom. Students were given the opportunity to form work groups in order to research self-selected events and times of interest in Canadian history and then to create multi-media products through which they could share their understanding with others.

In adopting this approach, Karen wanted to investigate what she saw to be the untapped potential of history—when compared with science—for exploration through inquiry rather than through the textbook-based study which tends to be the norm. Equally important, she wanted her students to understand that studying history requires one to take into account the multiple, often conflicting, aims and perspectives that are involved in any event, historical or present day. Karen hoped that, as students grappled with the interpersonal moral dilemmas inherent in their topics, they would be increasingly aware of multiple perspectives within their own classroom community. Further, she structured the activities and assignments in the unit so that, as her students struggled to create products that represented their group's shared understandings of their history topics, they would come to recognize and deal with the conflict that is inherent in the development of any community, and to make the connection between the experiences and decisions of the unknown "others" of history, and their own local, day-to-day issues.

When the unit ended, students voted it a huge success, mainly because it had allowed the multimedia production they enjoyed, along with long periods of time spent in the company of friends. However, from the perspectives of both historical inquiry and community development, she felt that the unit work had been less than satisfactory.

THE MULTIPLE PERSPECTIVES INHERENT IN HISTORICAL EVENTS

It is generally agreed that for historical inquiry to be successful, it should enable those involved to "attain an understanding of past human events *from the inside*" (original emphasis, Phenix, 1964, p. 239). In part, this means going "behind" the objectivized official account to the subjective versions of the events as they were experienced by those who were actually involved (Smith, 1990). However, this also entails recognizing not only that there are different versions, but that every version is colored by the way in which the teller was positioned with respect to the event and by his or her interest in its outcomes. In other words, it involves recognizing that there can be no account that is immune to contestation from another perspective, no version that is ultimately "correct."

This can be a difficult concept to grasp, as we see in a comment made by U.S. Senator Diane Feinstein, during the Congressional debate about whether or not the Smithsonian Institute should be permitted to display the *Enola Gay*, the military plane that dropped the first atomic bomb, along with photographs of "ground zero" at Hiroshima and Nagasaki:

> In the days when I studied history, the text...was essentially a recitation of fact, leaving the reader to draw their own analysis. Now what you see is a writer's interpretation of fact, which is different. (*Testimony by Diane Feinstein*, 1994)

Given the difficulty for adults to understand the multiperspectival nature of history, it is not surprising that it is equally difficult, if not actually impossible, for adolescent students. Not only do they tend to see issues in categorical terms—as right or wrong—but they are not helped to develop an openness to the ambiguity of events by the kind of resources that are readily available to them. As we observed earlier, rather than containing narratives that present alternative accounts, which might encourage students to see history as interpretive and perspectival, the majority of texts accessible to students are written in a synoptic register which serves to foster the misconception that an objective truth can be arrived at through examination of a body of historical "facts" that are independent of the author's perspective. So, although students were provided with a wide range of both print and nonprint resources, as well as the opportunity, in many cases, to conduct interviews with people who could offer firsthand perspectives, most student-created products were essentially compilations of predigested information.

For example, one of the topics chosen was the development of the Canadian railway. Both in their final report and in the videotape that accompanied it, the three boys who chose this topic mirrored the chronologic documentaries that they perceived as good reportage in history. When Karen suggested that they might want to include the differing perspectives of, for example, the government officials who wanted the railway built in a timely manner, contrasted with that of the men who had to work under intolerable conditions in order to meet that commitment, her students claimed that such perspectives weren't history unless someone had been there at the time recording their every word, and that even then it would be the perspectives of only two individuals and not at all representative of the larger group.

The classroom community didn't fare much better than the historical inquiry. A collective commitment to making progress in understanding more about Canadian history and in representing that understanding for others could have been a unifying force. However, students actively resisted repeated efforts to persuade them to connect their event or time period with another group's, even when this was made part of the assessment of their work.

For students to develop an understanding of historical events and for them to participate in a community, they must be able to manage conflicting perspectives and, rather than dismissing them all as equally valid or invalid, they must be able to recognize that there are supportable and insupportable interpretations that can be made from each perspective. However, by ignoring or glossing over this inherent characteristic of historical inquiry, each group was able to maintain an isolated focus on their own work and to complete it with the least discomfort and the most fun possible.

And that is no doubt how it would have ended, had the class not become involved in an impromptu dramatization of the building of the Canadian railway, animated by David Booth (1994), a renowned educator and champion of educational drama.

BUILDING THE CANADIAN RAILWAY:
TRANSFORMING INFORMATION INTO UNDERSTANDING

Although Karen was delighted when David accepted her invitation to lead a drama lesson, it was not without some trepidation that she introduced him to the class. With their prior drama experiences being limited to scripted school theater productions on the one hand, and unstructured student "skits" on the other, it was neither surprising nor alarming that the students should have variously anticipated that drama would be "fun", "stupid," "babyish," or "boring." However, the repetition of comments such as "Can we wear costumes?" and "Can this guy make faces like Jim Carey?" and "Do we get to kill anybody?" was less reassuring. What would they make of it?

Karen need not have worried. After a few minutes' discussion with the class about the difficulties people had in traveling from one part of the country to another before Canada was formed in 1867, David announced that the morning's work was to be about "the building of the first railway across Canada." Then, after more discussion about the differences between today, when there are many ways of keeping in touch with relatives who have moved to different parts of the country, and the days before the railway, when there were no easy means of communication, he launched into the drama.

> So our work today then is about this railway and this Canada and this problem of loneliness. And so we're going to begin our work right now. So what I want you to do is take a moment to think about the problem of this railway, getting it built. Now if we were people living in Ontario and we were government officials talking about why we need a railway—at this big conference we're having today—what might be some of the reasons we might say why we have to push through the railway?
>
> Just stand (to a group of boys). We'll be government officials. I'll call you "sir," all right? Sir, you can speak first.

From now on, the information David elicits from them will no longer be produced in the familiar mode of the "recitation script" (Tharp & Gallimore, 1988), but given strategically, "in role," as they begin to take on the stance and motivation of the character they have been assigned. This is not easy, in part because the experience is new to them, and in part because the relevant historical information they can draw on is patchy and not always accurate. However, David makes the most of every student's attempt and builds it into the fabric of the developing drama, simultaneously using it to help the students to recognize the multiple perspectives involved.

For example, one student, Paul, is a laborer asking for money to be sent back to his family in Korea. David, in the role of a local manager, responds:

David: You're not a citizen. You're a worker. And you'll get your money when your job is done, and we'll ship you back. But nothing is shipped back. We can't ship money back on boats! Half of you would go back. We can't do it.

Paul: Well...

David: You knew this when you came.

Paul: Pardon me?

David: You knew this when you came.

Paul: No, I didn't.

David: Yes, well you signed the paper right here. Can you not read?

Paul: No, I can't.

David: Then you should have had someone read it to you.

Then, stepping out of role, David makes the point explicit by asking the class, "What did you find out about a worker just then?" When a student offers that many were illiterate, he asks why so many would sign contracts they couldn't read, then leave their homes and families to cross an ocean to do dangerous work. The students begin by offering vague answers:

Indra: Because their families needed support. To support their families.

David: Why was their family needing support? Why all of a sudden did their family need support? What was going on in 1860?

Steve: 'Cause there was no work in Asia.

David: Why was there no work in Asia? People need farms in Asia. People need clothes. What are you talking about?

Then follows an extended dialogue in which students offer war, depression, disease, discrimination, hostile takeovers, natural disasters, nuclear meltdowns, and famine as explanations. After each offering, David acknowledges the thinking, gives examples of present-day instances of the problem, and encourages students to make personal connections by imagining something that might impoverish their families in the same way that the Asians were impoverished in 1860.

Then, having gotten the class involved, David divides them into work teams of four and charges each team with the task of preparing a report of problems encountered and the ways in which they had been solved. A little while later, he convenes a managerial meeting and calls on one member of each group to present a report. As the meeting progresses, the existence of a conflict begins to emerge between the managers who are charged with the responsibility of getting the railway built and the Chinese laborers whose lives are all too often being sacrificed as part of the managers' solutions. Here is how the theme emerged. Scott is one of the managers, giving his report to David, the "big boss":

> *Scott:* There was a few deaths when the liquid nitrogen was put into the Rocky Mountains.
>
> *David:* Here's why that's very bad. The minute people hear of deaths, they will not come. Now we've had a lot of trouble with the Americans taking our workers because in San Francisco they're building the very same railway. I want Canada to have it first. They've been taking the immigrants and offering them more money. We haven't got the money. We can't do it. So when they hear of deaths and that hits the newspapers... How did you keep it out of the newspapers?
>
> *Scott:* We didn't say anything about it. We did Morse code to China to tell their families that there was a tragedy.
>
> *David:* Where did you bury the bodies so that nobody would know?
>
> *Scott:* We buried it in the cemetery with another person.
>
> *David:* (*speaking as "teacher/producer"*) Listen carefully as two people talk about having heard in the night bodies being carried away.
> (*switching to the role of "Railway Official," he turns to another student*) What did you hear?
>
> *Bryan:* Nothing. (*some students laugh*)
>
> *David:* (*as teacher*) Why might he say "nothing" to start with?
>
> *Stuart:* He wants to, not to get in trouble or anything.
>
> *David:* Excellent. We'll go on.
> (*as "Official"*) You heard what I heard. We were both awakened. The tents have thin walls. You heard what I heard. When you say you heard nothing you betray your country and its people. You heard what I heard. They took away bodies. And you lie to me and I—(*someone whispers "liar"*).
>
> You know exactly what they took away. They took away dead people. They took away dead people without a burial, which means their spirits wander the earth. You know that and I know that and your family knows that. Why have you lied to me?
>
> *Bryan:* So that I won't get in trouble.
>
> *David:* The spirits that wander in anguish for the dead have not been in trouble? You will come with me to the boss, and we will tell the boss what happened, won't we?
>
> *Bryan:* Yes.
>
> *David:* Will you do it?
>
> *Bryan:* Yes.

Bryan's agreement to stand in support of his fellow laborers, to speak on behalf of the men carried away in the night, marked the beginning of a new phase in the drama.

ENRICHING HISTORICAL UNDERSTANDING: EMPATHY LEADS TO MORAL AWARENESS

Up to this point, students have been able to assume a role that is in a perspective other than their own and to defend it intellectually. However, for them to grow in historical understanding—and equally in the awareness of self that is necessary for developing community—they still need to recognize that there are multiple perspectives and that these perspectives are affective, as well as intellectual. They need, in other words, to develop empathy.

In history, empathy is defined as: "Learning to attribute causal explanations to human motivation and intention. The burden is on evidence and logical argument while simultaneously considering values and beliefs, both past and present" (Myers, 1994). By challenging students to take "action" in their roles, David introduced a new dimension into the drama. Now, not only were they providing information "in role," but some of them were being pushed to assume the responsibilities that their roles entailed and, as a result, finding themselves called upon to make moral decisions.

As the Director's meeting progresses, the issue of laborers being killed through accidents of various kinds occurs with increasing frequency. Eventually, in his role as one of the managers, Mike asks to speak to the meeting:

> *Mike:*   Our group is strongly opposed to the railroad because we feel there's too much risk to human life. We don't feel it's worth that risk.

This, of course, evokes strong counter-arguments from other members of the Board, including the Director. But, a few minutes later, David stops the drama for a moment to review what has just happened.

> *David:*   It took great courage saying he was worried about too many deaths. [But] I thought the attack by your group here, saying "Listen, there's been death before and there'll be death later" was very powerful. It was one of the most powerful things I've heard in drama in a long time.

Then, in order to explore this conflict further, David forms a line consisting of Mike, a couple of other managers who, he says, will support Mike, and four students to whom he assigns the role of Chinese laborers. He suggests that they rebel by refusing to build their part of the railway. David then warns the rest of the class, "If they don't get done, you don't get your bonuses and your money," and he lines them up in opposition to the small group. It's suggested by one of the latter that those who don't want to work be sent back to China, but another counters that they might spread word of the danger, making it difficult for Canada to find more immigrant labor. One of the managers offers to hire the workers for his team so they won't have to be sent back to China, but this doesn't solve the problem of a section of the railway not getting built.

Then, in a move that surprises everyone, the four laborers turn their backs on the bosses who have quit their jobs in order to save them, and plead for the opportunity to take their places. The managers discuss this, worrying over the possibility that the workers, because they aren't college graduates and aren't knowledgeable about finances, may still inadvertently prevent the completion of the railroad and thus the paying of the bonuses. Nevertheless, they decide to allow the workers the opportunity, and they collectively turn on the former bosses, claiming that Mike and his group have betrayed them, stopping them from achieving success and earning their bonuses. Neil wants them blackballed from working. Cody thinks they should have to pay extra if they ever want to ride the train. A couple want them executed.

However, Michelle, one of the workers turned bosses, makes the point that no reparation will compensate: "But it's too late. All of my family members' lives are dead." David reinforces:

> So they're saying, they're saying "It's too late." This is very powerful work. Hold it a moment. Listen to how powerful their work is. They're saying, "It's too late." No matter how they change. No matter what they refuse. You can execute them, but then their families have nobody to support them. See it's so easy to be simple. It's so better to be complex as she's saying. No matter how hard they now try. You can't forgive them, can you? That's very powerful work, women. That's very powerful. We've got the kids here, all goosey, want to say, "Let's just kill people." And you are saying, "When people are killed, no one forgives." That's what they're saying. That's deep work.

At this point, Paul, a manager, reiterates Mike's earlier point: "We need to realize how many deaths are occurring." David, back in role, challenges him to take a stand rather than equivocate:

David: Hold it! Are you saying the Board's at fault?

Paul: I'm not saying the Board's at fault.

David: Just a minute. You're one of the Board. Hold it! This means you four guys have done something here. You have actually forced this Board, one Board member. What did you just say? Repeat what you just said.

Paul: That we need to realize how many deaths are becoming.

David: Hold it. Hold it. *(said in response to loud disapproval from others in the class)* Very brave. You see what you [the class] have to understand is not the facetious response you're giving, but what he's actually said. What he's done is he's said that he has heard those men's voices.

Cody: And he's put down the Board.

Paul is rejected by the other managers, accused of putting down the Board by being a traitor. He tries to convince them by appealing to their interest in building their workforce:

Paul: We're supposed to be a free country where we let people from all over the world come to our country. If we don't care about other immigrants who come here to work and get killed. If we just say "Who cares? They're not from our country," people are not going to want to come here.

David takes a hard line with Glen who, throughout Paul's speech has been muttering that we should kill them all. Notice that in the face of Glen's challenge, Paul changes his explanation from a support of self-interests to a statement of morality, although it is morality defined externally by others' perceptions of us.

David: Okay. Stand up and answer him. You're meeting his challenge. Go ahead. *(Glen is silent)* He challenged you.
(to Paul) Want to repeat the challenge?

Paul: I say that we're a free country and we let immigrants from all over the world come, and I'm saying that if we don't care, if they die and we don't care, people will think we're racist and that we don't care about any immigrants at all.

David: Well? Has he got a point?

Glen: Yeah

David: He's got a point.

In spite of Paul's protestations, the Board decides that the railroad must be built. David tells them it's the first time in a long time that he has been in a situation where the heroes lose, and he turns to one of the managers to ask if he has any second thoughts:

David: Jeff has said again and again, "We've got to get this railway built."
          I think Jeff that you hold the responsibility on your shoulder
          today for these guys who have lost their jobs, for the death of all
          their family and relatives, for the careless work that these guys did
          and blamed others. What are you going to tell yourself, Jeff? You
          can say it had to get built.

Paul: We should have taken more time to make the railway safer.

David: You've got to somehow persuade the people in your class because
          right now they voted against you. So when I leave this school, I
          leave thinking that in this school, in the building of the railway,
          what didn't matter were the lives of people. That's the message
          you gave me.

Paul: That's what I'm saying.

David: And I'm saying to you, Phillip, are you the only one saying it? Jeff
          isn't saying it. Are you, Jeff?

Cody: Now I feel guilty.

David: You do? Then we've reached a very important point in this
          drama. Good work.

REFLECTIONS

The anxiety that had preceded the drama was succeeded by elation—for
the students as well as the teacher—after it had ended. There was no
doubt in anyone's mind that something incredible had just taken place
among the 37 students working for just two hours, without props or
advance preparation, in their school's large, empty, community-use
room. This feeling was confirmed by David in his parting remark: "In
my life of doing drama, this last two hours was absolutely the most powerfully complex work I've ever seen."

Given the students' prior knowledge of the development of the railway, mostly based on a Heritage Canada television commercial which
they recount as, "They sent this guy into the tunnel and then it blew up
and they thought he was dead, and then he came back alive," it's difficult to imagine how the work could possibly have been complex. However, building historical understanding is not simply a matter of piecing
together information about the chronology of events; it also requires an
immersion in the lives of those who were involved and an awareness of
the factors that impacted on their decisions:

> An event may be inwardly understood only as an outcome of deliberate
> human decision. Many factors enter into the outcome, in that each deci-
> sion concerns what to do given certain material and social circumstances,
> personal goals, and moral principles. The reconstruction of the past there-
> fore requires a considerable fund of knowledge. (Phenix, 1964, p. 241)

Throughout the drama students had been forced to think and respond in role in order to meet David's forceful demands; as chairman of the Board of Directors for the railway, he had pulled out all the stops. He was, as he said himself, "a very mean person," an exacting taskmaster who had no time for excuses or insurmountable difficulties. In this he completely upset the students' views of how they would be treated by him, and how they should respond. In journal entries written immediately following the drama, this point was made again and again:

> Mr. Booth was nothing like what I was expecting.... He made me think, and he did this all by playing an actor and setting the scene for us. *(John)*

> Mr. Booth is a good actor. I could never really tell when he was acting and when he was serious—that's how good an actor he is. *(Neil)*

> At some points he sounded pretty scary. You could never tell if he was acting or not. *(Paul)*

> When I talked back to him he really got mad at me. But I know he was pretending (I think!) *(Indra)*

For many of the students, the chance to be in role and to meet the challenges of that role supported them as they reached for abilities and language they didn't know they possessed. Scott explains:

> When Mr. Booth was talking to Richard I was beginning to get really worried because I didn't really know what to say that he wouldn't chew up and spit out. All my ideas came to me when Mr. Booth pointed at me. When I was done talking I knew that it was going to be a good morning because he didn't chew up what I had said.

As Scott and the others experienced the success of defending their given perspective as railway managers responsible for getting the lines built quickly and cost effectively, they were able to meet another criterion of historical inquiry, that of supporting their views with evidence and logical argument. This was evident when David, through a student, introduced the perspective that "there's too much risk to human life." Jeff, one of the students who had originally studied the railway for his small group history project, was quick to respond:

> *Jeff:* When the riot was held by Louis Riel. When it finally arrived to Ottawa, Cornelius Van Horne, the director of the railway, thought that it would be the chance to get the railway finally and completely built by sending troops by train to [inaudible], the nearest railway, to stop the Louis Riel riot. And that is exactly what happened, and although there was a break in the line and it

took ten days for them to get there and it stopped the country, which could have resulted in many more deaths than there would have been in the railway.

David: I must say that in hiring our next level of management, someone with that knowledge will be applicable. Do apply for that position because that knowledge…

(*to Mike*) You're talking a few deaths of people who aren't even Canadians. He's telling you how our army had to stop a riot that could have caused many more deaths. You hear that? This is wisdom. This is understanding what Canada really is.

Scott: (*to Mike*) Without the railway; yes, a few people will die and it's their fault for rustling with the dynamite, and how are you going to get supplies from Nova Scotia say into Ontario? Are you gonna walk them over there, or do you personally want to do that? It's saving us a lot of money and a lot of time and we don't even have the railway completed.

These students were among the most confident in class. But they were not the only ones who were enabled "to go beyond themselves" (Vygotsky, 1987) under David's skillful leadership. Take Michelle, for example, the worker-turned-manager who so forcefully brought home the point that no reparation can compensate for family members who have been killed. In everyday life, Michelle believes that the best defense is a good offense. She has spent most of her school life in one special education class or another, for various language and behavioral difficulties. Michelle doesn't let anyone, except maybe her best friend Sandra, anywhere near her. She doesn't often have the language to express it, but if she did, Michelle's philosophy of life would have some connection to "survival of the fittest" or "get the other guy before he has a chance to get you."

And yet now, in this drama, Michelle can step inside the skin of a worker who has lost those "he" loved to the railway, and who understands that revenge isn't going to change the outcome or erase the wound. The drama has allowed Michelle to behave differently, and to try on other possible responses to her life. Knowledge building can thus be seen, in its affective capacity, to be identity forming (Penuel & Wertsch, 1995). Further, the drama has given Michelle, a student labeled as "language disordered," a vehicle through which she can express these new possibilities.

Here is Michelle's journal entry about the drama:

I had fun this morning with David Booth. It was funny when he started to yell at the group because I didn't know a cool man like him could be so mean in action, and I like the part when me, Sandra, Natalie, we got even with the bosses. It was fun because I liked it. We got to have fun.

Those of us who don't have Michelle's language difficulties can only try to imagine what it must be like to repeatedly attempt communication and not be heard. But in this drama, Michelle was heard, and by one of the opposition.

However, the breakthrough was not only individual students finding the courage to speak out in front of the whole class and, in some cases, to adopt a stance that they knew would be unpopular. One of the conditions both of community development and of knowledge building is that there be progress towards a collective goal. In the drama, the goal was clearly stated as "Can this class build the railway across Canada?... Can this class at this school get this railway built?," and it was taken seriously by students, even after the event, as they mourned the fact that they "didn't get to solve the railway problem" (Stuart). Not only was this one of the first times in the year that students collectively focused on a goal but, even more noteworthy, they justified their behavior, both intellectually and affectively, in terms of the roles they were required to play, rather than as simply who they were. In other words, for the first time, students were able to conceive of the possibility that they could be different. The drama provided a safety net for testing out these possibilities, and the collective goal meant that there was community support for their efforts. Jeff comments on this:

> I liked...how the class had different opinions about everything. And what I never saw before was how the people took a stand for what they believed like Paul, the four bosses, the four workers, Cody, Neil, and others.

As Jeff recognized, there was a clear sense throughout the drama that students were both cognitively and affectively engaged. This was evident in the diversity of participation, and in the comments of the many students whose journal reflections after the event showed their ongoing interest in the underlying causes and principles of the conflict. Gerald is one of several that discuss content:

> I think that we should have built the railway even if it's the cost of some lives. It's not that I don't care but the railroad has saved more lives than it has taken. I still think that they should take the convicts and tell them if they want to work off the years in prison instead, then their sentence will be shorter. Even if police would have to guard the railway it wouldn't be that hard because instead of hiring and paying workers, you could pay Mounties.

Even more frequent were the entries that made clear how feelings had been engaged:

Close to the end of the role-play, Mr. Booth made me feel guilty about not caring if immigrants die. *(Neil)*

Our workers turned on us 'cause of the deaths we caused. But I thought we were saving their lives. *(Mike)*

John tells us in his journal:

I actually found myself being a slave owner and how he made me think in the way I have never thought. I really became that person and I really felt like an actor. Mr. Booth was right about doing mean things and saying mean things on the outside but in the inside I was thinking how can I say this? or what am I saying?

For some students, like John, the extent to which they had difficulty in justifying their actions was more than a little disconcerting. Perhaps for the first time they began to understand that, throughout history, people have been faced by moral dilemmas and have had to live with the consequences of their decisions.

HIROSHIMA: THE AFTERMATH

As we have suggested, the Canadian railway drama was one of those experiences that, in John Dewey's words, "live fruitfully and creatively in future experiences" (1938, p. 28). Drawing on what she learned from it, Karen has attempted to incorporate the power of multiple perspectives through story and drama into all subsequent work in history. The students too were changed. They started to really listen to each other and to grapple with making sense of perspective and value in history. This also had some impact on relationships within the classroom community. Nevertheless, when the going got tough, their tried and true methods of absolving themselves of responsibility, or even of empathy, still tended to come to the fore—at least initially.

This took various forms, from claims that, since there were so many perspectives and, therefore, so many possible interpretations, everyone should just believe whatever they wanted, to the argument that if they weren't involved as actual participants, it's got nothing to do with them. For example:

I think there's no right or wrong because there's two sides to the story, so how're you supposed to say who's right or wrong.... They should just have both sides of the story and you believe what you want to believe. *(Claire)*

Both these views were expressed following role-play around the *Enola Gay* issue that was referred to previously. Having heard the perspectives of the Smithsonian curator who wanted to mount the exhibit, a historian, a journalist, an American veteran pilot, and a Japanese mother whose child was born horribly deformed—all presented, in role, by members of the classroom community—the question under discussion was whether it was possible to decide who was right and who was wrong. In an effort to help students to move from their either/or, categorical thinking, Gordon suggested in the following dialogue:

> *Gordon:* The whole question of saying whether people are guilty or innocent is so simple minded isn't it? It's obvious that the pilot dropping the bomb on Hiroshima was "innocent," because he was following orders.... But as a thinking human being he was also, in some sense, "guilty" because he did actually do it, whether or not he was ordered to. He can't say, "Not guilty. I was ordered to do it, and I'll do whatever I'm ordered." You wouldn't do that, would you? Doing what you were ordered whether it was right or wrong? So we're all partly guilty, in a sense, and we're all partly innocent.
>
> *Claire:* Except we're not American in real life.
> *Karen:* So we're guilt free?
> *Claire:* Yup. Well, we are. Us, in this classroom.

Paradoxically, the most negative and, simultaneously, the most heartening comment came in one student's argument that the dramas, the conversations and, by extension, all of history was useless:

> *Alec:* There's no point. What's the point of telling stories? People are dead now. There's no point in telling stories.

The negative import of this comment is apparent. What cannot be shared in print, however, is the frustration in Alec's voice—a frustration at the recognition that the energy and commitment such as had not often been seen in this classroom before still led to no ultimate conclusion. Although depressing if taken at face value, we nevertheless see Alec's contribution as heartening because, compared with the class's starting point, it represents a profoundly felt conflict that can, if explored further, provide the basis for future growth. Like Michelle and John in the railway drama, Alec and others are perhaps beginning to recognize that, in the end, the stories of real people's lives are both the subject matter of historical inquiry and its *raison d'être*.

GETTING A GRIP ON KNOWLEDGE

As we stated at the beginning of this chapter, students typically embark on the study of history with a "schooled" view of knowledge—a view that is strongly reinforced by most textbooks and many teachers. According to this view, knowledge is fixed, authoritative, and immutable, and the task of students is to acquire and memorize it in order to be able to reproduce it on demand. To suggest to them, by contrast, that all knowledge is tentative and temporary, always open to correction and improvement, is often very disturbing. And to further suggest, as in the case of history, that there can be no final decision between alternative perspectives is doubly disconcerting.

The difficulty is that when you push students to recognize multiple perspectives, you're not only working against their training to seek correct answers in school, but are often, it seems, forcing them into a hopeless postmodernist view that simultaneously and rather paradoxically leaves them claiming that the facts do exist, but if we can't know them for sure, everything is just a matter of opinion.

However, the roots of the problem go much deeper, we would argue, and are to be found in the dominant conceptualization of knowledge that is pervasive in all subjects, as these are taught in schools. In our view, this conception is misguided in two important respects. First, it privileges theoretical knowledge over the kinds of knowledge that are involved in practical and aesthetic activities (Smagorinsky, 1995), and that provide the foundation on which theoretical knowledge is built. And second, it places more emphasis on knowledge as a collection of autonomous objects—facts, generalizations, and theories—than on the activity of knowing, in which these objects are collaboratively constructed and then used as tools to mediate further knowing in action (Wells, in press-a).

As we argue elsewhere, the current emphasis in education on the acquisition of knowledge objects as a form of individual intellectual capital (Freire, 1970) flies in the face of the way in which human knowing has developed, in all cultures, over many millennia; in the long term, it will probably be recognized for the aberration that it is—one of the short-lived manifestations of theoretical knowing as applied in industrial mass production. But, in the short term, it is this emphasis on knowledge objects, rather than on the activity of knowing, that is largely responsible for the conceptualization of education in terms of knowledge delivery and evaluation and for the prevalence of the "recitation script" as the means through which these objectives are achieved (Wells, in press-c).

For those brought up to accept the (false) certainty of authoritative knowledge that is implicit in the recitation script, the idea that there may be alternative perspectives and interpretations, each valid in its own terms, is initially very disturbing. It seems to leave no alternative to the "hopeless relativism" of postmodernism—a first glimpse of which was probably the basis of Alec's previous despairing comment. However, when the emphasis is placed, instead, on knowledge building as an active process in which both students and teachers are engaged together, and on individual understanding as constructed and continuously transformed in this process, learning-and-teaching becomes an ongoing, exhilarating dialogue in which knowledge is created and recreated "in the discourse between people doing things together" (Franklin, 1996). For, as Bereiter (1994) proposes, although there can be no ultimate certainty, in any community that is genuinely committed to collaborative knowledge building, one can engage in "progressive discourse" that, through the sharing, questioning, and revising of opinions, leads to "a new understanding that everyone involved agrees is superior to their own previous understanding" (p. 6). It is this sort of progressive discourse that, as members of DICEP, we are trying to achieve in our classroom communities of inquiry.

CONCLUSION: A ROLE FOR DRAMA IN INQUIRY

In the paper referred to above, Bereiter (1994) was describing knowledge building in science and it was theoretical knowing with which he was predominantly concerned. However, as we suggested earlier, theoretical knowing is only the latest to emerge of a range of modes of knowing that have developed sequentially over the course of human history, each embedded in different kinds of joint activity and mediated by different kinds of artifact (Wartofsky, 1979). Furthermore, although not in any simple form of recapitulation—since today's children are growing up in a culture that makes use of all the modes of knowing—there are strong grounds for arguing that each individual goes through essentially the same developmental sequence in mastering the modes of knowing and appropriating their associated values, practices, and artifacts (Egan, 1997).

In science, the value of starting with practical activities that recruit the instrumental, procedural, and substantive modes of knowing involved in experimentation and observation is well established (Driver, 1983; Gallas, 1995). Such "hands-on" activity provides a solid experiential basis on which to begin to engage in theoretical knowing, with its more abstract, synoptic explanations and equations. However, we would argue that the same principle applies in all subject areas and, as far as possible, with all ages:

> There should, wherever possible, be opportunities for gaining first-hand, practical experience of tackling problems in the relevant domain so that there will be a perceived need for the theoretical constructs that provide a principled basis for understanding those problems and making solutions to them. By the same token, since theoretical knowing should not be treated as an end in itself, there should also be opportunities to put the knowledge constructed to use in some situation of significance to the students so that, through bringing it to bear on some further problem, they may deepen their understanding. (Wells, in press-b)

As a general principle for an inquiry-oriented approach to the curriculum, this is fine. But what might it look like when translated into practice in a 7th- and 8th-grade unit on Canadian history? This was the starting point for the work that we have described in this chapter, where Karen's invitation to her students to create "multimedia products" as the outcome of their investigations was the first attempt to realize this principle in practice. However, as we discovered, while the students certainly found the work interesting and "fun," it did not lead to the engagement in historical knowledge building that had been our goal; the practical problems that the students found so engrossing did not give rise to the "perceived need for theoretical constructs" which, we argued, is the essential starting point for theoretical knowledge building.

What the Canadian railway drama made clear to us that the essential basis for this sort of knowledge building in history is not of this practical kind. Rather, it is activities that involve the aesthetic mode of knowing—activities that, through empathy and imagination, enable students to "attain an understanding of past human events from the inside," and to feel the conflict of perspectives and values that was inherent in the decisions and actions that brought about what are now seen simply as historical facts. This was the mode of knowing that was central to David Booth's role-playing activity and it was the dawning of this aesthetic mode of understanding that was expressed, or at least hinted at, in the journal entries that many students wrote after participating in it. What is more, as a result of this experience, the discussion that followed the *Enola Gay* role-playing activity gave rise to problems that really did generate a perceived need to grapple with some of the more difficult abstract issues that are at the heart of theoretical knowing in history.

The "spiral of knowing," shown in Figure 3.1, is one attempt to represent diagrammatically the relationships between inquiry, modes of

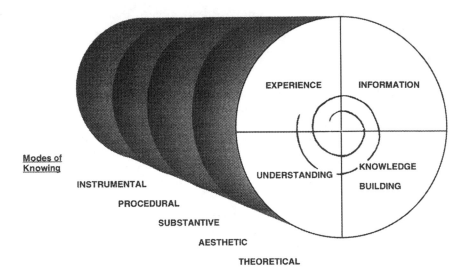

FIGURE 3.1.   The Spiral of Knowing.

knowing, and curricular activities that have been sketched in the preceding paragraphs. In terms of that diagram, the role-play activities discussed in this chapter can be situated in the second circle, that of aesthetic knowing, although, as we have seen, they both move into the theoretical mode and draw upon the earlier-to-emerge modes of knowing that are involved in the practical activities that were required in role. But it was when we looked at the railway drama in terms of the four quadrants in the diagram that we came to a full understanding of its significance.

Each student embarked on the railway building task with personal experience that was potentially relevant to the role that he or she would be asked to play. Each also had encountered at least some information—whether earlier in the unit or at some other time—that might contribute to the activity. What David's crafting of the drama did was to enable each student to bring his or her experience and information into the "theater" of knowledge building and, by engaging the students in the collaborative attempt to solve the problem of getting the railway built—despite the multiple and conflicting perspectives—to advance their individual understandings through the imaginative and empathetic efforts involved in using that experience and information to feel, act, and speak in ways appropriate to their different roles.

For the authors of this chapter, the attempt to describe and interpret the historical events through which the unit on Canadian history was enacted has also been an occasion of collaborative knowledge building. At the start of the unit, neither of us had recognized the potential of role-play for enabling adolescent students to enter into the discipline of history. But by reviewing the videotape of the railway drama, transcribing it, and selecting episodes for further analysis, then writing and discussing interpretations of them, each of us increased our understanding. And, as is the intention of conducting collaborative action research, the understandings gained through our inquiry are also informing our practice.

Although the railway did not get built (at least not as a result of our enactment of the events) and although Karen's two years with that group of students also ended without the resolution for which she had hoped, the drama was an important experience for all involved and one that we are convinced will live on fruitfully in the lives of each of us. As David Booth has written of role-play:

> The right choice and management of situations, contexts and stories relating to the environment…can provide young people with very authentic experiences of what it would be like to be in surroundings which might be far removed in time and place from their own. Drama deals with concrete and specific contexts—particular people in a particular relationship in a particular place at a particular time. (1994, pp. 48–49)

For Karen's students, role-playing the building of the Canadian railway enabled them to know this essential truth: The "facts" of history are always and inevitably rooted in such particular moments and relationships. And in this way it gave them an unforgettable way to understanding "past human events *from the inside.*"

NOTES

[1] These extracts are taken from Hux and Jarman (1987).

[2] See Martin (1989, 1993) for a much fuller treatment of the language of history and other textbooks.

[3] Of course, part of the trouble is that such textbooks are also vetted by government organizations for their "political correctness"; not surprisingly, they contain little interpretation and what there is is presented as nondisputable fact.

[4] DICEP is a collaborative action research group made up of school-based and university-based educators. Supported by a grant from the Spencer Foundation, the project has as its goal to promote an inquiry-oriented approach to learning and teaching and to seek to understand and improve the role of discourse in this process. Reports of some of the inquiries carried out by the group can be found at the project's homepage on the Internet at http://www.oise.utoronto.ca/~ctd/DICEP/

REFERENCES

Bereiter, C. (1994). Implications of postmodernism for science, or, science as progressive discourse. *Educational Psychologist, 29*(1), 3–12.

Booth, D. (1994). *Story drama.* Toronto: Pembroke.

Dewey, J. (1938). *Experience and education.* New York: Collier Macmillan.

Driver, R. (1983). *The pupil as scientist?* Milton Keynes, UK: Open University Press.

Egan, K. (1992). *Imagination in teaching and learning: The middle school years.* Chicago: University of Chicago Press.

Egan, K. (1997). *The educated mind.* Chicago: University of Chicago Press.

Franklin, U. (1996, May). Introduction. In U. Franklin (Chair), *Towards an ecology of knowledge.* Symposium conducted at the University of Toronto, Ontario, Canada.

Freire, P. (1970). *Pedagogy of the oppressed.* New York: Herder and Herder.

Gallas, K. (1995). *Talking their way into science: Hearing children's questions and theories, responding with curricula.* New York: Teachers College Press.

Hume, K. (1998). *Co-researching with students: Exploring the value of class discussions* [On-line]. Available: http://www.oise.utoronto.ca/~ctd/networks

Hux, A., & Jarman, F. (1987). *Canada: A growing concern.* Markham, Ontario, Canada: Globe/Modern Curriculum Press.

Martin, J. R. (1989). *Factual writing: Exploring and challenging social reality.* Oxford, England: Oxford University Press.

Martin, J. R. (1993). A contextual theory of language. In B. Cope & M. Kalantzis (Eds.), *The powers of literacy: A genre approach to teaching writing* (pp. 116–136). Pittsburgh, PA: University of Pittsburgh Press.

Myers, J. S. (1994). *Background to history essentials* and *Explanation and inquiry in history and beyond.* Papers presented at the Ontario Institute for Studies in Education's Second Annual Showcase of Research and Teaching, University of Toronto, Ontario, Canada.

Penuel, W., & Wertsch, J. V. (1995). Vygotsky and identity formation: A sociocultural approach. *Educational Psychologist, 30*(2), 83–92.

Phenix, P. (1964). *Realms of meaning.* New York: McGraw Hill.

Senate Testimony, 103d Cong., 2d Sess., Cong. Rec. S12968 (1994) (testimony of Diane Feinstein).

Smagorinsky, P. (1995). Constructing meaning in the disciplines: Reconceptualizing writing across the curriculum as composing across the curriculum. *American Journal of Education, 103*, 160–184.

Smith, D. E. (1990). *The conceptual practices of power: A feminist sociology of knowledge.* Toronto: University of Toronto Press.

Tharp, R., & Gallimore, R. (1988). *Rousing minds to life.* New York: Cambridge University Press.

Vygotsky, L. S. (1987). Thinking and speech. In R. W. Rieber & A. S. Carton (Eds.), *The collected works of L.S. Vygotsky, vol. 1: Problems of general psychology* (pp. 39–285). New York: Plenum.

Wartofsky, M. (1979). *Models, representation and scientific understanding.* Boston: Reidel.

Wells, G. (1998). Some questions about direct instruction: Why? to whom? how? and when? *Language Arts, 76*(1), 27–35.

Wells, G. (in press-a). *Dialogic inquiry: Towards a sociocultural practice and theory of education.* Cambridge, England: Cambridge University Press.

Wells, G. (in press-b). Dialogic inquiry in the classroom: Building on the legacy of Vygotsky. In C. Lee & P. Smagorinsky (Eds.), *Vygotskian perspectives on literacy research.* New York: Cambridge University Press.

Wells, G., Bernard, L., Gianotti, M. A., Keating, C., Maher, A., Maher, C., Moscoe, T., Orzechowska, E., Smieja, A., & Swartz, L. (1994). *Changing schools from within: Creating communities of inquiry.* Toronto: OISE Press; Portsmouth, NH: Heinemann.

part II

Conflict Resolution

O ften the goal of educational drama is to acquaint students with moral dilemmas that inhere in all social groups, but its side effect may well be to improve the interpersonal proficiency of the participants themselves. Because educational drama is, by its nature, a social medium, it usually improves the social health of its participants, even if the primary goal is to introduce moral dilemmas of a larger society or to help them master subject matter. Unlike most educational dramas, however, the dramas presented in the following two chapters have as their primary goal the improvement of conflict-resolution proficiency. Drama can show students an alternative to "fight or flight," namely, "collaboration through communication."

Conflict is the center of any drama, and, in fact, defines the genre. Unfortunately, conflict also characterizes far too much of the school and the personal lives of a great many students. Teachers, administrators, and community leaders are looking for ways to help these young persons learn better ways of resolving their conflicts, and in Part II of this book we present two detailed examples (Chapters 4 and 5), as well as a survey (Chapter 6) of quasi-experimental studies of drama's effect on attitudes, behavior, and moral reasoning.

Wolf and Heath show the problems that can arise when teenagers negotiate development of a drama for performance. These problems challenge them to develop conflict-resolution strategies in order for them to proceed with the making of the play. The researchers analyze two programs for youth who live in high-risk areas of their major metropolitan communities. The teenagers bring to the situation a genuine desire to create and perform plays, but minimal interpersonal skills to enable them to negotiate their individual visions. In the process of creating a play, they learn a great deal about how to negotiate and cooperate.

The drama that Giffin and Yaffe describe is quite different. The leader's goal is to teach conflict management directly, showing 2nd-grade students—through the course of the drama and in reflection sessions after the drama—techniques for listening actively and for dealing with anger. The leader, with the help of a teacher in role, sets up and directs all of the sessions, building identification with the characters and emotional investment in the conflicts that the teacher-in-role initiates.

In Chapter 6, I review studies of educational drama, concluding that it has a positive effect on the outlooks of student, particularly on self-esteem and on the attitudes toward oneself. Several studies show drama to be particularly effective in improving social behavior as well as attitudes, especially among emotionally disturbed or learning-disabled young persons. Studies of the effect on moral reasoning are not as conclusive, in part because of methodological shortcomings and the lack of comparable measuring instruments among the studies.

chapter 4

When Resolution Comes in Stages: How Drama Makes Good Use of Conflict*

Jennifer Lynn Wolf

Shirley Brice Heath
Stanford University

> The depths of human acting...are about survival.
> Victor Turner

I t is hard to imagine any conversation among adults these days when the topic of *youth* does not soon provoke a companion focus on *conflict*. Adults will quickly recite ways that young people fight with their parents, express violence in their own group relationships, and threaten the safety of communities. Media polls routinely report that youngsters themselves say they fear conflict and violence and want places of safety.

These views paint conflict as entirely negative; yet positive views of conflict now figure centrally in theories of development for the young (Shantz & Hartup, 1992), and cognitive psychologists point out how conflict is a central factor in developmental change and how dissonance and discord heighten learning (Brown & Campione, 1990). What is it

---

*Data for this chapter are drawn from two multiyear studies of the lives of young people in community youth organizations, including those centered around drama. Directors of these projects have been Heath and Milbrey W. McLaughlin. Senior research associates include Wolf, in addition to Kim Bailey, Ali Callicoatte, Merita Irby, Juliet Langman, and Shelby Wolf. Publications that summarize the larger context for the data used in this chapter include Heath and McLaughlin (1993), McLaughlin, Irby, and Langman (1994), and Heath (1993, 1995).

then about conflict that makes it such a two-headed coin—negative and feared, yet positive and fundamental? And how does "staging" management of conflict enable young people to learn experiential and text interpretation strategies, oral and written language skills, planning and time management, and technical and interpersonal knowledge?

This chapter builds from a comparative framing of conflict resolution and drama. Frequently introduced in both schools and community youth-based organizations in the 1990s, both of these role-playing frameworks offer youth the opportunity to step out of their designations as "just kids" into roles that society usually reserves for adults. Moreover, both of these frameworks enable young people to achieve, not just as individuals, but as collaborative group members with a quasi-professional identity. Not surprisingly, conflict-resolution steps and dramatic creation stages parallel each other, and both stress highly similar skills and responses, as Table 4.1 illustrates.

Conflict resolution, a form of drama, moves interactants away from the heat and fray of emotions and into the listening-mediated safety of reflecting on past events, planning future strategies, and being attuned to others' needs, as well as one's own affective state. In some school and probation programs, and in many after-school youth programs, young people receive training in conflict resolution and then function as peer counselors. These programs give young people extensive opportunities to participate in activities very similar to those used in dramatic training: mirroring, improvising, and mediating the interactions of others. Following such training, youth mediate actual conflict resolutions among their peers. Such programs have captured the learning potential of conflict and the numerous benefits of establishing frames in which young people can safely take on the conflicting emotions, expectations, and norms that surround personal identities and interpersonal relations.

Such role-playing provides protected zones of practice for key roles that young people have now and will continue to experience as adults. Their entry into dramatic roles can come through conflict-resolution programs in schools or through dramatic arts programs, either in schools or after-school community programs. Such participation and

TABLE 4.1.
Stages of Conflict Resolution and Dramatic Creation

Conflict Resolution	Dramatic Creation
1a. Stating the Conflict	1b. Creating the Play
2a. Listening to Others	2b. Playing Roles
3a. Analyzing Solutions	3b. Rehearsing the Play
4a. Resolving the Conflict	4b. Performing the Play

learning tell us that *knowledge about social life comes much more from performance than from information*. Drama and the playing of roles in conflict offer opportunities for reflective performances that ensure the buildup of skills and knowledge centrally called for in current educational reform: the abilities to plan, to step back and consider, to work collaboratively, and to take risks in communication and with new ideas and processes of learning (Sizer, 1984).

DISSONANCE IN EDUCATION

For many years, American schools included opportunities, even classes, that allowed students to perform—under adult directors—scripts written by adults (and often for adult audiences). The most popular plots at the heart of these plays involved major conflicts that thrust family loyalty against patriotic duty, individual pursuits of pleasure against familial responsibilities, and murderous greed against altruistic benevolence. Students played out these scripts, often spending hours discussing various possible interpretations and comparing the assumed emotions of the character they were to play with their own similar experiences and feelings. Outside of schools, community theaters for children depended not only on scripts from playwrights, but also allowed young people to improvise and create their own written texts. These improvisations and original texts, more often than not, reflected contemporary portrayals of age-old types of conflicts that centered around aspiration, opportunity, battle, and disappointments in love.

By the late 1980s, when many states removed funding for the arts, including drama, from public schools, teachers committed to drama had to become more and more creative in order to retain it in the curriculum or even in extracurricular programs. Some high school English departments allowed teachers to substitute a course in drama for an advanced English literature class; other schools permitted seniors to take over directorship of school plays, recruiting and training their own actors and technical crew. Increasingly, as schools dropped drama study, community-based youth programs added drama to their programs. Boys and Girls Clubs incorporated teen drama programs; job training programs for youth centered around theater; and parks and recreation departments for major cities asked community youth theater groups to provide entertainment for the children at their summer day camp programs. Within these nonacademic sites for drama, youngsters turned not only to prepared play scripts, but also to their own script building and improvisations.

In the late 1980s, several research projects focused on the learning environments young people judged effective in fostering their social and academic learning and persistence. They found drama and role-playing to be a component of 90% of these organizations. The vast majority of youth organizations that young people in inner cities considered most effective included either conflict-resolution segments or performance drama. Only in rare cases were these youth-chosen learning environments in community drama linked to traditionally conceived school theater programs. Here, we include as cases two groups: the first, a youth-based community program that centers around drama as job preparation; the second, a public high school-based theater touring company serving communities locally and throughout the state.

Both of these programs attract youth who live in high-risk areas of their major metropolitan communities. Adults deal drugs on corners they pass each day; friends and family tempt them with alternative paths; their classrooms offer few consistent opportunities for building collaborative skills, identifying and resolving problems, and practicing language skills as they engage in projects they regard as authentic. Many of these youngsters live with conflicts around them that can and do erupt into physical and verbal violence. When they move from these environments into classrooms, they often find matters important to school personnel or other classmates trivial and petty compared to the concerns they face at home or in their neighborhoods. Numerous accounts from social scientists, journalists, and educators document these "real" conflicts.[1] The following matter-of-fact report is from a young boy, calling himself "Tree Frog," who participates in a youth media program that puts young people in the media arts and also into roles as news commentators and writers, illustrates background conflicts he mediates through his youth program and numerous role-playing strategies on the street. Tree Frog responds to questions, asked by a local journalist, as a "young old man."

Q: *Why do they call you Tree Frog?*
A: Because I'm always hopping around from place to place.
Q: *Where do you live?*
A: In San Francisco, with my mother.
Q: *Can you describe home?*
A: I'm never home because it's dirty. My mother don't care about nothing. She's always shooting up her needles with her nasty-looking boyfriends, who mess up the house more.
Q: *How long have you known your mom to use drugs?*
A: Since I can remember. She didn't always shoot needles. She used to smoke crack when I was young.
Q: *When you were young?*

A: Yeah. When I was young. Age ain't nothing but a number. I've been though hell—in my life. I saw homies die right before my eyes. I saw a whole bunch of dope fiends overdose and die off of all kinds of drugs. Right now my mother isn't taking care of me, I'm taking care of her. I gotta deal with me, her, and the game.

Q: *The game?*

A: The game is the art of making money on the streets. I gotta buy all my food and clothes and pay rent, so I sell whatever I can sell—sometimes weed and sometimes rocks, and sometimes I deliver pistols for this baller [someone living lavish in the game] I know. (see Wallace, 1995)

Tree Frog, though not in school with any predictable regularity, participates actively in the youth program in his community, which involves youngsters in conflict resolution, playing roles ranging from editor to writer to planner for their media arts projects.

Within youth organizations (as well as in school drama programs that allow sufficient time, range of expression, and performance opportunities) such as that in which Tree Frog participates, young people negotiate their home and community conflicts, as well as those that arise in the course of accomplishing the work of their youth group. But they do more than examine their own lives and environments; they interpret a range of texts (literary, managerial, journalistic), write several genres (play scripts, reviews, stage directions), and participate in management and technical tasks necessary to keep the group functioning. Conflicts do much of the work of moving actors into and through scripts and improvisation in these settings. The time-worn notions of protagonist and antagonist come alive out of actual conflicts that young people bring into their language and then into their roles, complete with gesture, costume, and sound effects to create theater, written scripts, and video productions, as well as staged rehearsals of meetings with potential funders, evaluators, and clients. Their texts emerge out of experience, struggle, and emotion often submerged in other situations, but now allowed expression, explication, and exploration to positive ends.

What follows is a comparative case study of two programs, one a community service theater company run out of a public school program, and another an outside-of-school, community-based work skills and drama program. We offer for each an indepth analysis of the process of using conflict and channeling it through role-playing and dramatic arts.

THE CENTRAL TOURING THEATER

On an October afternoon, the advanced acting class of Jan Mandell, teacher and director, gets under way in a bare-bones, black box theater in the basement of Central High School in St. Paul, Minnesota.[2] A group of juniors and seniors who know one another well from previous years of beginning and intermediate drama classes come together in a circle in the middle of the stage, while someone plays some Motown music on a tape deck. The students lead one another through a series of physical and vocal warm-ups, state their dedications for the day, and then get down to the business of identifying the topic for the year's play. The class, meeting for the last two periods of the day, will improvise, rehearse, revise, and finally, tour its original play to schools, businesses, and community institutions in the Twin Cities and surrounding Midwest. In fact, when they first meet, many of their performance dates are already scheduled with audiences that have learned over the years to get on their performance calendar early.

In a school that regularly self-segregates along racial, economic, and academic lines, Mandell's class includes an unusually diverse assortment of students who know that they possess a unique status and reputation at the school. Moreover, they have Mandell's theater classes in which to explore the issue of how to break stereotypical barriers. During the first month of the school year, they have taken a field trip to Penumbra, the local, nationally acclaimed African American theater company, where they have seen the staging of a new play about a young black teen dealing with issues of racism and self-doubt. They have also had a private audience with the playwright and three intensive workshop days with the play's leading actor. They have collected newspaper articles and tapes of news broadcasts about issues of segregation in their community, read Maya Angelou's poetry on the topic of race relations, and brought issues from the school's hallways into their classroom as the basis for improvisation exercises. Today they decide to borrow Angelou's poem title, "I Shall Not Be Moved" (originally borrowed from the spiritual), to use as the title of their play, and begin to discuss situations that will best illustrate and explore their chosen theme.

Jan Mandell will spend the next few weeks designing exercises to help the students improvise scenes for the play. As some small groups of students develop scenes they like, the rest of the class will watch, compare, contrast, and reimprovise. Mandell will fashion the strongest scenes into a sequential play and the students will then rehearse it to memorization. For these students, memorization comes from doing, and the script of a play is generally not written down until after it has been performed. It is then illustrated with photographs and excerpts from positive reviews, copied, and distributed to ensemble members as a theater yearbook that members sign. When finished, their Angelou-inspired play, *I Shall Not Be Moved*, will contain eight open-ended scenes, each of which portrays a different version of the conflict between feeling pressure to adhere to stereotypes, and developing inner strength to break free of stereotypes.

LIVE NOW

The second group we focus on in this chapter works in another Midwestern city. In a loft of an abandoned school, young people, between the ages of 13 and 21, come together to begin planning and preparation for a show they will work up in a few months to perform at school and community events throughout the city. The temperature hovers in the mid-90s, with humidity only a few points lower, and the young people show their anxieties as each new person arrives. They have auditioned with the arts director by reading or performing a piece of their own writing. Most do not know each other; few come from the same schools, and most have traveled by bus or subway to reach the site. Because their families all qualify for public aid, all youngsters will receive pay for their work through a job training program fund. In order to receive their pay, however, they must appear on time, be fully participating within the group, and be there for all performances.

The arts director stimulates their talk in the first few days of working together by throwing "outrageous" statements at them and then moving them through relaxation routines, theater exercises, and improvisation games. Often during relaxation routines, he reads to them from texts fundamental to their central concerns, such as Cornell West's *Race Matters*, or the latest poetry of Jimmy Baca. A tape recorder sits in the middle of the group as they work in a large circle, and each night the arts director transcribes portions of their talk, so that the next day texts previously spoken by each individual are redistributed for others to play. Hence, the original speaker becomes the character study for the appointed actor on the next day. Portions of practice time go to youngsters working together in small groups to create separate pieces that they perform for the group as a whole. Later, some of these group works merge to become a unified whole under a theme chosen by the young people.

This particular summer, as the group worked together for the first few occasions, the fact emerged that several actors had asthma and often felt they had to "breathe in a box." As the preparation period moved along, this theme for their lives became central, and their final production—encompassing a range of "boxes" from gang rivalries, federal housing projects, family conflicts, disrespectful classrooms, too-tight cliques, and even boy-girl relationships—illustrated how these enclosures worked in their lives.

STATING THE CONFLICT AND CREATING THE PLAY

The work of collaboratively creating a play in each of these two cases depends on conflicts, and the process parallels the steps of conflict resolution. In both of the cases presented in this chapter, just as in conflict resolution, the first step is to bring the issue out into the open. As Susan Heitler (1990) says, "Someone needs to say out loud what s/he wants" (p. 31). Youth clients of conflict-resolution programs are typically asked to begin by sitting down together with a peer mediator to describe what has happened and explain in their own words events of the conflict. Communication must be honest, nonviolent, and free of insults and put-downs. Mediators enforce adherence to these guidelines and keep the discussion focused on determining the conflict that will be the most productive to define and resolve.

Teens in original-work drama groups learn that compelling plays require a conflict explored; their best source of information and interpretation in script development and acting rehearsals is often the drama of their own lives. Members of these ensembles explore their own lives for conflicts that both fascinate and frustrate them, acknowledging these as both problems to be solved and solutions to the problem at hand—a play to be written. Adults and teens work together in mutually dependent collaboration: Teens need adult expertise, direction, and performance technique; adults need teens to supply realistic and compelling material for performance. Diversity is a source of both misunderstanding and inspiration, and of both conflict and resolution. When performing, teens must both maintain their individual identities with pride and also perform as members of an ensemble, in which no one member is any more or less important than any other. In most of their plays, all performers share the stage throughout the play, thus, in order to perform conflicts, teen actors cannot be creating or fueling conflict backstage. Unlike the volatility of their off-stage lives, which often encourages aversion and camouflage, the play requires and rewards clear, effective, and cooperative communication. Ensemble members must represent the harshness of their lives so that audiences can hear and understand. Participants in a conflict-resolution session must present their conflicts in a way that is both honest and respectful, and also honest and poetic in the creation of their plays. Being *honest* is essential because clichéd unidimensional conflicts ring false and lose an audience's trust; being *poetic* is central because the reality of the young performers' lives depends on the softening effects of figurative expressions of metaphor, symbolism, and literary allusion. These plays reveal that drama can demonstrate to teens how to take a proactive approach to conflict, imagining conflicts before they break out, discussing them, and envisioning and performing the resolutions.

LISTENING TO OTHERS AND PLAYING ROLES

Conflict resolution requires disputing parties to listen carefully to each other. Once each party has stated its version of the conflict to the mediator, each one states the same to each other, and then repeat back what they have heard. The mediator guides them through a process of comparing what was heard with what was said. Are people hearing what was said, what has been said in the past, or what they wish would be said? To prevent misunderstanding, resolution encourages two specific types of listening: (1) cooperative listening for what is right and helpful, rather than judgmental listening for what is wrong; and (2) empathetic listening, which attempts to place the listener in the speaker's position (Heitler, 1990). From the beginning, both parties know that they are working toward a mutually beneficial solution, a goal that demands careful listening first to establish commonalties, then, to understand the other.

Actors know how to find commonalties between themselves and the characters they play. The core of traditional dramatic training, called "method acting," instructs actors to search for a "kinship between the actor and the person he plays" (Stanislavsky, 1936, p. 49). Theater scholar Barranger's (1995) description of how and why actors must find a kinship in language is reminiscent of conflict resolution:

> Through the development of self-discipline, observation, relaxation, and total concentration his actors learned to recall emotions from their own lives that were analogous to those experienced by the characters they played.... What mattered to Stanislovsky was the *actor's truth:*... Actors learned to experience what their characters experienced *as if* it were actually happening to them. (original emphasis, p. 229)

Drama, then, asks young actors to combine their powers of observation and imagination to bring the characters of their plays to convincing life on stage.

Some observers of contemporary drama groups ponder whether asking students to perform the characters and situations of their own lives is as demanding a characterization task as asking them to perform scripted characters from settings outside of their own experiences. While performing life-based characters may not require students to search as far to find "kinship" with their characters, it may intensify the incentive to bring their performances to accurate and convincing levels. Because young actors in original-work groups are asked to recreate characters of their own lives for community audiences, the accountability stakes are high and immediate. Teen actors in these ensemble groups frequently switch and share characters, and are often asked to take lines or scenes written by or about another ensemble member to protect privacy and allow the original author to direct for authenticity. Therefore, with original, life-based dramas, acting risks are two-fold: Can you act well enough to convince your audience that you have become someone other than yourself? Can you convince them that you have become people they know well? A third challenge is embedded in performing original work: Do you have the courage to say things on stage as a recreation of yourself that you might not say off stage? This, too, can be seen as an aspect of conflict mediation—not just finding commonalties with the person to whom you are listening, but also presenting your own self in such a way as to invite your listeners to empathize with you.

In the Central Touring Theater's play *I Shall Not Be Moved*, the time-worn advice "to take a walk in the other person's shoes" is used to structure a scene examining the conflicts that the ensemble sees existing between light- and dark-skinned African American students at their school. The scene begins with two girls stating their conflict with one another over skin color and proceeds with their learning to listen to what the other is saying:

Both Girls:	Who are you? No, I asked you first. Who are you? (*look at each other with admiration*) I wish I could...
Tonicia:	Braid my hair like yours.
Khulia:	Have straight hair like yours.
Both:	You're so beautiful! You look like...
Tomicia:	An African queen.
Khulia:	A model.
Both:	You don't want to be me.
Khulia:	I said you don't want to be me!
Tonicia:	I said you don't want to be me! So you think it's easy being light-skinned?
Khulia:	Yeah, I want to be light-skinned.
Tonicia:	You ain't got a clue.
Khulia:	If I was light-skinned...(*Enters a fantasy which begins with black men telling her she's beautiful, but ends with dark-skinned women telling her, "Girl, get if you don't get your high yellow ass out of my face with your nasty weave. You may think you're all that, but you are still black."*) So you think it's easy being dark-skinned?
Tonicia:	Yeah, I wanna be dark-skinned.
Khulia:	Girl, you ain't got a clue.

> *Tonicia:* If I was dark-skinned... *(Enters a fantasy which begins with black men treating her with respect and discussing politics with her, but ends with some light-skinned girls telling her, "My friend and I just wanted to tell you that we think you use your assets to their fullest potential. You're pretty, for a dark-skinned girl.")*
>
> *Both:* I don't get it.
>
> *Khulia:* They say I'm too dark for beauty.
>
> *Tonicia:* I say by whose color spectrum?
>
> *Khulia:* They say my hair is too short and nappy.
>
> *Tonicia:* I say by whose rule, and whose comb?
>
> *Khulia:* I wonder when I'll be just right for them. Black, but not a jigaboo.
>
> *Tonicia:* White, but not a wannabe. Sister, I have just one question for you.
>
> *Both:* Who are "they" anyway?

The dramatic structure of the scene does much to encourage these two characters to cooperate and empathize. The girls begin and end by speaking the same lines simultaneously; they follow parallel speaking structures; they finish one another's sentences; they use and switch off parts in the refrain, "So you think it's easy?" The girls begin by stating their conflict to one another, but the process of repeating back what they have heard manifests a glitch in communication: "You ain't got a clue!" Simply telling one another about the problem does not convince, and so the device of trapping one character in the other's situation is employed. Here, each actor has to perform two conflicting characters at the same time, a challenge which suggests that the two characters are really two aspects of one person, responsible for understanding both aspects of the self. In the beginning of the scene, the question they ask simultaneously—"Who are you?"—is directed to the other and points to a lack of understanding, but by the end their shared question—"Who are "they" anyway?"—is rhetorical and points to a mutual understanding. It is this cooperative and empathetic listening on the part of both the actors and their characters, or "the actor's truth," that leads to this mutual understanding.

Teen actors achieve the mark of learning "to experience what their characters experienced *as if* it were actually happening to them" in Live Now's *Learning to Breath in a Box* as well. In the following scene, actors explore one of the boxes in which they are learning to breath: the housing projects in which they live.

> *Tennile:* Here's a number: 1150 North Sedgwick. I live in the same project my Grandma does. Let me give you a little description of my project building. It's tall.

Shalinda:	A lot of the windows are out.
Tennile:	Most windows are in, 16 floors.
Shalinda:	Gate on porch, bars on the window.
Tennile:	Writing on the wall, one new elevator…
Shalinda:	And one old… (*jumps down from chair*) elevator.
Maria:	I walk up to my run-down Foster-Walker building. The building itself gives off a germified odor and so do most of the people who live there. The odor isn't something you smell, but something you see. The people are from a lonely and lost world with stereotypical slaves of society. As I walk it seems like everyone is watching me. I'm usually in a hurry. I can hear their enchanted whispers. It sounds like a song. (*ensemble whispers the following lines*) "Why is she always rushing? She act like she white? What school she go to? Is that her man? What's up?"
Tennile:	We always have heat in the winter though. Got to keep the windows open it's so hot in there.
Shalinda:	Playground with lots of glass, no swings, kids everywhere, dope dealers under the building scurrying like rats, hypes always standing in line for their high, a straight line of hustlers going door to door selling merchandise to get rock (*ensemble lines up in straight line, as hustlers*).
Damarcus:	Ah, man, you got a rock! O.K., line up, I want no food stamps, no change, no merchandise, just dollar bills. I want no lip, no…
Earl:	Daddy's [sic] has a favorite glass pipe. He tells us not to look at him while he talks to it. Daddy is crazy about his glass pipe.
Damarcus:	Ah, man, you got a rock!
Earl:	No one can make me stay here in this suffocating glass covered pipe. Life is this. Life is that. For me, it's hard to look beyond the deep roots of poverty, pain, and stupidity when you have two people you love blowing smoke filled with death into your eyes. Eyes that are already blinded by the sights of becoming a failure. I live to save my little sister from my Daddy's smoke.

Before coming to the stage, the writer-actors of Live Now have listened carefully to the characters in the real-life drama of the projects: walkers and watchers, dope dealers, hypes and hustlers, children and parents, brothers and sisters. This scene provides the actors with a vehicle to express their frustration with those who make project life harder, but not before they first explore this life from their point of view. The scene begins by setting the conflict of opposition between those who want to leave before they become "run down" by life in the projects, and those who have already become "stereotypical slaves" to it. Maria explains her opinion that the Foster-Walker projects are "germified" by the people she sees there, but then imagines what her critics think about her as she rushes past: "Why is she always running? She act like she white. Is that her man?" Shalinda states her criticism of the dealers and addicts as scurrying rats who spread the plague of drugs in her project, only to have Damarcus immediately portray the dealer as a disciplined businessman who can both exert military-like control when others cannot ("Line up...I want no lip") and get money out of project addicts ("No food stamps, no change, no merchandise, just dollar bills"). Earl adds a third characterization—that of a father who is both seduced and suffocated by his addiction. The character Earl presents reveals that he has listened carefully to his actual father (by eavesdropping on his conversations with his crack pipe) and that he has found commonalty through the "deep roots of poverty, pain, and stupidity" that affect them both.

ANALYZING SOLUTIONS AND REHEARSING THE PLAY

For those who progress through the first stages of the conflict-resolution process—stating the conflict and listening to others—the next stage is offering and analyzing solutions. Those in conflict with one another imagine together how a proposed solution might work, identifying its benefits and deficits, rather than dividing to "tally up" pros and cons and then reporting back with objections. John Burton (1990), in his book entitled *Conflict: Resolution and Prevention*, which works toward a theory of conflict resolution, argues that conflict resolution "must be analytical," because it is both "concerned with identifying causes" and "requires a new synthesis of knowledge...and changes in conceptualization of a problem" (p. 202). This mutual analysis of options leads parties back to the sources of their conflict, while at the same time projecting them into the future to envision consequences and benefits, requiring a blend of concrete and imaginative thinking skills.

Scholars and mediators alike have turned to game theory for help in facilitating and analyzing satisfying resolutions. Fisher, Ury, and Patton (1991), in their text about negotiation, *Getting to Yes*, point out that any interaction between two people can be defined in terms of a game, when a game is defined as a situation in which each participant has, at specific times, a range of choices of action. Games are categorized according to how the total "points" earned add up, as shown in Table 4.2.

During the analysis stage of conflict resolution, it is the mediator's job to help opposing parties play a positive-sum game. They work to broaden and deepen the understanding of the situation and prevent blinding attachment to any one solution, without relieving participants from the responsibility of analyzing and agreeing to their own solutions. They ensure that each alternative is evaluated by standards of mutual

TABLE 4.2.

Zero-Sum Game:	Payoff to players is "0" One player's gain is the other's loss Example: Competitive sports
Positive-Sum Game:	Payoff to all players is positive One player's gain is the other player's gain Example: Business partnerships, Marriage
Negative-Sum Game:	Payoff sum to all players is negative One player's loss is the other's loss Example: War

benefit, by asking such questions as: What value does it enable each side to attain? Does it meet the needs of each player? It is in this evaluation that both sides are required to move forward through analyzing—evaluating, comparing, contrasting, and predicting—rather than stagnating by simply restating opinions.

Original-work drama is evaluated as successful when it is played as a positive-sum game. All actors must cooperate in order to enjoy a successful performance, which in turn is the winning outcome to be enjoyed by all involved. Original-work plays are custom built and balanced with an ensemble cast, and when one actor either hogs the spotlight or fails to give a full effort, the whole performance suffers. When this happens, the performance has been played as a zero-sum game, with the stage-stealing actor winning at the expense of the rest of the ensemble; or worse, as a negative-sum game, with the stage-stealer so damaging the structure of the play that it no longer communicates its messages, and everyone loses. Rehearsal is the stage of artistic creation which requires actors to analyze their performance. Is it balanced? Is it showing off all ensemble members in their best light under the goal of showing off the play and its message in its best light? Will it have the planned effect on the audience?

In order to answer these questions, actors must do the same as conflict-resolution participants—revisit the original intentions of the play while they simultaneously predict how it will appear to future audiences. Rehearsal, like conflict resolution, means imagining, comparing, and contrasting. It also means trying on as many options as possible, viewing each one with a critical eye and against an agreed-upon standard goal, until the best one emerges clearly. Because the analysis inherent to the rehearsal process requires perspective, a director is essential as a third party to mediate between various interpretations and to keep the ensemble on the course of the play's intention and message. Whereas traditional theater often looks to the director to interpret and then prescribe the meaning, look, and style of a scripted play, original-work theater cannot, by its definition, take this kind of direction. In this genre, the director instead functions as "a guide [who] creates an atmosphere in which actors dig, probe, and investigate the whole fabric of the play" and rehearsals "are used to search out, to listen, and to yield to suggestions" (Barranger, 1995, p. 249). And because the actors are also the playwrights, the play is a flexible, growing vehicle throughout the rehearsal process. Bringing lines to life, especially repeatedly, brings up questions of authenticity and validity not envisioned in the earlier creation stage. Can performances retain strength over time? Are performances serving the vehicle of the play? Are characters and the interactions between them believable, respectful, and entertaining? It is the director's job to pose these analytical questions, but it is always and ultimately the ensemble's job to answer them. As with conflict resolution, success in this creative theater is contingent upon young actors taking responsibility for themselves.

THE CONFLICT GOES ON IN RESOLUTION

The final stage in the resolution process is agreement—both parties agree on the solution to the problem that will most benefit everyone, agreeing that the solution will be adhered to in good faith in the future. The tenets of conflict resolution—honest communication and mature tolerance—follow the parties after resolution, as they have agreed to remember what they have learned and to use it. Audiences who watch "final" performances of ensemble drama groups that are the result of the four-part cycle—stating/creating, listening/playing roles, analyzing possibilities/rehearsing, and resolving/performing—may judge the fourth phase as central. Youth in most programs, however, begin the cycle again as they reach the performance stage. They see their plays as openings and not closures, but what is there in the opening is further learning, through exploration of differences and variations in points of view, of the same issues they have raised in their roles and through their performed text.

At the end of performances, the young people engage directly with the audience, often by moving back on stage in character and addressing questions directly to certain audience members. These questions challenge audience members to identify with the key issues of the play and to talk about how they see youth *they* know as responding to circumstances similar to those of the play. Variants on this continuation of conflict by opening a new "play of ideas" may also involve the actors coming on stage as themselves, giving brief autobiographies of how they came to be in this drama and how work in theater relates to their survival through the struggles of their daily lives. When performing for commissioned audiences, the Central Touring Theater divides the ensemble into pairs of actors and also, divides the audience into small groups. The actors then take on the responsibility of leading their audience group in an improvisational continuation of a scene or issue from the play that particularly intrigued them. Improvisations are then shared, and lively discussions follow as a result of transforming the audience from viewers to participants in conflict. Some theater companies deliberately write and perform their plays with open endings and then invite audience members to come up on stage, take on a character, and improvise a resolution to the play and its conflict (Boal, 1979).

The dance of discord and accord, of conflict and resolution, and of destruction and creation offers significant relational processes in youth development—processes that depend on learning how to articulate and express nonverbal emotions (positive and negative) that can carry high risks in daily interactions. Within the fervor of a theater production, and the high tension and drama of such events as dress rehearsals and final production, young people can feel comfortable with close body contact, exuberant hugs, tears of joy and disappointment, and voicing, through another character, thoughts that may well be one's own.

Young people, within such programs as the public school offering of Mandell's program and the community-based program of Live Now, have not only the few hard and fast rules that adults set for the group, but they also develop their own. For example, even when adults do not specifically mandate a "no drugs or alcohol" rule, young people themselves "make" such a rule so that agreement by players is explicit. If group members smoke, the group sets rules about when and where smoking is appropriate. These group-generated rules inevitably safeguard against conflicts within their immediate settings, and also offer practice for developing rules and conflict-resolution strategies for use in contexts distant from the school or actual drama program.

When do young people put to work what they have learned through drama? How does their experience in dramatic arts carry over into managing conflict in other situations? A case in point comes from Living Women, a small performing arts and college-preparatory youth group in San Francisco. They wanted to illustrate their belief that when offered an inadequate education system, students can choose to learn by their own book and teach by it as well. In a scene titled "The Report," one of the actors tells the story of how she rewrote the book on book reports.

The Report

(Lead-in music: "You Remind Me," by Mary J. Blige. Sage moves stage left, play-
ing Mr. Dingo, Maya moves center, everyone else moves stage right in
staggered rows, as in rows of desks.)

Maya: I can't remember who my report was on, but I do know that it was
about an author. First I wrote the main points about my author on
the board, so that the class would be able to take notes *(all other*
girls act as students, taking notes, except Mr. Dingo, with his own notes).
Then I stood behind the podium and waited for the class to copy,
staring out at all of the papers stapled to the walls.

I wasn't nervous when I started to give my report, because I had
done this once before. But about half way through my presentation, certain people in the class, like Alana, just started in singing
that song by Mary J. Blige—"You Remind Me." *(everyone begins to*
sing along) All of a sudden, the whole class was singing along *(sing*
a little louder)—even me! We sang loud *(everyone stops singing)*, but
we didn't sing that long because we could tell we were upsetting
Mr. Dingo.

Sage (as Mr. Dingo, wearing a sweater and glasses, in a calm, firm voice): Everything you say will be documented.

(Students stop singing, look disgusted, groaning.)

Kat (to Mr. Dingo, in disbelief): Whoo—you clownin'!

Sage: I do not wear a red nose or big floppy shoes—I am not a clown.
But your behavior will be documented.

Maya: He keeps a referral on each person in the class and he took them
all out and wrote down what each person did *(Sage does this)*. With
the class laughing and Mr. Dingo documenting, I finished my
report. I know we shouldn't have behaved like that, but there was
something about it that made me feel good, and a little proud. So
I decided to document it myself.

This scene provided the cast of eight girls with a multitude of analytical decisions to make as they rehearsed it. Primary among these was the
question of fairness to Mr. Dingo (a pseudonym very close to his real
name)—an actual teacher several of them had at the same time they
were working on the play. They had promised each other at the outset
that they would, in the words of their program (and of conflict resolution), "balance the good and the bad of going to school in the city;
being realistic while breaking down stereotypes." Did their script present
Mr. Dingo as a stereotype or as he really was? What should Sage do during her performance to prevent stereotyping? While Sage's initial performance of Mr. Dingo struck the rest of the cast as very funny, the
actors decided to observe Mr. Dingo carefully and separately for a
period of a week in and out of class. Also, since others in the cast had

also been present during the original book report, they were asked to write their version of what happened.

Armed with this research data, the girls were ready to rehearse the scene again. Reviewing the data they collected, they decided that Mr. Dingo was indeed a poor teacher, quick to fill out referrals rather than talk with his students. In addition, they all agreed that his monthly oral book report assignments were too rigid and rote to equal productive learning. They asked Sage to try her performance of Mr. Dingo once more, keeping the clown line since those were his actual words. They wanted their performance to show that he was a clever person; they asked Sage to slow down the words and not play the scene for laughs, but rather for accuracy, and to highlight his intolerance as they saw it. In addition, the cast admitted that their original version of the scene did not show how badly the class members had acted during the singing revolt. Alana was asked to sing out the first line of the song much more dramatically, and Kat was pushed through several rehearsals to play up her clowning line until it clearly illustrated rude behavior. With these two parts further dramatized, the rest of the ensemble agreed that they had to play along and act more rebellious or the scene would fall flat. They analyzed that in order for Maya's final lines—"I know we shouldn't have behaved like that, but there was something about it that made me feel good, and a little proud"—to carry the full impact of irony, she had to have a strong scene of misbehavior on which to reflect. The cast wanted their audience to be so moved by her monologue that they would ask themselves if misbehavior in a class is ever justified, and if it ever serves a beneficial purpose.

Once the girls had rehearsed the scene this far, the director asked them to push their analysis of the scene to an even deeper level: Would they be willing to perform the scene as it was if Mr. Dingo were in the audience? They were planning to perform for an audience of their school friends and teachers, and while it was unlikely that Mr. Dingo himself would attend, others who knew him well certainly would. This question sent Sage back to her original characterization of Mr. Dingo; the actors asked one another why he might treat students as he did. They improvised scenes in which he tried to do a better job but was still treated rudely by students, who were making racist remarks to him about his Asian American heritage. The result of their deeper character-ization of Mr. Dingo heightened the hostility between him and the rebellious students, drawing the scene even further away from comedy. When the director pointed out this shift to the actors, they agreed it was worthwhile. The more they thought about it, the less funny the whole scene became. That Mr. Dingo was a burned-out teacher was not really funny, and neither was the fact that his students were burned out on learning because of his poor teaching.

DRAMA AS KNOWING

Illustrations of transfer of knowledge and skills speak more loudly than testimonies. Nevertheless, if we ask what young people learn through drama, they have ready and numerous answers. Why do they agree to the long hours and hard work required in mounting a production and taking risks before friends and strangers? Their responses indicate learning of skills and information, as well as gaining experience about other groups and types of people not otherwise available within their communities or schools. Table 4.3 summarizes assessments given by youth in not only the two programs detailed in this chapter, but in 20 other youth-based programs involving conflict resolution through role-playing and/or dramatic productions for either live or video performances.

In addition to these general skills and areas of knowledge, almost all of which offer preparation for handling dissonance and dissent positively, individual players speak often to the philosophical and psychological merits they see in taking part in conflict resolution and/or drama programs. Such terms as "therapeutic," "releasing," "opening," and "liberating" appear most often in their discussions of what attracts them to these programs. But what do these terms mean, and are there

TABLE 4.3.

Personal Skills	Interpersonal Skills	Academic and Life Management Strategies
• Stress control	• Meeting new people	• Note-taking for events in progress
• Time management	• Making friends through work	• Ability to read and interpret other's writings
• Sense of individuality	• Risk taking with peers	• Script preparation
• Accomplishment within a group	• Verbal and body language communication	• Voice projection and enunciation
• Cure for boredom		• Vocal interpretation
• Preventative for trouble		• Stage movement
• Body image confidence		• Cost projection
• Confidence in presenting before an audience		• Travel planning for daily and special events
• Learning technical skills in theater (e.g., makeup, costumes, lighting)		

differences in the power they achieve in conflict-resolution programs and theater projects? Any release or liberation cannot be complete, as social constraints will always prevail, but learning to work with and building toward discovery of oneself within these restrictions often results from, and is accelerated by, conflict. Practicing for these *before* they occur or build to the intensity of self-despair, violence, or separation becomes possible within the theater, whereas in conflict-resolution projects, these consequences have already occurred.

Within the theater, youth work on handling conflicts and, thereby learn—through modeling and actual safe practice—numerous skills and strategies necessary in both academic performance and life management. The conflicts of time-honored literature, as well as of daily life, come in the love, honor, pity, compassion, sacrifice, and pride risked in the theater. It is the process by which individuals create and recreate their comprehension and compassion of the human condition, enabling the critical practice of putting oneself in the place of the other, necessary in handling conflicts off the stage.

Vaclav Havel, artist and political leader, sums up the role of theater in thoughts that parallel those of young people involved in the creating, listening, playing, and analyzing roles of conflict resolution and drama. In a period in which governmental bodies have increasingly cut support for the arts in schools, while persisting in calling for improved communication and collaboration skills addressed to the identification and solution of problems, drama in education stands as a necessary art.

> The role of theater...is not to make people's lives easier by presenting positive heroes into which they can project all their hopes, and then sending them home with the feeling that these heroes will take care of things for them.... If I can goad someone into realizing, with heightened urgency, that there are some arrangements to be made, then I've done my job, which is to remind people of their dilemma...to demonstrate that there really is something to be settled here. Only the solutions a person discovers himself will be the proper ones. They will be his, they will be an act of his own creation and his self-creation. (Havel, 1990, p. 97)

NOTES

[1] See, for example, Lefkowitz, 1987; Kotlowitz, 1991; Johnson, 1992; Goodwillie, 1993; and Anderson, 1990.

[2] Because the Central Touring Theater has been the subject of extensive regional and national media coverage over the last 15 years, the actual names and facts of the program are used in this chapter.

REFERENCES

Anderson, E. (1990). *Street wise: Race, class, and change in an urban community.* Chicago: University of Chicago Press.

Barranger, M. S. (1995). *Theater: A way of seeing* (4th ed.). San Francisco: Wadsworth Publishing.

Boal, A. (1979). *Theatre of the oppressed* (C. A. McBride, Trans.). London: Phitto.

Brown, A., & Campione, J. (1990). Communities of learning and thinking, or a context by any other name. *Human Development, 21,* 108–125.

Burton, J. (1990). *Conflict: Resolution and prevention.* New York: St. Martin's Press.

Fisher, R., Ury, W., & Patton, B. (1991). *Getting to yes: Negotiating agreement without giving in* (2nd ed.). Boston: Houghton Mifflin.

Goodwillie, S. (Ed.). (1993). *Voices from the future: Our children tell us about violence in America.* New York: Crown Press.

Havel, V. (1990). *Disturbing the peace: A conversation with Karel Hvizbala.* New York: Knopf.

Heath, S. B. (1993, Summer). Inner-city life through drama: Imagining the language classroom. *TESOL Quarterly, 27*(2), 177–192.

Heath, S. B. (1995). Race, ethnicity, and the defiance of categories. In W.D. Hawley & A. Jackson (Eds.), *Toward a common destiny: Educational perspectives on improving race and ethnic relations* (pp. 39–70). San Francisco: Jossey-Bass.

Heath, S. B., & McLaughlin, M. (1993). *Identity and inner city youth.* New York: Teachers College Press.

Heitler, S. (1990). *From conflict to resolution: Skills and strategies for individual, couple, and family therapy.* New York: W. W. Norton.

Johnson, L. (1992). *"My posse don't do homework": A funny and inspiring story of teaching.* New York: St. Martin's Press.

Kotlowitz, A. (1991). *There are no children here: The story of two boys growing up in the other America.* New York: Doubleday.

Lefkowitz, B. (1987). *Tough change.* New York: Doubleday.

McLaughlin, M. W., Irby, M. A., & Langman, J. (1994). *Urban sanctuaries: Neighborhood organizations in the lives and futures of inner-city youth.* San Francisco: Jossey-Bass.

Shantz, C. U., & Hartup, W. W. (Eds.). (1992). *Conflict in child and adolescent development.* New York: Cambridge University Press.

Sizer, T. R. (1984). *Horace's compromise: The dilemma of the American high school.* Boston: Houghton Mifflin.

Stanislavsky, C. (1989). *An actor prepares.* New York: Routledge. (Original work published 1936)

Wallace, E. (1995, May 26). 12 going on dead. *San Jose Mercury,* p. 13b.

OTHER RESOURCES

Abdennur, A. (1987). *The conflict resolution syndrome: Volunteerism, violence, and beyond.* Ottawa, Ontario, Canada: University of Ottawa Press.

Bray, E. (1991). *Playbuilding: A guide for group creation of plays with young people.* Portsmouth, NH: Heinemann.

Bush, R. A., & Folger, J. P. (1994). *The promise of mediation: Responding to conflict through empowerment and recognition.* San Francisco: Jossey-Bass.

FreeStreet Programs. (1994). *Learning to breathe in a box.* Unpublished play.

Gatto, J. T. (1992). *Dumbing us down: The hidden curriculum of compulsory schooling.* Philadelphia: New Society.

Hapgood, E. R. (Ed. & Trans.). (1994). *An actor's handbook by Constantine Stanislovsky: An alphabetical arrangement of concise statements on aspects of acting.* New York: Theater Arts Books.

Hare, A. P. (1985). *Social interaction as drama.* Beverly Hills, CA: Sage.

Holman, C. H. (1972). *A handbook to literature.* New York: Bobbs-Merrill. (Original work published 1936)

Lightfoot, S. L. (1983). *The good high school: Portraits of character and culture.* New York: Basic Books.

Matthew, J. (1988). *Escalante: The best teacher in America.* New York: Henry Holt.

Polti, G. (1977). *The thirty-six dramatic solutions.* Boston: Writers.

Project Co-Arts. (1993). *Safe havens: Portraits of educational effectiveness in community art centers that focus on education in economically disadvantaged communities.* Cambridge, MA: Harvard Project Zero.

Rose, M. (1989). *Lives on the boundary: A moving account of the struggles and achievements of America's educational underclass.* New York: Penguin Books.

Schutzman, M., & Cohen-Cruz, J. (Eds.). (1994). *Playing Boal: Theatre, therapy, activism.* New York: Routledge Press.

Scimecca, J. A. (1991). Conflict resolution in the United States: The emergence of a profession? In K. Avruch, P. W. Black, & J. A. Scimecca (Eds.), *Conflict resolution: Cross-cultural perspectives* (pp. 33–51). New York: Greenwood Press.

Weeks, D. M. (1992). *The eight essential steps to conflict resolution: Preserving relationships at work, at home, and in the community.* New York: Putnam.

Wolf, J. L. (1997). Balancing act: Using drama to even the exchange of information in the classroom. In J. Flood, S. B. Heath, & D. Lapp (Eds.), *A handbook for literacy educators: Research on teaching the communicative and visual arts* (pp. 67–75). New York: Tomson Press.

Yarrow, C. H. (1968). *Quaker experiences in international conciliation.* New Haven, CT: Yale University Press.

chapter 5

Using Drama to Teach Conflict Management

Holly Giffin
Katherine Yaffe

INTRODUCTION

Throughout the United States, educators are becoming increasingly aware that teaching the skills of conflict resolution must become part of the school curriculum. Principals and teachers are seeing greater numbers of children arriving at school with higher levels of social and emotional needs and lower levels of skill with which to deal with them. Thus, children's conflicts erode time available for traditional content learning (Prothrow-Stith, 1991). In addition, our understanding of intelligence has been expanded to include a wider range of human endeavor. Personal and interpersonal competencies are increasingly recognized as intelligences in their own right and the legitimate responsibility of quality public education (Gardner, 1991).

Conflict Management in Schools

Over the years, several programs have been developed for teaching skills related to conflict management. Although emphasis varies from program to program, conflict is usually defined as a struggle or disagreement between people who are in a relationship with each other and thus, to some degree, interdependent. Skills taught include listening, observing, perspective-taking, empathizing, expressing and identifying feelings, clarifying needs, managing anger, cooperating, and problem-solving (Lam, 1989).

Some of the earliest conflict-resolution curricula geared toward the regular classroom situation were influenced by the affective education movement of the early 1970s (Judson, 1984). By the mid-1980s, new curricula concerned with conflict resolution in schools derived from three additional sources: (a) organizations concerned about global peace began to look more closely at the need for interpersonal conflict-resolution training; (b) human resource trainers and mediation specialists began to see the potential of training students in the skills of mediation; and (c) the rise in violent crime among youth generated a strong concern for violence prevention as a public health issue (Prothrow-Stith, 1991). Concurrently, literature from the fields of guidance counseling and psychology continues to provide theoretical and practical support in prosocial skills training, which is directly related to conflict management (McGinnis & Goldstein, 1984).

Most current conflict-resolution programs rely, at least to some extent, on role-play as a teaching strategy. Schmidt and Friedman (1985) explain that "Role-playing provides opportunities for students to respond to conflicts and become aware of how those responses escalate or de-escalate a conflict situation. Role-playing allows students to take risks and practice new responses within a non-threatening environment" (p. vii). Friedman and Yarbrough (1985) add, "Role-play often is used to follow up a didactic message at a point where there must be progression from knowing to doing" (p. 130).

McGinnis (McGinnis & Goldstein, 1984) notes that "research impressively demonstrates the value of role-playing for behavior and attitude change" (p. 13). However, Friedman and Yarbrough (1985) caution that problems with self-consciousness and awkwardness can occur, sometimes resulting in rejection of the activity itself. Children may play their roles in an unrealistic way, for example, by "hamming it up." They may distort the intended thrust of the role-play by adding elements to the character's lives that are not applicable. They may hit an impasse in their interaction or move quickly to the most disastrous outcome, ending the scene abruptly. Or children may move too quickly and smoothly to resolution, not dealing realistically with the emotional complexities of conflict.

In this chapter, we shall describe a program that leads children into an extended improvised drama. One of the significant differences between the role-play used in some other conflict-resolution trainings and our extended group drama is the amount of time and attention given to generating emotional involvement in an imaginary conflict. This engagement builds a deeper commitment to conflict resolution.

The program, called Building Bridges™, part of the Colorado Educational Theatre Company, depends upon a multiframed, often allegorical situation developed over time. It is designed and conducted by drama specialists with the specific goal of improving conflict management in children from kindergarten through grade 8.[1]

This approach is strongly influenced by the work of Dorothy Heath-cote, a British drama educator. She defines drama as "a social art where people are and do, and other people may see them doing and being.... Drama seeks to examine the nature of social life" (1984, pp. 130, 140). As a method, drama seems particularly appropriate to the study of con-flict resolution in three ways: through *as-if* experience, reflection, and negotiation.

The first concern of the drama leader is to engage the whole class in "living through" a shared dramatic event. Together, the teacher and the class explore and resolve problems as they emerge. Sessions are struc-tured to build on each other, generating over time an authentic emo-tional experience. The goal is that students act and feel as if they really are the persons confronted with the problem of the drama. To the extent that participants experience real emotion, the conflict-resolution skills of empathy and emotional management can be most effectively tested and honed.

Second, at key moments throughout a drama session, the flow of *as if* action can be stopped. Then, participants who have just had an experi-ence in the drama can reflect upon it (Heathcote, 1984). And, as with a role-play technique, the children are invited to discuss their feelings and evaluations of the events and choices involved in the previous action. Participants in the drama learn to psychologically step outside of the frame of the conflict situation in order to reflect upon it. Sometimes stu-dents reflect upon the events as themselves; however, sometimes they are framed by the drama as persons who have a particular interest in the event. For example, in the drama we describe here, children are framed as citizens who are faced with a problem posed by a mysterious new stranger who is stealing their vegetables. They are invited to take up the burden of solving this social dilemma. The dramatic framing provides the perspective from which children will, through identification with problem solvers, construct new insights on the effects of antisocial behavior on a community.

Third, drama is a collaborative process. The drama leader sets up the dramatic structure and acts more as a facilitator than as an instructor. The participants construct their own meanings derived from the experi-ence generated by the structure. The direction the drama takes is deter-mined, in part, by a succession of agreements negotiated with the class. The drama session itself rests on the fundamental shared agreement to participate sincerely in the *as-if*. As new events are encountered, partici-pants must choose how to respond. Each decision generates new direc-tions and further agreements to be negotiated. At each step, the drama leader must be prepared to structure the *as-if* circumstances so that par-ticipants can experientially explore the consequences of their choices.

In summary, a classroom drama process includes: (a) experiencing a problem situation as if it were really happening; (b) reflecting upon the experience; and (c) negotiating with others about the choices presented in the process.[2] These characteristics of the classroom drama process relate closely to significant conflict-resolution skills. These inherent similarities suggest that classroom drama might be an even more effective method for facilitating the development of conflict-resolution skills than traditional role-play.

The question is: What does a drama structured to develop conflict-resolution skill actually look like? What specific drama strategies can be chosen? How do these strategies relate to learning the specific content of a conflict-resolution curriculum?

Drama Strategies and Conflict-Resolution Objectives

To explore these questions, we focus here on a second-grade program in order to identify selected drama strategies and describe how these relate to specific objectives in a conflict-resolution curriculum. Four classes of second graders representing two demographically contrasting schools were observed as they participated in the Building Bridges program over the 1993–1994 school year. The program covered essentially the same dramatic episodes and process for each of the four classes.

The program for any of the grades is designed to be meaningful and accessible to children of widely diverse abilities and cultural backgrounds. It is usually limited to eight weeks of one hour per week for each classroom.

The second-grade drama series is conducted by a main drama teacher (Katherine) and a supporting actor-teacher (Hugo). The drama scenario concerns a neighborhood and the conflicts that develop within it. The second graders are framed as experts in conflict resolution. Hugo, in role as Mr. Penny, owner of the neighborhood store, asks the second graders for help in resolving problems in his neighborhood. Katherine, as drama facilitator, moves in and out of a "transitory role" as Mrs. Penny. Each lesson revolves around a new problem, sequenced to gradually introduce increasingly advanced concepts and skills.

Ultimately, the goal of the program is to introduce specific prosocial norms of behavior so they might be integrated into the culture of the classroom, school, and community. The second grade sessions initially focus on building students' beliefs in the world of the drama in order to generate an authentic emotional experience of the conflict. Once emotional investment is attained, the objective is that students learn to resolve conflict constructively, meeting individual needs, while at the same time preserving relationships. This is accomplished through a sequenced series of lessons to introduce peacemaking skills.

The strategies described below are not necessarily discrete but may be used simultaneously. They may overlap and recur, and are designed to bring the class closer to the practical objectives of the program: experiencing the conflicts within the drama and assimilating the skills to resolve them.

STRATEGIES TO GENERATE EMOTIONAL INVESTMENT

Identification with an Imaginary Neighborhood

> *Katherine:* What do the people in the green house grow?
> *Child with green name tag:* Corn and spinach.
> *Katherine:* They're famous for corn and spinach. And the people in the orange house?

The first session of the program is partially dedicated to establishing the neighborhood. This is begun visually, with the children sitting on the floor directing Katherine as she creates a map, placing paper cutouts of houses of different colors and unusual shapes on a large sheet of white paper. The realistic elements, such as the houses, are made distinctly unusual in shape and color in order to define the neighborhood as pretend. Katherine elicits the ideas of the children: "Where are the houses located? Where should the park be? Can this be a very important tree? Is there a lake? Where is Mr. Penny's store?" She draws in the details with markers. The children are invited to add to the map during free time over the next week.

Before the first session, the children are given name tags in different colors. They begin to identify with their homes as they pick out their colored-paper houses. "Someone wearing a yellow name tag, what shape are the windows in the yellow house?" asks Katherine. Katherine introduces the concept that the houses have gardens and the people that live in each house bring their produce to Mr. Penny's store. Because gardening is a familiar concept to the children, this provides a comfortable point of entry into the drama. Small groups of children with name tags of the same color are associated with the house with the corresponding color. They meet to decide what kinds of fruits or vegetables to grow.

The map must reflect the children's own experiences of what a neighborhood is like, and yet also depict a shared imaginary world. In creating the map together, the class builds a collective image of the neighborhood. Looking together, they see the whole and identify their own parts within the whole. Speaking and listening to each other, the children move from isolated individual perspectives to a shared understanding. The children's investment in creating the neighborhood is evident from their enthusiastic volunteering.

Later in the session, the children meet in small groups in their respective "homes" and take time to physically delineate the space in their houses, establishing the place for their beds, the fireplace, etc. This time, they are using the classroom space, not the space on the map, as their territory. This gives them the opportunity to identify both personal space and group space. They interact with each other spontaneously, and collectively construct an imaginary scene, much as young children do in uninhibited, pretend play.

This dramatic play time gives them the opportunity to develop more of a sense of individual and collective ownership of the drama. It also provides Katherine with a chance to observe the social health of the class. Some questions that guide her observations: Can they work in cooperative groups, or do they immediately get bogged down in conflict? Are they able to be self-directed, or do they depend on an adult for direction?

A magical, fantastical quality is deliberately evoked. The children are enchanted when Hugo, as Mr. Penny, appears dressed in a bright blue coat and a bright blue grocer's apron. This eye-catching fantasy draws the children in. The magic of their own belief keeps their attention focused on the drama, yet the fantasy also allows them to maintain an objective eye, which is fundamental to productive problem solving.

Teaching through metaphor leads children to explore the possible connections between the content of the lessons and their own life experiences. The neighborhood metaphor is chosen to provide an image for thought about the real community that is the classroom and the school. The drama moves intentionally toward conflict within the context of community. At first, the children are encouraged to imagine what a peaceful neighborhood might look and feel like. "Peaceful" may include productive, active, and cooperative, as well as happy and content. They practice identifying themselves as members of a peaceful community. Ultimately, the goal of the program is that this image carries over as an ideal for the real world of school.

Negotiating Commitment to the Drama

> Katherine: Could everyone agree that when Hugo comes in the door he'll be a special visitor from the neighborhood?
>
> Class: Yes!
>
> Katherine: I wonder what questions we might ask him?

In each session, the contract to enter the world of the drama is made explicit. The drama leader negotiates with the class at each level: "Can we agree that Hugo will act as if he were Mr. Penny? When Mr. Penny puts on Jabber's hat, he will show us what Jabber did on the day the conflict happened. Can we help Mr. Penny by showing what the neighbors did?"

The children have chosen—and no one has been tricked—to enter the imaginary world. There can be no willing suspension of disbelief unless participants have agreed of their own free will. The distinction between drama and reality is made clear.

Negotiation opens the door to belief. By making an overt agreement to enter the world of the drama, the children explicitly accept responsibility for taking on their roles in a truthful way. The drama leader does not get trapped in a position of low power because the contract acknowledges the drama frame explicitly. If the children's behavior disrupts belief in the drama, the leader can step outside of the drama frame, remind them of their agreements, and let them try again.

Although the drama is guided by a session plan developed by the leader, the plan must be continually subject to renegotiation throughout the session in response to the emergent needs of the group. One of the major goals is to empower the students to take ownership of the drama. In one session, for example, a child decided that he could facilitate the problem-solving discussion under the Big Tree, a task usually performed by Katherine. She accepts his suggestion, allowing him to lead the meeting in order to validate his belief in himself and to empower the group. Therefore, the children took the drama in their own direction. As with effective negotiation in other arenas, people will commit to an agreement, to the extent that they have been included in the decision-making process.

Balancing the objectives of the session with the commitment to negotiating the process is crucial. Allowing too much negotiation can hopelessly sidetrack the session so that important goals, such as using specific conflict-resolution skills, are not reached. However, if the leader does not allow enough input from the class, he or she risks not generating adequate emotional investment in the drama.

Children as Experts

Hugo is in role as Mr. Penny at the beginning of the active-listening session:

> *Mr. Penny:* I've heard that you are all very good problem solvers. Is that true?
> *Class:* Yes!
> *Mr. Penny:* Well, the reason I am here is that there is a very big problem in my neighborhood.

The class interviews Mr. Penny the week after the active-listening session, when they all were troubled by Jabber's constant talking and not listening.

> *Gertie:*   What's going on in the neighborhood?
> *Aaron:*   Are they doing any better?
> *Alison:*   Did Jabber think about the stuff we taught him?

After the children, as neighbors, have had to experience the frustration Jabber caused, they take on a different role. This time they are framed as advisors, experts who know how to resolve conflict peacefully and justly. Hugo, in role as Mr. Penny, and Katherine, as Mrs. Penny, come to these consultants to ask for help, hearing that they are good problem solvers. How the children interpret their role is directly influenced by how the facilitators present their roles as Mr. and Mrs. Penny. They must treat the second graders as if the children are indeed experts. By withholding their expertise, the adult leaders empower the children to draw upon their own knowledge and intuition in order to help Mr. Penny, thus reversing the standard real-life roles of teacher/expert versus child/learner.

In order for the children to develop through their interaction with the teachers-in-role, the characters must also be approachable, familiar, and needy. Hugo plays Mr. Penny as a soft-spoken gentleman who is upset and frustrated by conflict in his neighborhood. He is presented as a physically nonthreatening person in need of help. Mr. Penny's low-power status thus empowers the students in their role as experts. The characters of Jabber and Grabber, which Hugo also plays in order to demonstrate the conflict, are likewise nonthreatening. Wearing a striped t-shirt and baseball cap, Hugo protrays Jabber and Grabber as friendly but thoughtless troublemakers. They are not evil, but rather rambunctious, good-hearted persons who make mistakes—a type that is familiar in many classrooms. In this progam, the leaders do not want to label the person who presents the problem as a truly dangerous or even sinister person because he or she might then be beyond responding to the kind of helpful conflict-resolution strategies the second graders could use, and a more appropriate response might be to remove that person from the neighborhood.

The emotional level of the situation is thus pitched to be appropriate to actual day-to-day interpersonal conflict in the children's classroom or school, which can be alleviated by common conflict-resolution skills. The children are induced to access and develop the common sense responses that are likely already in their repertoire of skills, thus increasing their sense of personal competency. The children's self-esteem is further reinforced as Mr. Penny reads letters that report that his neighbors have successfully used the children's advice and thank them for their help.

There are several reasons for employing the strategy of giving children the role of experts. It is easier to help children build belief in something they enjoy believing, and they relish a power they don't often have as children. Furthermore, they become aware of their legitimate expertise. Playing this prosocial role heightens the children's awareness of the interpersonal skills they already have and generates interest in using those skills. In enacting the role, they verbalize social and moral understanding, which they probably do not act upon consistently in everyday life. Children often can reason morally before they find the will to act that way (Lickona, 1991). The role of expert elicits a sense of ownership and inspires practice.

Framing the children as expert advisors elicits truthful enactment. The children help Mr. Penny by accurately recreating the events in order to understand them. The children are not acting with sincerity in order to please the teacher (which is all too often only perfunctory), but because truthful acting is intrinsic to meeting their own objectives.

The drama framework also facilitates critical thinking, while providing psychological protection. It anchors a context in the children's minds (right now we aren't the neighbors like we were yesterday; we're expert problem-solving consultants) to which the class can return throughout the sessions, in order to objectively reflect upon the situation. Particularly with this emotionally charged content—for example, the examination of what might be considered bad behavior—the framing protects the children emotionally. They are not the ones who create the conflict and make poor choices. Rather, they are the ones who know better. As experts, the children are able to look without guilt or defensiveness at behavior that may be similar to their own. This allows them to be both compassionate and critical.

Generating Experience of Interdependence

People from the green house are harvesting their apples as a storm approaches.

> *Luis:* Jabber will you help us?
> *Jabber:* Yeah, I'll help you. *(distractedly)* Hey! Is that a new haircut?
> *Emily:* Jabber, there's a storm coming and we need to get our crops to Mr. Penny!
> *Jabber:* Oh! Look at that airplane!
> *Rosa:* Jabber, we need help! We need to pick our apples!

Jabber: Oh! I love to eat apples!
Ricardo: Pick them! Not eat them!
Jabber: Where did you get that haircut?
Ricardo: Ah-h-h! You're hopeless!

Creating a sense of interdependence is key to generating an emotional investment in community and in conflict. Community depends upon people needing each other and helping each other work toward individual and collective goals. Conflict is experienced when people do not meet each other's needs and/or actively interfere in the attainment of each other's goals (Hocker & Wilmot, 1989).

The first step toward generating experience of community is to create a relationship of interdependence between the neighbors and Mr. Penny. Through the device of narration, Katherine establishes that Mr. Penny depends on the neighbors to bring in produce and products to be sold in his store. The neighbors depend upon Mr. Penny to market their products. As in any small community, their interdependency extends beyond mere economics to the meeting of mutual social and emotional needs.

In the drama to teach active listening, each house has crops to harvest (e.g., apples to pick, carrots to pull, etc.). In the session to teach anger management, each house has a product to make (e.g., skateboards to sand, paint to mix, apples to press for cider, etc.). The drama is slowed down to allow the children to mime their work. Small motor activities are chosen in order to promote concentration and build kinesthetic knowing. Katherine encourages them to imagine their actions in detail. The more the children use their imagination, the more genuinely invested in the drama they become. In role as Mrs. Penny, Katherine enhances the children's sense of interdependence by asking such questions as "What time should I send the truck for your apples?" Speaking to the children as if they were really the neighbors, she heightens their commitment to that role, as well as their obligation to Mr. Penny.

For conflict to be authentic, the children must sense that the character Hugo plays interferes with their attaining their goals, and he fails to recognize their interdependence in the neighborhood. Once the children are committed to the goal, they are emotionally ready to experience conflict with the problematic person played by Hugo.

Another conflict occurs when the people from each house attempt to elicit help from the character named Jabber. "Then the people in the blue house went out to their garden to harvest their crops. They saw Jabber walking by," Katherine narrates. The neighbors need Jabber's help. They try asking politely, then ordering, and, finally, yelling. Conflict is generated as all attempts to get Jabber to help are futile. Jabber won't listen long enough to know how to help. He interrupts, changes the subject, and misunderstands the directions, all the while talking incessantly. Katherine heightens the tension by introducing a further dimension of interdependence in the neighborhood. In role as Mrs. Penny, she worries aloud, "Mr. Penny needs those vegetables! We have orders to fill! People have been phoning the store."

The session on anger management depends upon interference to generate conflict. A character named Grabber (played by Hugo) enters the houses when the occupants are not home. He carelessly but unintentionally damages products the neighbors were making to sell at the store. The children's identification with their work is critical to the success of the drama at this point if the children are to experience the conflict on an emotional level. As Grabber mimes borrowing their property without permission, the children are dismayed.

Again, Katherine, in role as Mrs. Penny, heightens the tension. She confronts the neighbors, complaining loudly that she needs their products at the store immediately. As the neighbors, the children become aware of how Grabber's thoughtless, self-centered actions affect them, their relationship with Mr. and Mrs. Penny, and the attainment of their goals, which then result in genuine outrage.

Community depends upon the maintenance of relationships. Constructive conflict management both resolves a problem and builds a relationship. It is, therefore, very important that the problematic roles, Jabber and Grabber, are not played as bad guys. They have to be annoying enough to evoke genuine feelings of frustration and anger among the children, but friendly enough so that the children want to change them rather than banish them. The teacher-in-role must create enough of a positive relationship with the neighbors to justify the effort involved in dealing constructively with the conflict. On the other hand, he must also be enough of a problem that the children want to admonish rather than please him.

Opportunities for Observation

> *Katherine:*   Now people in the orange house, each of you find your special window.... I wonder what might cause the people to look out of their windows?
>
> ***
>
> *Luis (looking in Jabber's window):* He's sad. I know why he's sad. Because we asked him to help but when we ask him he keeps on fooling around. So when we leave, he's lonely.

During the initial house-setting time each child is asked to find a window that will look out at the park. The window works both metaphorically and practically throughout subsequent events in the session. Metaphorically, it anchors the idea of looking out of one's own perspective and of becoming aware of the frame or limitations of that perspective.

The window also represents the opening: a way for others to see you as well as for you to see out to the world. Dramatically, this allows the drama leader to spotlight each group. The window provides an entry into the imaginary world of the house. While the children are miming their work in their houses, Katherine, donning a shop apron to signal a change in role, becomes Mrs. Penny. She looks in on the neighbors with appreciative comments and questions: "My, what beautiful skateboards! Do you have any supersonic ones? I've always wondered how you make them…. When will you have them ready to sell?" By talking to the neighbors about their work, she as teacher-in-role can heighten the drama and direct it from within.

Practically, within the drama, the window gives each child an orientation from which to be an observer when not directly involved in the action, watching other groups as the session progresses. The creation of the window also emphasizes the observer as an integral, if not active, part of the drama. It helps to direct and enhance the collective focus of the class.

Experience of the conflict is deepened through repetition and observation. As Katherine narrates, the people in each house encounter the problem, in turn. The people in the other houses observe from their windows. For example, in the Grabber session, the pattern is that the people from one of the houses take a break from their work and go to the park. Meanwhile, Grabber enters the empty house and messes with their work (e.g., eating the blueberry pies, playing with the new skateboards, etc.). The people return to find their work destroyed or missing. The children experience the conflict as both observers and participants. The rhythm of each house, in turn encountering the same problem, reinforces the experience of the conflict. The repetition creates a tension of prediction and discovery which refines observation skills and provides information for subsequent problem solving in the session.

The effectiveness of the discussion depends upon what the children observe. Hugo's task as teacher-in-role is to demonstrate behavior and thinking which lack interpersonal communication skills and awareness. In the ensuing reporting and discussion, the children must be able to identify these problem behaviors. For example, in the active listening lesson, in order for the children to identify the problem as poor listening, Jabber must demonstrate, in the course of interaction, specific types of nonlistening, such as not looking at the speaker, changing the subject, or interrupting. A possible solution to the problem would be teaching Jabber to listen.

In addition to reviewing the conflict, observing from the windows allows the class to overhear the thinking process, which guides the behavior causing the conflict. Grabber self-talks as he rationalizes his theft. "They have a lot. They won't miss this. They told me to come by any time." Observing this enables the children to identify the faulty thinking that is the source of the problem behavior. It steers them away from good or bad character judgments, which can impede productive conflict resolution. Misunderstandings can be impacted by problem solving; innate qualities cannot.

STRATEGIES TO TEACH CONFLICT RESOLUTION SKILL

Establishing a Tradition for Problem Solving

Katherine (in role as Mrs Penny): Why haven't you brought any strawberries for me? People are waiting for their strawberries!

Mike: Jabber! We've been asking him if he could help us but he's just playing all around and he keeps on doing wrong stuff!

Katherine: And where are your apples? You have a lot growing and I need them for the store.

Aaron: They were too high and Jabber wouldn't help us!

Katherine: You know, I think we need to have a meeting under the Big Tree in the park. Do you think you could come to a meeting?

Children: Yeah!

Katherine: Would you ask the other neighbors?

Mike (to rest of class): Come on! We're having a meeting under the Big Tree in the park!

***

David: We should tell him how we feel.

Ricardo: I just felt, you know, like banishing him out of this neighborhood. He's driving me nuts!

Katherine (as Mrs. Penny): Well, we have some choices. We could banish him from the neighborhood or we could tell him how we feel. Can you think of any other choices for how to solve this conflict? Honestly, I can't think of any!

The culmination of the conflict in most sessions is the neighborhood meeting under the Big Tree. The image of the Big Tree was chosen because it is a universal symbol of peace and growth. In the drama, it represents a forum for the public airing of grievances, discussion, and problem solving, traditional in many communities.

Katherine drapes a green cloth over a tall chair and asks, "Can we say that this will represent the Big Tree?" As the children accept the meeting, they accept discussion as the neighborhood policy for dealing with conflict. In the culture of the neighborhood, "When we have a problem, we talk about it." Ideally, this meeting under the Big Tree in this drama models a tradition that will be translated into the culture of the school.

In role as Mrs. Penny, Katherine facilitates the meeting. Again, she deliberately withholds expertise in order to allow the children to draw on their own ideas and experience. From within the role she helps the children clarify and embellish their reactions to the situation. The children emotionally reinvest in the drama as they report on the events and validate each other's experience. Katherine's goal at this point is to facilitate the shift in the children's involvement from emotional reacting to critical thinking. Directing through questions, Katherine steers the discussion to identify the problem, challenging the children to pay attention to what they actually observed and experienced. She does not allow them to rest on unexamined solutions which, in their past experience, may have gained teacher approval. For example, when one child suggests that "We can talk nicely to him," Mrs. Penny counters, "But you did talk nicely to him! I heard you!" She pushes the children to confront the complexity of the situation.

As the community tries to decide upon solutions, Katherine guides them to consider choices of action, predict consequences, and evaluate effectiveness. She may deliberately model responses that dysfunctionally escalate conflict, thus infusing tension and forcing the class to confront their options. For example, as Mrs. Penny, she often will be first to endorse the idea of banishing him from the neighborhood. This is not the thinking of a responsible teacher but of a frustrated character in the drama. The neighbors are jolted out of their anger to reconsider what their goals really are. Do they really want Jabber to go away, or do they just want him to change?

Similarly, in a Grabber session, Katherine translates the neighbors' urge to angrily confront the thief by pounding on Grabber's door, threatening, "Grabber, you come out this minute! We want to talk to you! You come out or else! " The conflict is clearly escalated as Grabber emphatically refuses to face the group. Mrs. Penny asks the group to assess the interaction and diagnose what was wrong with that strategy. What would be a better approach? In this example, she elicits directly from the children the idea of being calm before a confrontation, a key concept in problem solving.

Stepping out of the Drama for Direct Teaching

> *Katherine (as teacher talking to second graders):* What else was he doing that was bad listening?... What does a good listener do?... I brought in a poster that says some of the things you talked about. Remember how you decided that everyone should look at the speaker?

Essentially, the entire thrust of each session is to develop within the children a readiness to learn specific conflict-resolution skills. This is done by stimulating an authentic emotional experience of conflict. At this point, the roles of observer and expert, which were carefully implanted at earlier stages, are evoked to distance the children from that emotion. The children are invited to reflect analytically on the behavior and identify specific skills.

Addressing them as experts, Katherine, no longer Mrs. Penny, attempts to elicit the children's own collective knowledge. In doing this, she honors the inherent wisdom of the children. However, part of her role as teacher is to elevate their knowledge through the supply of terminology, the clarification of concepts, and the identification of skills. As actual second graders they have much to learn.

The teaching objective is to train children in specific conflict resolution skills, for example, restating, I-messages (statements of how the speaker feels), and brainstorming for solutions. The program also promotes a specific model of steps for problem solving that provides a practical guideline for resolving conflict in the classroom and on the playground. These concepts must be taught directly.

The ability to move in and out of the frame of the drama allows for both experiential and more teacher-directed forms of teaching and learning. Thus, a spectrum of learning styles from affective/experiential to cognitive/direct is addressed. The drama convention of frame allows teachers to engender an authentic discovery process and yet teach a predetermined content. By stepping outside of the drama entirely before she directly teaches, Katherine avoids behaving incongruently to the context. After all, as Mrs. Penny, she's not supposed to have a clue! In the reality of the second grade class, however, she is the teacher. They are, once again, the students. The roles are clear and the relationship is appropriate.

As neighbors, the children authentically experience the conflict. As experts, they authentically mined their own wisdom. Now, as second graders, they are open to learning precisely because it can enrich their roles when they return to the drama. The list of skills becomes knowledge that the children can draw upon when they return to being experts.

Learning through Teaching

Katherine: Can you tell Jabber what he's doing right now that's poor listen-
            ing?
Bobby (to Jabber): You're interrupting.

***

Ricardo: Jabber, I think you are really improving and I like that.
Maria: I think we've been teaching Jabber a very good lesson. And now
            he's doing a very good job.
Jeb: I think Jabber been listening a lot and he been nice. And he
            been watching whoever has the feather now and being quiet.
            He's a nice person.

When the children re-enter the drama, they are once again bearers of
what Heathcote terms the "mantle of the expert" (Heathcote & Bolton,
1995). The session culminates in a ritual in which the children, as experts,
teach the problem-role the skills they themselves have just learned. Here,
the job of the teacher-in-role is to learn the skills, but not too quickly. For
example, children practice the skills of I-messages, clearly stating what
they feel, what Jabber or Grabber did, and how they want him to change.
A sense of completion is achieved when, after listening to several of the
children, the problem character acknowledges the conflict-causing behavior and commits himself to change. Recognizing the problem-role's need
for the skill, teaching the skill to him, and enjoying success when he
learns it, reinforces the children's ownership of their new knowledge.

The sessions are designed to end with a sense of closure, achievement,
and satisfaction. Sometimes a final session is closed with an affirmation
circle. In one class that had difficulty listening, Katherine, as Mrs. Penny,
explains that she has found a feather in the park by the Big Tree and wonders if it can help the neighbors listen to each other. The neighbors pass
the feather around the circle. As each child/expert receives the feather, he
or she addresses Jabber and summarizes what has been successful about
the teaching experience. While this is also a listening exercise, in the context of the drama, the ritual gives every child an opportunity to affirm
what he or she has learned. The authority imbued by the feather elevates
each child and heightens the imperative for respectful listening. A cumu-
lative positive expression of "who we are as a community" is generated.
The children move out of the drama with a sense of triumph.

Transference to Life

Transferring what is learned in drama to the reality of childrens' lives is
the ultimate objective of the program. The connection is drawn
throughout the sessions. In out-of-drama discussion at the end of every
session, Katherine directs attention to how the skills investigated in

drama apply to real life. "What ideas did we use today to make the neighborhood a peaceful place? Can you use those ideas in your classroom? Which ones? What do you think you could do the next time you feel really angry? Let's think about what you taught Grabber."

In one session on anger management, Hugo (out of role) coached two boys who were tussling for space on the floor to use I-messages and restating:

> *Hugo:* Juan, can you give Carl an I-message?
> *Juan:* I feel bad when you just pick my foot up because if you had asked me I would have moved it.
> *Hugo (to Carl):* What did you hear him say?
> *Carl:* He feels bad because I pushed his foot out of the way.

This real-life experience demonstrated to the class that using the simple skills of listening and sharing perspective can defuse conflict.

The focus of the final drama sessions is specifically on helping the children transfer the skills learned in the previous sessions to their own lives. In these sessions Mr. Penny tells the stories of conflicts among neighbors. People from the green house accuse people from the yellow house of throwing litter in the park. People from the blue house won't let people from the orange house help build their snowman because the orange-house people are bossy. The conflicts are the type that many children have experienced in their own lives. Now the children, as members of the community, play both sides of the dispute, responding to each other, rather than to an actor in role. The scene is played out until the issues and the escalating behaviors are clear. Modeling the observer perspective, Katherine coaches them to pay attention to what is happening and to remember their skills.

> *Katherine:* What did you notice?
> *Children:* They were yelling at each other.
> *Katherine:* What other choices do they have?

In this way, she leads them in practicing the steps of stopping and calming down. People of the disputing houses then meet, under the guidance of the drama leader, to create a mutually acceptable solution to the problem. Here they practice using I-messages, active listening, and brainstorming ideas—skills they learned from their encounters with Jabber and Grabber. It is an opportunity to practice what they have learned. They need to demonstrate to Mr. Penny what they now know about productive conflict resolution.

The next stage of the transference process is indeed to introduce direct role-play of real-life conflict. They role-play to rehearse newly acquired skills applied directly to the context of child life. They "help Mr. Penny" by showing him examples of how they might solve conflicts at school. Descriptions of types of conflicts that children have actually observed or experienced at school become the basis for demonstration role-plays by small groups. For example, Darryl, Bill, and Angela refuse to let Jim and Tonya play on the climbing equipment unless they will play their game.

Coaching from the adult is very appropriate and will continue to be until the students mature in their conflict-management abilities. An adult facilitator coaches the children in each group through the conflict-resolution steps. It is unrealistic to expect that second graders will be competent immediately. In the process of working even awkwardly through the steps, the children begin to integrate the cognitive observation and critical thinking skills introduced in previous sessions into their spontaneous responses. They discover how to use these skills to defuse emotionally charged content and solve problems in their everyday lives.

Much of the actual transference work must be left to the classroom teacher, who deals with the conflicts that spontaneously arise from day to day. The drama program, when successful, has generated an awareness of and appreciation for the skills of conflict management. The skills themselves can only be acquired through repeated practice over time. These last sessions model for the teacher how to use the shared drama experience as a reference point and a structure for helping children understand and resolve conflict.

For example, when disputants in a conflict are all talking at once, the teacher might say, "Remember what a problem Jabber caused when he wouldn't listen? What could we do to listen better?" In a situation when disputants are yelling angrily at each other, the teacher might refer to the drama by saying, "Remember how Grabber was too scared to talk to us when we yelled at him? Do you think Nick feels this way when we yell at him?" The teacher is encouraged to help the children consider what they learned from being in the imaginary neighborhood that could be used on the playground. He or she can then help the children practice those skills in role-play.

ASSESSMENT

Dear Mr. Penny,
I felt bad when you got mad at us.

When we made the wrong things. But you didn't tell us to make sleds.

From Hanna

P. S. I like making houses out of our desks. I learned that you shouldn't get mad at someone if they do the wrong thing.

December 6, 1993

Dear Mr. Penny,
I felt bad wen you got Mad at us.

Wen we mayd the rog things. But you Dinint tel us to mac sleds.

From Hannah.
P.S. I like making housis awt of are desks. I lrnd that you shudint get man at sumwun if thay Duw the rog thing

We are constantly trying to assess how much of the content is in fact assimilated through the drama method. Behavior in the drama and in role-playing provides information on what the children are learning. In addition, drawings, inspired by the drama and by writing (such as journal entries or letters to Mr. Penny), indicate the children's comprehension of the material. Pictures of Jabber, the one who always talked, show big mouths full of teeth. Letters to Mr. Penny demonstrate carefully composed I-messages.

Katherine also interviewed the children and teachers directly. For example, in returning to one second grade nearly two months later, she found that the class could recall the conflicts in the neighborhood and the good feelings they had when they successfully resolved them, but had a hard time remembering how they had gotten to resolution. However, when reminded, they were quick to identify the steps.

Nearly a year later, Katherine worked with third graders that had participated in the conflict-management program in second grade. She noticed that the class had a common understanding of both drama and conflict management vocabulary. They were able to move into role-play more easily than groups with no previous experience, also portraying more complex ideas through role-play. In group discussion, the children were extremely forthcoming in their remarks and specific in their use of language to describe emotions and conflict management techniques, such as I-messages.

> *Jerry:* I remember lots of things. We met a man with lots of friends who came to his shop. He spilled paint on the skateboards. We had conflict in the neighborhood.
>
> *Alison:* We learned how to solve conflicts by being in the neighborhood together. You talk it over. We learned to help out and be with each other.
>
> *Dennis:* We did drama.... Learned to stop, calm down, count to ten.

One child described angry feelings as "you want to combust and hit." Katherine sensed a higher "level of willingness to verbalize conflict issues and feelings" in these children than she had seen in similar groups who have not had this training.

SUMMARY AND CONCLUSIONS

In describing the goals and teaching strategies of the second grade program of Building Bridges, three important characteristics of drama emerged as being especially pertinent to the teaching of conflict-management skills: (a) emotional authenticity; (b) frame flexibility; and (c) drama as a method that models the process of conflict resolution.

Emotional Authenticity

A concern for those teaching conflict-resolution skills is how to evoke emotional authenticity in a training situation. Much of the initial effort in real-life conflict resolution focuses on breaking through the emotional impasse that usually exists between disputants. Most training programs rely extensively on role-playing to simulate actual conflict. However, when emotional investment is low, as it often is in one-dimensional hypothetical role-play scenarios, the resolution of conflict can be made to seem too easy. When players are not emotionally invested in the problem or the relationship, there is no impasse, and also no challenge. Without challenge, conflict-resolution skill cannot be demonstrated or practiced effectively.

Many role-plays in other conflict-management programs are performed after a brief verbal planning session and last only a few minutes. However, most of the strategies employed by our second-grade program are designed to immerse the children for an extended time in a complex drama rich in details and interrelationships. Belief is built over the span of several sessions through mapping, mime, encounters with teacher-in-role, etc. Conflict is generated as the logical extension of the interplay of relationships, as it is in real life. As neighbors, the second graders experience the spectrum of emotions—hope, pride, frustration, and outrage—generated in living through the event. The drama is carefully structured to systematically generate an authentic experience of conflict and a desire to resolve it. The evidence of our experience suggests that, as a method, extended informal classroom drama may be more likely than short-term role-play to produce a readiness to learn and retain conflict-resolution skills.

Frame Flexibility

In order to resolve conflict productively, people must be able to acknowledge the significance of feelings, yet not respond to each other in an emotionally reactive way. Feelings are significant facts in any conflict situation. They signal when there is a problem and when a solution is truly achieved. Yet behavior that is fueled by feeling without thinking is likely to escalate conflict rather than resolve it. The skills of calming oneself, reflective listening, and I-messages taught in Building Bridges sessions are key interpersonal techniques. They enable disputants to distance emotionally from the conflict situation while communicating about it. We call this "frame flexibility," the ability to move out of one context and into another. Psychologically, a person steps, at least with one foot, outside the frame. In conflict, this enables disputants to step back from the immediate event and communicate assumptions and expectations. This generates an awareness of other perspectives and alternative interpretations of events. It also enables disputants to see how behavior choices escalate or de-escalate the conflict, and to consider alternative choices.

Our second grade Building Bridges program creates multiple, nesting frames, each establishing a greater emotional distance from the innermost frame, the conflict. The frame of the neighbors' conflict is set within the frame of advisors consulting with Mr. Penny, which in turn is set within the frame of the social reality of the second grade. Drama strategies guide children into and out of the various levels of framing, establishing different perspectives from which to consider the conflict. As neighbors, they struggle with Grabber; as advisors, they empathize with Grabber and teach him necessary skills; and as second graders, they consider how to build a bridge in real life with their classmates.

The emphasis on fantasy in the second grade drama has significant implications for teaching conflict-resolution skills. The imaginative nature of this drama helps participants remain conscious that the events transpiring in drama time are not really happening, even though the meanings gleaned from the experience may be very real. In the drama, the children know that they are playing, and have agreed to play, and thus are aware of the frame. The result of this conscious agreement is that players are able to move easily between definitions of reality. Theoretically, because they can move out of frame, they can distance themselves from the emotions of their initial perspective and are freed to consider the emotional reality of the other side of the story. They are able to move outside of their own role to empathize with another. Based on the information from such multiple perspectives, they are able to generate and evaluate possible solutions to conflict. Our experience suggests that frame flexibility, fundamental to skillful conflict resolution in real life, is effectively engendered in extended whole-class drama.

Method Models Conflict Resolution

Drama as a teaching method assumes a collaborative relationship between teacher and students. As the Building Bridges program demonstrates, while the drama leader begins with a plan, the method assumes that the plan will evolve in interaction with the students. Thus, the drama process is based in constructive negotiation: considering multiple choices, listening to different points of view, working to reach collective agreements, etc.

Drama is by nature a creative and cooperative group activity, structured so that participants enter the world of the play as a group. They encounter the problems in the as-if world and must work together to solve them. The focus of drama is in setting up conditions in which students work collectively to solve problems and arrive at their own conclusions. The drama work, which requires people to create fictive relationships and solve fictive problems, provides practice in the creative synergy required for maintaining real relationships in real problem solving.

What have we learned? In terms of teaching conflict-resolution skills, the extended whole-class drama method enables students to experience interpersonal conflict subjectively and affectively, while reflecting and negotiating objectively and cognitively. The strategic use of frame allows the drama leader to generate the balance of cognitive and affective involvement, optimal for learning conflict-resolution skills. Full group drama is a particularly appropriate method for developing the mental flexibility and emotional fluency necessary for successful conflict resolution.

Furthermore, identifying this fit between drama and conflict-resolution skill may have implications for our understanding about the nature of both drama and conflict resolution. One theoretical proposition could be that drama, in all its incarnations, including dramatic play, role-play, and theater, is fundamentally a method for understanding and expressing how human beings construct their personal and interpersonal realities. Drama then could be recognized as the inherent symbol system for the exploration and expression of interpersonal intelligence (Gardner, 1983), of which skill in conflict resolution constitutes a major part.

NOTES

[1] See the *Building Bridges Handbooks for Primary Grades and Intermediate Grades*, ©1991. Colorado Educational Theatre Company, 3606 Silver Plume Lane, Boulder, CO 80303.

[2] See pp. 132–135 for an elaboration of these three characteristics of drama process.

REFERENCES

Friedman, P., & Yarbrough, E. (1985). *Training strategies from start to finish*. Englewood Cliffs, NJ: Prentice-Hall.

Gardner, H. (1983). *Frames of mind*. New York: HarperCollins.

Gardner, H. (1991). *The unschooled mind*. New York: HarperCollins.

Heathcote, D. (1984). From the particular to the universal. In L. Johnson & C. O'Neill (Eds.), *Dorothy Heathcote: Collected writings on education and drama* (pp. 103–110). London: Hutchinson.

Heathcote, D., & Bolton, G. (1995). *Drama for learning: Dorothy Heathcote's mantle of the expert approach to education*. Portsmouth, NH: Heinemann.

Hocker, J., & Wilmot, W. (1989). *Interpersonal conflict.* Dubuque, IA: William C. Brown.

Judson, S. (Ed.). (1984). *A manual on nonviolence and children.* Philadelphia: New Society Press.

Lam, J. (1989). *The impact of conflict resolution programs on schools: A review and synthesis of the evidence.* Amherst, MA: National Association for Mediation in Education.

Lickona, T. (1991). *Educating for character.* New York: Doubleday Dell.

McGinnis, E., & Goldstein, A. (1984). *Skillstreaming the elementary school child: A guide for teaching prosocial skills.* Champaign, IL: Research Press.

Prothrow-Stith, D. (1991). *Deadly consequences: How violence is destroying our teenage population and a plan to begin solving the problem.* New York: HarperCollins.

Schmidt, F., & Friedman, A. (1985). *Creative conflict solving for kids.* Miami Beach, FL: Grace Contrino Abrams Peace Education Foundation.

OTHER RESOURCES

Bateson, G. (1972). Toward a theory of play and fantasy. In G. Bateson (Ed.), *Steps to an ecology of mind* (pp. 177–193). New York: Ballentine. (Reprinted from *Psychiatric research reports, vol. II*, pp. 39–51, 1955, Washington, DC: American Psychological Association)

Goffman, E. (1974). *Frame analysis.* Cambridge, MA: Harvard University Press.

Kriedler, W. (1984). *Creative conflict resolution.* Glenview, IL: Scott Foresman.

Prutzman, P. (1988). *The friendly classroom for a small planet.* Philadelphia: New Society Press.

Sternberg, P. (1998). *Theatre for conflict resolution in the classroom and beyond.* Portsmouth, NH: Heinemann.

chapter 6

Attitudes, Behavior, and Moral Reasoning

Betty Jane Wagner
Roosevelt University

E ducators and drama theorists have long claimed that improvisational role-playing in the classroom is a powerful way to improve:

- self-expression, particularly for students who have trouble showing
  their emotions in other situations;
- self-understanding, through talking about feelings with others;
- empathy and understanding of others;
- and behavior and interpersonal relations.[1]

Participants should gain in self-confidence as well, because all ideas are
accepted in a drama and all honest effort valued.

EFFECT ON ATTITUDES

Heathcote (Johnson & O'Neill, 1984) asserts that engaging in drama
helps us explore the feelings of an experience, thus decreasing any anxiety we may have toward that experience, and thereby increasing our
control over it. Bolton asserts that the effect of drama is long-term:
"sensitivity, commitment, confidence, self-assertion, eagerness to learn,
the development of positive thinking and the acquisition of wisdom is a
kind of natural outcome of drama" (Bolton, 1990, p. 11). In their meta-
analysis of empirical studies, Kardash and Wright (1987) found that creative drama appears to have a positive effect on self-esteem. Research in
the field is in a state of methodological flux, so the studies reported in
this book represent both quantitative studies of the effects of educational
drama and qualitative analyses and interpretations.

Two recent doctoral dissertations (Fischer, 1991; Halladay, 1994) have explored parallels between participation in drama and what Csikszentmihalyi (1990) has extensively identified, namely optimal experience, or "flow." This comes when a person chooses a goal in which to invest psychic energy and keeps the energy focused on the goal. Action merges with awareness, and the individual is totally involved in a process that excludes outside distractions. Halladay (1994) found that both creative drama and actor training have significant theoretical parallels to components in optimal experience. The congruence between drama and flow is the most obvious when the activities involve a physical manifestation.

Perhaps because of this total mental and physical engagement, drama can effect opinion change. King and Janis (1956) compared the effects of improvised versus non-improvised role-playing on opinion changes and found that the degree of improvisation positively affected the amount of opinion change. They concluded that in inventive improvisation, a person's psychological resistance was lowered whenever he was forced to assume different ideas and roles; this made him or her more amenable to change in attitude. Renaud and Stolovitch (1988) found that simulation games that included role-playing improved the attitudes and behavior of five-year-olds toward traffic safety.

Five empirical studies report that educational drama changes attitudes toward the self (Gourgey, Bosseau, & Delgado, 1985; Hedahl, 1980; Noble, Egan, & McDowell, 1977; Pisaneschi, 1977; Rosen & Koziol, Jr., 1990); and two others do not show a significant effect (Barrager, 1980; Huntsman, 1982). A study by Miller, Rynden, and Schlein (1993) shows improvement in being considered a friend by one's peers. Two studies (Gimmestad & DeChiara, 1982; McLaughlin, 1990) show drama changes attitudes toward different racial or ethnic groups, but one does not (Greer, 1986). Bramwell (1992) reports a change in attitude toward the elderly; Feinberg (1977) sees a movement away from sex role stereotyping; and Jackson (1993) and Buege (1991) note a change in attitude toward emotionally disturbed peers.

When Rosen and Koziol, Jr. (1990) compared oral reading, dramatic activities, and theatrical production, they found that drama had a positive influence on attitudes toward the self ($p < .01$). The sequence of theater production activities led to an in-class staging of scenes from a play. Rosen and Koziol, Jr., concluded that "drama had a greater influence on oral communication skills and self-esteem whereas theater production had a somewhat greater influence on knowledge and comprehension of the play" (O'Farrell, 1993, p. 29). Their findings confirmed Pisaneschi's (1977) finding that drama has a positive effect on self-concept. After only six hours of informal drama experiences, 20 lower socioeconomic urban seven-year-olds were significantly better able to describe themselves verbally and nonverbally and were more self-aware (Noble, Egan, & McDowell, 1977).

Hedahl (1980) compared a course in creative drama with a course in creative drama that included filmmaking, and with a course in creative writing and oral interpretation. The children were fifth and sixth graders from two middle-class, parochial schools. After 15 classes and again 22 weeks later, using the Piers-Harris Children's Self-Concept Scale, Hedahl found that immediately following the classes, students in both the creative drama and the drama with filmmaking courses made greater improvement in self-concept than those in the writing and oral interpretation class. The boys improved significantly in both drama conditions, but the girls' improvement was only marginally significant ($p <$ .10) in the drama-plus-filmmaking course. Twenty-two weeks later, only the boys continued to show improvement in self-concept. Students of one of the two teachers had more positive influence on self-concept than the other teacher.

Gourgey, Bosseau, and Delgado (1985) found that six months of role-playing and story making or playwriting, as well as improvisational exercises, significantly ($p <$ .001) improved self-expression, trust, acceptance of others, self-awareness, and awareness of others, but not self-acceptance and empowerment. Their student population was made up of 141 lower socioeconomic Black and Hispanic students in the fourth, fifth, and sixth grades. They also found that reading achievement significantly improved, which "may have been the result of the program's strong emphasis on individual and group story making and story telling" (p. 14), since these activities may have developed skills directly applicable to reading comprehension.

Barrager (1980) found that Heathcote-type drama was significantly effective in improving a group of sixth and seventh graders' self-esteem when compared (a) with a group of students who read plays, wrote reports, completed papers, discussed and analyzed plays, and did play readings, and (b) with two control groups. All four groups had thirty 45-minute sessions. Students were tested on the Self-Esteem Inventory and the Children's Self-Concept Scale. The Heathcote-type drama group improved significantly more ($p <$ .05) than the main control—which received no drama at all—on the Self-Esteem Inventory, but not better than the play reading group (p. 32). There were no significant differences between the groups on the Children's Self-Concept Scale, although mean changes were in the direction of favoring the Heathcote-type drama group. The small sample size (54 students in four different groups) make it difficult to generalize from this study.

Huntsman (1982) found that 30 first-year college students significantly improved in self-actualization ($p <$ .05) but not in self-worth or the ability to relate to others. The experimental group participated in 22 two-hour sessions of creative drama activities. These included voice and body exercises, puppetry, dramatic play, original theater games, and Spolin's (1963/1985) improvisational theater games. The control group did not receive any special instruction. Huntsman used as tests the California Psychological Inventory, the Personal Orientation Inventory, and the Self-Report Inventory.

Miller, Rynden, and Schlein (1993) compared dramatic games with noncompetitive games with 24 regular and special education fifth-grade students. He found that after drama games, the mentally retarded students were more highly regarded as friends than those who played the noncompetitive games.

Drama can also enhance cross-cultural understandings, improve human relations, and reduce racial and ethnic tensions (McLaughlin, 1990). In an experimental study, Gimmestad and DeChiara (1982) found that students in two public schools in New York who were exposed to plays and activities focusing on Black, Puerto Rican, Jewish, and Chinese ethnic groups improved in social distance and knowledge of the cultures. The control group students did not show similar gains.

Greer (1986) concludes that research on the effect of simulations or role-playing activities have had fair success in positively affecting the racial attitudes of Whites toward Blacks. However, Greer's own study did not confirm this conclusion. He compared a two-week role-playing unit, stimulated with a multimedia kit, "Log Cabins and Great Houses," with a traditional social studies unit on South Carolina history. Greer's subjects were a mixed group of 79 White and Black eighth-grade students. He measured the effect on racial attitudes of the White students in this group with the Social Distance Scale originally developed by Emory Bogardus, and with the Gough, Harris, Martin, and Edwards Prejudice Index. He measured student attitudes toward social studies with the Estes Attitude Scale. Greer found that the role-playing did not significantly affect the racial attitudes of the participating White eighth-grade students, nor was their attitude toward social studies on the Estes significantly different than the control group. However, the students did find the unit stimulating and interesting, according to a post-test questionnaire.

Bramwell (1990, 1992), the winner of the 1991 American Alliance for Theater and Education Research Award, examined the attitudes of fifth graders toward aging and elderly people both before and after a three-month program of drama education. Her qualitative and quantitative examination showed improvement in the attitudes of the two groups that engaged in drama ($n = 22$ and $n = 29$) in comparison to a control group ($n = 19$). The goal of the drama program was to help students develop an attitude closer to *agape*, or brotherly love of other persons. Because people cannot love what they do not know, a stance of agape imposes a responsibility to come to know the other—in particular, to come to know the other's goals and means. The goal is not to behave *ideally* toward others, because in so doing, persons run great risks as they consider the subjugation of their own wants and needs by taking into account the goals and means of others. As Bramwell notes, respect for persons includes, indeed demands, equal respect for the self and requires a continuous balancing act which generates tension, both within the person making the judgment and among persons involved in the outcome.

Drama is particularly effective in changing attitudes because it "holds the real experiences of its participants in mind at the same time that it creates an imagined world in which characters are engaged in struggling with the central paradox" (Boal, 1979, pp. 7–8). Bramwell (1992) points out that any "investigation of topics through drama is primarily the investigation of the norm and the ideal in the attitudes and values of participants through an action-reflection dialectic" (p. 10). As students engage in drama, they try on the moral stances of imagined characters and in the process identify with them. Through this fusion of participants' and characters' concerns, a persona can emerge through negotiation with others in honest action and reflection both inside and outside the drama. This process nudges the participants toward the normative; in the process, they reflect on what might be ideal behavior under such circumstances. Participants in a drama are always referring to their experiences in the real world and the logical consequences of events. However, actual change in behavior is difficult to measure, because it often comes much later than the experience with the drama.

Bramwell (1992) had two experts in the depiction skills of children and psychological assessment, respectively, measure the children's change in attitude from pre- to post-tests using the Children's Attitudes Toward the Elderly Test (created by Jantz, Seefeldt, Galper, and Serock), consisting of a blind assessment of pre- and post-drawings. They sorted the drawings first into strong and weak depictions, then into positive, neutral, and negative depictions. Both found a clear improvement in attitude on the part of the groups that had engaged in drama, and the improvement was greater for the strong depictions than for the weak ones. An analysis of the journals children kept as part of the drama showed that the children believed their attitudes toward old people had changed as a result of the drama. Some of them realized that drama had caused them to revalue people in their own lives. The findings of this study were confirmed in an ethnographic analysis of interviews with the co-researchers and with the teacher.

Bramwell (1992) found that the positive change consisted of not only more knowledge and feeling for the elderly, but also a disposition to act more positively toward them in the future. The quantitative study did not show a change in the children's fear of aging, but a reduced fear of aging showed up on qualitative examination in one case. In a subsequent unit of study on "transformations and explosions," the children became fascinated with the process of aging and showed a sense of wonder about such changes.

Feinberg (1977) showed that a creative dramatics inservice program for teachers and students effectively liberalizes sex role stereotyping more than an inservice program without drama. Two studies showed that social interactions using creative drama improved attitudes toward emotionally disturbed children (Buege, 1991; Jackson, 1993). Jackson's investigation of the effects of creative dramatics participation on the reading achievement and attitudes of elementary school children with behavioral disorders found a significant improvement in attitude, as measured by the Piers-Harris Self-Concept Scale. However, he did not find significance in the improvement of reading comprehension. Buege found that normal fourth graders improved their attitudes toward emotionally disturbed children, and the disturbed children improved in their self-concepts after 32 half-hour weekly sessions involving creative drama and social skills training. She made two videotapes of each of the 32 sessions; other sources of data were the teacher's log and student journals, interviews with individuals after the program was over, and indepth informant interviews with the teacher, the student teacher, and the parent volunteer who operated the camcorder.

Three studies show that drama can be effective in changing attitudes toward the curriculum or toward the idea of attending a university (Norton, 1973; Ridel, 1975; Simons & Hughes 1991). Ridel showed that a six-week exposure to creative drama in an average ninth-grade language arts class of 25 effected a significant difference ($p < .01$) over pretest scores in attitudes toward the class and enthusiasm for drama, using participant observation and the Torrance Test of Creative Thinking, Verbal Form. The creative drama program, based on Spolin's (1963/1985) theater games, was led by a teacher inexperienced in drama one day a week for a semester. Ridel also found improvement in the creative writing ability and originality of the students. As there was no control group, it is impossible to know how much of the difference could be accounted for by the maturation that took place in the four months between the first and the second writing sample. Ridel's conclusion is that creative dramatics can aid the development of the imagination and communication, even with a teacher inexperienced in drama. Norton (1973) found that second graders improved in their attitude toward the curriculum, their interpersonal skills, and their self-perception after a twice-weekly, 55-minute creative drama unit over a 12-week period, when compared with a matched nontreatment control group.

Drama can also change students' attitudes toward a new experience that might seem overwhelming or even frightening. Simons and Hughes (1991) took on the daunting task of encouraging a group of 33 students from a rural high school to seek access to the University of Sydney as their right. The University, founded in 1850, is an imposing structure, with its grand main quadrangle and medieval architecture. The sheer size of the student body is the same as the total population of the town in which the students lived. The students toured the University as part of their four-day drama excursion to Sydney, and it was clear they found it to be a "profoundly new and foreign environment" (p. 36.)

After a discussion of what it is like to leave a country town and go to a huge university and what they had seen on the tour, they prepared, in groups of six, *tableau vivants*, depicting various imagined stages of a student's progress through university life; they were also instructed to include internal conflict. The small groups presented their depictions chronologically, ending with graduation in the Great Hall. The whole group analyzed the body language, attempting to identify the emotional content of each scene, and then reflected on university life.

Then the drama began. Each student was issued a contract—emblazoned with the university crest and a Latin motto—indicating that he or she was specifically selected for a cadetship, with full tuition, board, a weekly allowance of $200, and a guaranteed job upon graduation. The Latin motto was a clause signing over intellectual property to the University Foundation. They all signed their contracts.

Then the teacher-in-role as a TV interviewer doing a documentary about Australia's most brilliant young students, asked them about their character and their work. They divided into groups depending on their major interests or career goals, and they were told that in their final year they were to develop a group project which would better humanity. After they developed their solutions to problems, they presented them to the group. For example, the medical scientists discovered a process to allow paraplegics to recover, and the architects created a domed city to counteract the greenhouse effect.

The teacher-in-role as an official of the University Foundation, listened, but was skeptical. She warned the students not to release their findings to anyone else, drawing attention to the Latin clause in the contract. They were confronted with a dilemma: they would agree to the contracts they had signed, accepting that they would *not* share their discovery with humanity, or they would lose their scholarships and be prevented from graduating. In the reflection that followed the drama, the students discussed the choice between individual benefit and the good of society.

Draping the students in the metaphorical "mantle of the expert" lifted them to a more universal problem than the quandary of university students. The effect of the drama was to move rural students from an awe-struck and intimidated state to a feeling of "at-homeness" in the Great Hall. They even took the Hall over to present a group of songs, reveling in the sound of the Hall and their own talent. The "drama session enabled the students to realize that they could manage change and that the new environment of the University was not one to be feared.... [It] had ceased to belong to someone else; it had become part of their culture and a possibility for their future" (Simons & Hughes, 1991, p. 38).

EFFECT ON SOCIAL BEHAVIOR

Because drama is a group art, it is not surprising that drama theorists have long recognized its efficacy in promoting social growth.[2] Changes in attitude are part of any change in social behavior, but in this section of the chapter, we survey only those studies that focus on changes in the way persons behave in interactions with others.

Several quasi-experimental studies have shown that classroom drama has a positive effect on self-confidence, self-concept, self-actualization, empathy, helping behavior, cooperation, and the development of social competence.[3] However, Elder (1983) and Ziegler (1971) were not able to establish such a relationship.

In this chapter, we report on 10 studies that show a positive relationship between drama and social behavior.[4] The last four of these are with emotionally disturbed or learning disabled students. Finally, we report on Elder's (1983) study, which shows no correlation between drama and improved social behavior.

Connolly and Doyle (1984) found positive correlations between pre-schoolers' sociodramatic play and several measures of social competence. Shmukler and Naveh (1980) showed that training in sociodramatic play results in gains in social skills, such as cooperation.

In a study of third-grade students, Fischer and Garrison (1980) found that qualitative changes in social relationships occurred after group experiences involving discussion, role-playing, and role training. The students were more direct and honest in their communication, which included expressing their needs and feelings. They accepted introverts and rejectees and included them in their activities more often, showing greater respect for individual differences.

Kranz, Lund, Pruett, and Stanley (1982) found improvement in inter-personal relationships and self-concepts of gifted fifth graders. They improved statistically significantly in their sense of personal worth, feeling of belonging, personal adjustment, family relations, social adjustment, cooperative behavior, and leadership; and they demonstrated significantly fewer instances of withdrawal, nervous symptoms, and antisocial tendencies.

Backstrom (1988/1989), in an ethnographic study, found improved self-concept, according to the Piers-Harris Self-Concept Scale, after eighth graders read stories and used role-playing to re-enact scenes from the literature in an eighth-grade curriculum. Students showed improved attendance, grades, cooperation, and attitudes toward the teacher and other students, as well as toward reading. They also improved in reading comprehension and in their ability to remain focused on tasks. Backstrom observed that students grew in self-confidence, became more independent learners, and volunteered more often. Results were based mainly on classroom observation, student/teacher interviews, and journals. Additional data were pre/post interest and self-concept surveys, unit quizzes, and parent questionnaires. Backstrom also found that when students read stories and then reenacted them, their reading comprehension improved.

Danielson (1992) investigated the effect of role-playing, script writing, and improvisation on two classes of rural, "low ability" tenth graders. He observed growth in social skills and the creation, through theater games, of an environment allowing nonthreatening group interaction.

We now look at the four studies that show drama to be effective with emotionally disturbed or learning disabled students. Goodwin (1985) studied the effects of creative drama—including side coaching, in-role improvisation, pantomime, narrative mime, and exercises in movement, rhythm, and the use of hand puppets—with 11 residents of a home for individuals with socially unacceptable behavior. Using a case study method, she looked at the effect of 10 creative drama sessions of 30 to 45 minutes each. Goodwin concluded, after observations and analyzing videotapes of the sessions, that 10 sessions were not enough to effect a change in behavior, especially among the lower-functioning participants. However, the dramatic activities did make a definite impression on them.

In a study with emotionally handicapped students, Miller, Ward, and White (1969) found that long-term, simulated-environment treatment through elementary and junior high school is significantly more effective than conventional instruction, in terms of improving personal and social adjustment, but not in terms of academic achievement in social studies.

Batchelor (1981) found that creative dramatics and theater arts increased the self-esteem and social skills of nine adolescents who were diagnosed as severely socially and emotionally handicapped. He introduced the group of nine, attending the Wiltwyck Alternative School in New York, to warmup exercises, relaxation techniques, theater games, and improvisations. His descriptive accounts of their moment-by-moment interactions with each other and with him, the drama director, illuminate the challenges drama educators face with such students, who moved from rebelliousness and indifference to commitment and cooperation in a final improvisational performance for their parents.

For six months, Batchelor directed this group, consisting of those who had previously had abusive or destructive parents, and who lived in a neighborhood of poverty, blight, hopelessness, and crime, compounding their physical and emotional misery and deprivation. Several had sometimes lived on the streets or had been in retention centers and prisons. Their school lives were nomadic, transferring from school to school. Batchelor reported, "Two had violently attacked a teacher. Some had been diagnosed as manic-depressive, and there were suggestions that they could turn homicidal" (1981, p. 123).

Batchelor's (1981) observations and firsthand narrative accounts make a strong case for drama as a way to enhance self-esteem. He showed how these disturbed students moved from belligerent, antisocial behavior, which caused episodes of "acting out," to a sense of group cohesion and better self-concepts. At the beginning, the students were hostile toward each other and disrespectful and suspicious toward the director/investigator, who was just another dubious authority figure to them. In the six months of creative dramatics, the students learned how to concentrate, to respond helpfully to one another, and to care about their own welfare, as well as each other's.

There is some promising evidence that the changed attitudes and behavior took root in their lives, even if the roots were fragile. Some examples: Their attendance at other Wiltwyck classes that spring showed improvement as they began to perceive the entire school in a new light, as a place of proven value to them; during the summer...five of the drama students served as peer counselors in Wiltwyck's summer orientation program for new students. Also, two worked in a summer arts education program and were accepted in a beginners acting workshop. All nine were considered by their teachers and placement counselors to be sufficiently socialized to be accepted as regular students in other high schools.

Vogel (1975) found that creative drama with children who had learning disabilities showed significant improvement in social adjustment, as measured by the California Test of Personality. However, Vogel found no significant difference between them and the control group in reading ability, as measured by the Metropolitan Achievement Test.

Educational drama can improve students' attendance, achievement, self-discipline, and self-esteem (Gourgey, Bosseau, & Delgado, 1985; Ingersoll & Kase, 1970). In Ingersoll and Kase's study, on the effects of creative dramatics on the learning and retention of fifth and sixth-grade students, females tended to benefit more than the males did.

"Developmental drama," as Widdows (1996) termed it, resulted in more consistent positive behavior on the part of 20 secondary students. In her action research, using a triangulated case study, Widdows reported that students widened their areas of reference and modified the way they related to people. The data for the study came from Widdows' detailed research diary as action researcher, participant observer, and teacher; and from an outside observer, a nondrama specialist, who observed a different student for one lesson each week, using a structured observation sheet, checking the key areas in educational drama and drama therapy: cooperation, listening, adaptability, and analyzing. In addition, the observer asked the students: "What emotions did you feel in the drama? Which parts of the contract [a contract of acceptable behavior agreed upon by the class before the drama began] have you achieved? Were the feelings in the drama different from those in the contract? How do you get yourself to feel these emotions?" (p. 69). Students also kept a notebook answering the questions: "What were the most powerful moments in the drama for you?" and "What do you need to improve upon for future work?" (p. 69). There were three 55-minute lessons of drama per week during the school year.

The developmental drama Widdows (1996) describes "combines educational drama and drama therapy theories and it aims to achieve a healthy psychological state by which pupils are empowered to solve problems and make decisions" (p. 65). In the drama, students are involved in group decisions that require the social skills of cooperation, concentration, and commitment. As they engaged in the drama, their confidence and self-esteem increased. This counteracted their negative behaviors, so the students became more personally effective.

The results of Elder's (1983) investigation contrasts with those reported above. She did not find correlations between either role-playing or sociodramatic play and prosocial behavior during free play. The 89 first graders who participated in this study were randomly assigned to one of five experimental groups: (a) role-playing with prosocial content (b) induction with prosocial content (c) sociodramatic play (d) stories and discussion, and (e) no intervention. The training intervention for each group, except the no intervention group, consisted of nine 20-minute sessions on alternate days over a three-week period.

MORAL REASONING

To play any part well, you have to put yourself inside the skin of another person, to view the world from a different perspective, and to develop empathy. What better training ground for living in a democracy, which is at bottom legislated empathy—a constitutional recognition that all persons are worthy of the same rights and protections? To develop empathy is to achieve what John Dewey argued was the central purpose of schools: to prepare citizens to function effectively in a democratic society.

Morality is the unavoidable concern of actors, playwrights, and audiences. As Dewey (1934/1959) put it, "a person's ideas and treatment of his fellows are dependent upon his power to put himself imaginatively in their place" (p. 348). As drama participants struggle to reconcile their own views of the world with those of the characters they are playing, they grow in moral reasoning. Thus, the aim of drama is the same as that of writing. As Elbow (1986) argues, we come to construct the concepts we have about the world by gaining "as many different and conflicting knowings as possible" (p. 242). Many "important insights and breakthoughs end up as a movement of thought from one frame of reference...to a larger one. There appears to be a contradiction...but the original one can finally be understood as a subset of the larger one" (p. 251, as cited by Edmiston, 1992, p. 24).

To illustrate how drama can facilitate this larger perspective, let us look at a drama based on the dilemma faced by Nathan in the novel *Weasel* (1991) by Cynthia De Felice. The students stopped reading the novel at the point where Nathan is faced with the opportunity of killing his enemy, Weasel, the man who was responsible for taking the Indians from their land and for the disappearance of the children's father. As long as he was at large, he would continue to kill and perhaps destroy Nathan's family. The teacher took on the role of Nathan, and the children formed a circle surrounding him, coming up with arguments for Nathan's killing Weasel. Then they stopped and repeated the activity, but this time each person had to come up with a reason not to kill Weasel. Finally, the students lined up in two rows facing each other to form a "Conscience Alley." Then the teacher, in role as Nathan, picked up a stick as his gun and walked slowly down the alley. The students voiced their opinions as his conscience as he walked along. By the time 'Nathan' reached the end of the alley, he threw the 'gun' on the floor. Then the children discussed the reason for his decision, and clearly their own attitudes had changed. They learned that a moral decision is not necessarily black and white. Then they went back to the author's book.

When students are placed in situations where they can view issues through the lens of another person, both their empathetic understanding and their moral attitudes are affected positively Because they are able to picture what they otherwise might never see, they find themselves examining their values and behavior (Dapice, Cobb, Hutchins, & Siegal, 1988). We have no way of testing or knowing whether this experience will change the students' moral behavior in real-life situations, but certainly experiencing the "grayness" of all true moral dilemmas should help prepare students for decisions in the future.

Bell and Ledford (1978) noted that, after sociodrama, elementary school boys showed a positive change in attitude before they made any observable changes in behavior. They also found that the effects of sociodrama lasted over a long term. The "against others" behavior of the boys continued to decrease after the completion of the sociodrama activities. Thus, they concluded that the process of behavioral change is gradual.

Bauer (1979) found that creative drama experiences were not as effective as small group discussions of moral dilemmas in promoting growth in moral reasoning and the reduction of dogmatism among college students. Forty-two students participated in creative drama, 46 participated in small group discussions, and 33, selected randomly from other communication skills sections, served as control subjects. They were measured with Rest's Defining Issues Test and Rokeach's Dogmatism Scale. Small-group discussions of moral dilemmas were significantly more effective ($p < .008$) in the growth of moral judgment than the creative drama activities. Although both the drama and discussion groups decreased in dogmatism, the difference between them was not significant.

Although Kardash and Wright's (1987) meta-analysis found that creative drama appears to have a positive effect on moral reasoning, in Kurdek's (1978) extensive review of the many studies of the relationship between perspective taking and moral judgment, the results were inconsistent. He attributes this to methodological shortcomings and the lack of comparable measurement instruments among the studies. Thus, even though there is some evidence that role-playing increases perspective taking and this ability seems to be a necessary prerequisite for mature moral judgment, one cannot prove this leads to more mature moral judgment or behavior; the findings of the large body of literature on moral development does not as yet shed much light on the relationship. Chandler (1973) found that training through role-playing in social perspective taking decreased the rates of delinquency among adolescents, but we do not know if that was the only cause of the change in behavior. Kurdek recommends that future investigators "conceive of both perspective taking and moral development as multidimensional constructs" and "devise reliable and ecologically valid assessments of these constructs" (p. 23).

As we have seen in this chapter, a number of studies show that drama can affect a positive change in opinions and attitudes toward oneself and others, and an improvement in socially accepted behavior. However, studies of the relationship of drama to moral reasoning are not consistent enough for us to generalize from them.

NOTES

[1] McCaslin, 1981; Rubin, Piche, Michlin, & Johnson, 1984; Verriour, 1984.

[2] Giffin, 1984, 1990; Heathcote & Bolton, 1995; Heinig, 1977; McCaslin, 1980, 1981; Moffett & Wagner, 1992; Siks, 1977; Wagner, 1976/1999, 1983; Ward, 1947; Way, 1972.

[3] Clore & Jeffery, 1972; DeCourcy-Wernette, 1977; Garner, 1972; Johnson, 1975.

[4] Backstrom, 1988/1989; Batchelor, 1981; Connolly & Doyle, 1984; Danielson, 1992; Fischer & Garrison, 1980; Goodwin, 1985; Kranz, Lund, Pruett, & Stanley, 1982; Miller, Ward, & White, 1969; Shmukler & Naveh, 1980; Vogel, 1975.

REFERENCES

Backstrom, E. L. (1989). The effects of creative dramatics on student behaviors and attitudes in literature and language arts (Doctoral dissertation, University of California, Los Angeles, 1988). *Dissertation Abstracts International, 49*(11), 3243A.

Barrager, P. W. (1980). The effects of Dorothy Heathcote's informal drama in influencing self esteem of pre-adolescents. *Empirical Research in Theatre, 6,* 5–35.

Batchelor, R. (1981). Creative dramatics and theater arts among socially and emotionally handicapped inner-city adolescents: A description and analysis of a drama project. *Dissertation Abstracts International, 41*(12), 4886A. (University Microfilms No. 81-11499)

Bauer, L. J. (1979). Moral reasoning and the decrease of dogmatism in the communication classroom: Small group discussions and creative drama as methods of instruction (Doctoral dissertation, Northwestern University, 1979). *Dissertation Abstracts International, 40*(06), 2980A.

Bell, S., & Ledford, T. (1978). The effects of sociodrama on the behavior and attitudes of elementary school boys. *Journal of Group Psychotherapy, Psychodrama, and Sociometry, 31,* 117–135.

Boal, A. (1979). *Theatre of the oppressed* (C. A. McBride, Trans.). London: Phitto.

Bolton, G. (1990, November). Four aims of teaching drama. *London Drama*.

Bramwell, R. J. T. (1990). The effect of drama education on children's attitudes to the elderly and to aging (Doctoral dissertation, University of British Columbia, 1990). *Dissertation Abstracts International, 53*(09), 3165A.

Bramwell, R. J. T. (1992). Drama education and children's attitudes toward aging and toward the elderly. *Youth Theatre Journal, 6*(4), 7–11.

Buege, C. J. (1991). The effect of creative dramatics and social skills training on attitude and self-concept (emotionally disturbed). *Dissertation Abstracts International, 52*(04), 1190A. (University Microfilms No. D81-12054)

Chandler, M. J. (1973). Egocentrism and antisocial behavior: The assessment and training of social perspective-taking skills. *Developmental Psychology, 9*, 1–6.

Clore, G. L., & Jeffery, K. M. (1972). Emotional role playing, attitude change, and attraction toward a disabled person. *Journal of Personality and Social Psychology, 23*, 105–111.

Connolly, J. A., & Doyle, A. (1984). Relation of social fantasy play to social competence in preschoolers. *Developmental Psychology, 20*, 797–806.

Csikszentmihalyi, M. (1990). Literacy and intrinsic motivation. *Dedalus, 119*(2), 115–140.

Danielson, T. R. (1992). *Evaluating the ability of drama-based instruction to influence the socialization of tenth grade English students labeled as "low ability"* (Report No. EDD001). Washington, DC: National Endowment for the Arts. (ERIC Document Reproduction Service No. ED 367 000)

Dapice, A., Cobb, L., Hutchins, E., & Siegal, G. (1988). Teaching and learning values. *Educational Horizons, 66*(3), 107–110.

DeCourcy-Wernette, E. E. (1977). Defining, implementing, and assessing the effects of human focus drama on children in two settings—drama workshops and a social studies class. *Dissertation Abstracts International, 38*(08), 4451A. (University Microfilms No. D77-19755)

De Felice, C. (1991). *Weasel.* New York: Avon.

Dewey, J. (1959). *Art as experience.* New York: G.P. Putnam's Sons. (Original work published 1934)

Edmiston, B. W. (1992). The dramatic art of theatre and drama. *The Drama Theatre Teacher, 4*(2), 21–24.

Elbow, P. (1986). *Embracing contraries.* New York: Oxford University Press.

Elder, J. L. D. (1983). The relationship between role-taking, prosocial reasoning and prosocial behaviour. (Doctoral dissertation, University of Western Ontario, 1982). *Dissertation Abstracts International, 43*(08), 274B.

Feinberg, R. M. (1977). *The modification of sex-role attitudes of students through teacher in-service education using creative dramatics.* Unpublished doctoral dissertation, Boston University School of Education.

Fischer, I. (1991). DIE paedagogish psychische bedeutung vot schulspiel: Moeglichkeiten zur foerderlung einer progressiven personalisation in de schule. (Doctoral dissertation, Universitaet Salzburg, Austria). *Dissertation Abstracts International, 54*(04), 273C.

Fischer, R., & Garrison, C. (1980). Transactional analysis and role training in the classroom: A pilot study. *Journal of Group Psychotherapy, Psychodrama, and Sociometry, 33,* 88–91.

Garner, R. C. (1972). Effects of a simulation learning game on student attitudes and on the learning of factual information. *Dissertation Abstracts International, 33*(02), 662A. (University Microfilms No. D72-22775)

Giffin, H. (1984). The coordination of meaning in the creation of a shared make-believe reality. In I. Bretherton (Ed.), *Symbolic play: The development of social understanding* (pp. 73–100). New York: Academic Press.

Giffin, H. (1990). To say or not to say. *Youth Theatre Journal, 5*(2), 14–20.

Gimmestad, B. J., & DeChiara, E. (1982). Dramatic plays: A vehicle for prejudice reduction in the elementary school. *Journal of Educational Research, 76*(1), 45–49.

Goodwin, D. A. (1985). An investigation of the efficacy of creative drama as a method for teaching social skills to mentally retarded youth and adults. *Children's Theatre Review, 34*(2), 23–26.

Gourgey, A. F., Bosseau, J., & Delgado, J. (1985). The impact of an improvisational dramatics program on students attitudes and achievement. *Children's Theatre Review, 34*(3), 9–14. (ERIC Document Reproduction Service No. ED 244 245)

Greer, L. (1986). The impact of an experimental eight-grade social studies unit on the attitudes of white students toward black people. *Dissertation Abstracts International, 47*(06), 2109A. (University Microfilms No. 86-19636)

Halladay, J. (1995). The potential for optimal experience in creative drama an actor training. (Doctoral dissertation, University of Utah, 1994). *Dissertation Abstracts International, 55*(07), 1745A.

Heathcote, D., & Bolton, G. (1995). *Drama for learning: Dorothy Heathcote's mantle of the expert approach to education.* Portsmouth, NH: Heinemann.

Hedahl, G. O. (1980). The effects of creative drama and filmmaking on self-concept. (Doctoral dissertation, University of Minnesota, 1980). *Dissertation Abstracts International, 41*(03), 851A.

Heinig, R. B. (1977, April). *Creative drama as an aid in children's development of communication strategies.* Paper presented at the annual meeting of the National Conference on Language Arts in the Elementary School, Phoenix, AZ. (ERIC Document Reproduction Service No. ED 090 541)

Huntsman, K. H. (1982). Improvisational dramatic activities: Key to self-actualization? *Children's Theatre Review, 31*(2), 3–9.

Ingersoll, R. L., & Kase, J. B. (1970). *Effects of creative dramatics on learning and retention of classroom material* (Grant No. G-1-9-08055-0105 010). Washington, DC: National Center for Educational Research and Development.

Jackson, J. T. (1993). The effects of creative dramatics participation on the reading achievement and attitudes in elementary level children with behavioral disorders (Doctoral dissertation, Southern Illinois University at Carbondale, 1993). *Dissertation Abstracts International, 53*(10), 3412A.

Johnson, D. W. (1975). Cooperativeness and social perspective taking. *Journal of Personality and Social Psychology, 31,* 241–244.

Johnson, L., & O'Neill, C. (Eds.). (1984). *Dorothy Heathcote: Collected writings on education and drama.* London: Hutchinson.

Kardash, C. A. M., & Wright, L. (1987). Does creative drama benefit elementary school students: A meta-analysis. *Youth Theater Journal, 2*(1), 11–18.

King, B. T., & Janis, I. L. (1956). Comparison of the effectiveness of improvised versus non-improvised role-playing in producing opinion change. *Human Relations, 9*, 177–185.

Kranz, P. L., Lund, N. L., Pruett, T., & Stanley, F. (1982). The use of psychodrama with gifted children. *Journal of Group Psychotherapy, Psychodrama, and Sociometry, 35*, 88–98.

Kurdek, L. A. (1978, January). Perspective taking as the cognitive basis of children's moral development: A review of the literature. *Merrill-Psalmer Quarterly, 24*(1), 3–28.

McCaslin, N. (1980). *Creative drama in the classroom.* New York: Longman.

McCaslin, N. (1981). *Children and drama.* New York: Longman.

McLaughlin, J. (1990). *Building a case for arts education.* Lexington, KY: The Kentucky Alliance for Arts Education and the Kentucky Arts Council.

Miller, H., Rynden, J. E., & Schlein, S. I. (1993). Drama: A medium to enhance social interaction between students with and without mental retardation. *Mental Retardation, 31*(4), 228–233.

Miller, R., Ward, E., & White, R. R. (1969). *Educational programming in simulated environments for seriously emotionally handicapped junior high school students.* Baltimore: Maryland State Department of Education. (ERIC Document Reproduction Service No. 027680)

Moffett, J., & Wagner, B. J. (1992). *Student-centered language arts and reading, K-12* (4th ed.). Portsmouth, NH: Boynton/Cook Heinemann. (Original work published 1968)

Noble, G., Egan, P., & McDowell, S. (1977). Changing the self-concepts of seven-year old deprived urban children by creative drama or videofeedback. *Social Behavior and Personality, 5*, 55–56.

Norton, N. J. (1973). Symbolic arts: The effect of movement and drama upon the oral communication of children in grade two. *Dissertation Abstracts International, 34*(04), 1491A. (University Microfilms No. 73-23589)

O'Farrell, L. (1993). Enhancing the practice of drama in education through research. *Youth Theatre Journal, 7*(4), 25–30.

Pisaneschi, P. Y. (1977). Creative dramatics experience and its relation to the creativity and self concept of elementary school children. *Dissertation Abstracts International, 37*(12), 7648A. (University Microfilms No. 77-13583, 115)

Renaud, L., & Stolovitch, H. (1988). Simulation gaming: An effective strategy for creating appropriate traffic safety behaviors in five-year-old children. *Simulation and Games, 19*(2), 328–345.

Ridel, S. J. H. (1975). An investigation of the effects of creative dramatics on ninth grade students. *Dissertation Abstracts International, 36*, 3551A. (University Microfilms No. 75-26811, 238)

Rosen, R. S., & Koziol, Jr., S. M. (1990). The relationship of oral reading, dramatic activities, and theatrical production to student communication skills, knowledge, comprehension, and attitudes. *Youth Theatre Journal, 4*(3), 7–10.

Rubin, D. L., Piche, G.L., Michlin, M. L., & Johnson, F. L. (1984). Social cognitive ability as a predictor of the quality of fourth-graders' written narratives. In R. Beach & L. Bridwell (Eds.), *New directions in composition research* (pp. 297–307). New York: Guilford.

Shmukler, D., & Naveh, I. (1980). Modification of imaginative play in preschool children through the intervention of an adult model. *South African Journal of Psychology, 10*, 99–103.

Siks, G. (1977). *Drama with children.* New York: Harper and Row.

Simons, J., & Hughes, J. (1991). Drama for access: Demystifying the university. *The National Association for Drama in Education Journal, 15*(3), 36–38.

Spolin, V. (1985). *Improvisations for the theater: A handbook of teaching and directing techniques.* Evanston, IL: Northwestern University Press. (Original work published 1963)

Verriour, P. (1984). The reflective power of drama. *Language Arts, 62*(2), 125-130.

Vogel, M. R. L. (1975). The effects of creative dramatics on young children with specific learning disabilities. (Doctoral dissertation, Fordham University, 1975). *Dissertation Abstracts International, 36*(03), 1441A.

Wagner, B. J. (1983). The expanding circle of informal classroom drama. In B. A. Busching & J. I. Schwartz (Eds.), *Integrating the language arts in the elementary school* (pp. 155–163). Urbana, IL: National Council of Teachers of English.

Wagner, B. J. (1999). *Dorothy Heathcote: Drama as a learning medium.* Portland, ME: Calendar Islands Publishers. (Original work published 1976)

Ward, W. (1947). *Playmaking with children from kindergarten to college.* New York: Appleton-Century.

Way, B. (1972). *Development through drama.* New York: Humanities.

Widdows, J. (1996). Drama as an agent for change: Drama, behaviour and students with emotional and behavioral difficulties. *Research in Drama Education, 1*(1), 65–77.

Ziegler, E. M. (1971). *A study of the effects of creative dramatics on the progress in use of the library, reading interests, reading achievement, self concept, creativity, and empathy of fourth and fifth grade children.* Washington, DC: Educational Resources Information Center.

OTHER RESOURCES

Allan, J. A. (1977). The use of creative drama with acting-out sixth and seventh grade boys and girls. *Canadian Counselor, 11*, 135–143.

Arbuthnot, J. (1975). Modification of moral judgment through role playing. *Developmental Psychology, 11*, 319–324.

Bellman, W. M. (1974). The effects of creative dramatic activities on personality as shown in student self-concept and achievement of fifth and sixth grade students (Doctoral dissertation, University of South Dakota, 1974). *Dissertation Abstracts International, 35*(09), 5668A.

Bennett, O. G. (1982). An investigation into the effects of a creative experience in drama on the creativity, self-concept, and achievement of fifth and sixth grade students (Doctoral dissertation, Georgia State University, 1982). *Dissertation Abstracts International, 43*(06), 1809A.

Blatner, A. (1995). Drama in education as mental hygiene: A child psychiatrist's perspective. *Youth Theater Journal 9*, 92–96.

Burke, J. J., Jr. (1980). The effect of creative dramatics on the attitudes and reading abilities of seventh grade students. *Dissertation Abstracts International, 41*(12), 4887A. (University Microfilms No. 81-12054)

Carlton, L., & Moore, R. (1966). The effects of self-directive dramatization on reading achievement and self-concept of culturally disadvantaged children. *The Reading Teacher, 20*(2), 125–130.

Carlton, L., & Moore, R. (1968). *Reading, self-directive dramatization and self concept*. Columbus, OH: Charles E. Merrill.

Csikszentmihalyi, M. (1975). *Beyond boredom and anxiety*. San Francisco: Jossey-Bass.

Curran, M. J. (1991). *Creative drama in a correctional center for youth*. Unpublished master's thesis, Arizona State University, Tucson.

Dunn, J. A. (1977). The effect of creative dramatics on the oral language abilities and self esteem of Blacks, Chicanos, and Anglos in the second and fifth grades. *Dissertation Abstracts International, 38*(07), 3907A. (University Microfilms No. 77-29908)

Dunn, M. A. H. (1974). An exploratory study of the effects of a college level creative drama course on creative thinking, risk-taking, and social group acceptance (Doctoral dissertation, Southern Illinois University at Carbondale, 1974). *Dissertation Abstracts International, 35*(04), 2431A.

Edmiston, B. W. (1995). Discovering right actions, forging ethical positions through dialogic interactions. In P. Taylor & C. Hoepper (Eds.), *Selected readings in drama and theatre education, the IDEA Papers* (pp. 114–125). Queensland, Australia: National Association for Drama in Education Publications.

Faires, T. M. (1976). The effect of creative dramatics on language development and treatment progress of children in a psychotherapeutic nursery (Doctoral dissertation, University of Houston, 1976). *Dissertation Abstracts International, 37*(04), 1958.

Gibbs, P. A. (1982). A descriptive study on the use of educational drama techniques to develop empathy in social work students (Doctoral dissertation, West Virginia University, 1982). *Dissertation Abstracts International, 43*(03), 647A.

Habermas, J. (1990). *Moral consciousness and communicative action* (C. Lenhardt & S. W. Nicholson, Trans.). Cambridge, MA: MIT Press.

Hall, N. (1988). Playing at literacy. *London Drama, 7*(5), 11–15.

Heiden, J. M. (1991). Creative dramatics: A moral education strategy. *Journal of Humanistic Education and Development, 30*(2), 61–72.

Irwin, E., Levy, P., & Shapiro, M. (1972). Assessment of drama therapy in a child guidance setting. *Journal of Group Psychotherapy, Psychodrama, and Sociometry, 25*, 105–116.

Johnson, X. S. (1978). The effect of three classroom intervention strategies on the moral development of pre-adolescents: Moral dilemma discussion, creative dramatics, and creative dramatics/moral dilemma discussion (Doctoral dissertation, Northwestern University, 1978). *Dissertation Abstracts International, 39*(08), 4597A.

Komar, P. R. (1992). Drama therapy and students with learning disabilities. *Masters Abstracts International, 32*(03), 787. (University Microfilms No. 89-1523)

Lardo, N. P. (1982). Examining changes in self-concept and other selected variables in seventh and eighth grade students participating in a creative and performing arts magnet middle school program (Doctoral dissertation, University of Pittsburg, 1982). *Dissertation Abstracts International, 43*(06), 1837A.

McCall, E. M. B. (1981). Creative dramatics, plus creative dramatics/parental intervention: Strategies for developing moral reasoning skills in pre-adolescents in a church setting an experimental study (Doctoral dissertation, Brigham Young University, 1981). *Dissertation Abstracts International, 42*(07), 2938A.

Milner, S. C. (1982). Effects of a curriculum intervention program using fairy tales on preschool children's empathy level, reading readiness, oral language development and concept of a story. *Dissertation Abstracts International, 43*(2), 430A. (University Microfilms No. 83-13664)

Saab, J. F. (1987). Creative dramatics experience and its relation to creativity and self-concept of elementary school children (Doctoral dissertation, West Virginia University, 1987). *Dissertation Abstracts International, 48*(10), 2538A.

Saltz, E., Dixon, D., & Johnson, J. (1977). Training disadvantaged preschoolers on various fantasy activities: Effects on cognitive functioning and impulse control. *Child Development, 48*, 367–380.

Vojta, B. (1997, Summer). Making a difference in students' self-esteem needs. *Stage of the Art, 9*(4), 23–26.

Whitman, L. M. (1994). Drama as a therapeutic intervention with behaviourally disturbed adolescents in alternative school programs (Master's thesis, University of Victoria, 1994). *Masters Abstracts International, 32*(03), 783.

Winston, J. (1998). *Drama, narrative, and moral education*. London: Falmer Press.

Woody, P. D. (1974). A comparison of Dorothy Heathcote's informal drama methodology and a formal drama approach in influencing self-esteem of preadolescents in a Christian education program. *Dissertation Abstracts International, 35*(05), 3163A. (University Microfilms No. 74-25466)

Zoellner, R. (1969). Talk-write: A behavioral approach for composition. *College English, 30*, 267–320.

part III

Drama as Entrée to the Written Word

I n this part of the book are two very different kinds of studies: an interpretive analysis of a drama in which Dorothy Heathcote led a group of children into valuing written records, and a quasiexperimental study of the impact of drama on writing. Although writing is the focus of both of these very different types of studies, the teacher's goals were quite different. Heathcote's goal was to help children understand how written records become important, and how a community comprised of a religious order becomes responsible to recording its experiences and preserving written relics of the past. My goal, as reported in Chapter 8, was to see if even a few minutes of role-playing would help students write better persuasive letters.

Carefully developed improvisations, like the one described in Chapter 7, help build the social communities in which students have an opportunity to face moral issues head on, and, in the imagined context, experience the consequences of impulsive or selfish behavior. In the process of the drama led by Heathcote, the children's language became more formal, their diction more lofty, and their seriousness more profound. I analyzed the ways in which the activities of the drama paralled critical elements in the writing process.

In Chapter 8, I examine the effect of 30 minutes of role-playing on the quality of persuasive letters written by fourth and eighth graders. Because the results show a statistically significant improvement in the degree to which the writers took account of the feelings, beliefs, or concerns of the person they were trying to persuade, this study provides convincing evidence for the power of even a few minutes of dramatic activity in a classroom. The results of this study are important for policymakers and curriculum specialists who are looking for scientific and replicable research as evidence of the effectiveness of a particular pedagogy.

In the field of drama research, the empirical paradigm is waning in favor of exploratory and interpretive studies like the one discussed in

Chapter 7. However, for some research questions, such as mine, a quasiexperimental design is appropriate. The question I asked was: Does role-playing have an effect on persuasive letter writing?

As shown in other chapters in this book, writing is not necessarily the most powerful way to express a response or to react to a text or to a learning experience. When students respond with their whole bodies and their speech, they often plunge more deeply into the heart of an event, whether imagined or real.

In typical classrooms, writing is the most conventional and privileged mode of response to learning. Teachers need to know that writing is better if it is infused with an active aesthetic response. This makes for a richer experience and more expressive writing. As Peter Smagorinsky (1995) puts it:

> Research suggests that an exclusive focus on writing as a mode of learning limits, rather than enables, students to construct meaning...and that students would benefit from having more flexibility in the media through which they express and develop their understanding of conceptual knowledge in school. (p. 164)

Although Janet Emig (1977), among others, has argued that writing is unique among sign systems in its power to enable the construction of meaning through the production of linguistic texts, "Witte and others have questioned whether writing's supremacy comes through its inherent powers or its privileged status" (Smagorinsky, 1995, p. 165). In the next two chapters, I explore the relationship between role-playing and writing.

REFERENCES

Emig, J. (1977). Writing as a mode of learning. *College Composition and Communication, 28*, 122–127.

Smagorinsky, P. (1995). Constructing meaning in the disciplines: Reconceptualizing writing across the curriculum as composing across the curriculum. *American Journal of Education, 103*(2), 160–184.

chapter 7

Building a Community That Values Historical Documents[*]

Betty Jane Wagner
Roosevelt University

BUILDING A COMMUNITY THAT VALUES HISTORY

The cloth was very long, and when we finally unrolled the cloth we found a very old parchment. And there was string around it in the shape of a cross. Brother Doric called the monks from the field to see. Inside the wrapping there was a parchment that said there was a story that was very old and preserved for a long time. I was very awed.

Words like "preserved" and "awed" are not common in the ordinary conversation or writing of American 9- to 13-year-olds, but this is the way one child in an improvised drama of monastic life recorded his feelings. On the day he gave this account, he and his classmates, in role as modern-day monks, had found, opened, and unrolled a manuscript they had chosen to believe was a relic of the 5th century. In their role as monks, these children created a community whose moral obligation was to honor and preserve a written document from the past.

Dorothy Heathcote, widely recognized for her effectiveness in using drama in the classroom, was the teacher, in role as Brother Doric in this improvisation, which is aimed both at raising the group's consciousness about the importance of written records and introducing the life and

---

[*]This chapter is adapted from Wagner's (1985) article, "Elevating the Written Word Through the Spoken: Dorothy Heathcote and a Group of 9- to 13-Year-Olds as Monks," *Theory into Practice*, 24(3), 166–172.

times of King Arthur. The first goal, making a historical written relic important, is the topic for this chapter.

Like most children their age, the participants in this drama came to the teacher using language in a casual manner. One of Heathcote's challenges was to get them to realize that certain occasions call for them to keep accurate written records, using precise and formal language. The drama that she set up framed the class as a brotherhood of disciplined, contemporary monks who not only kept careful written records, but also, quite by accident, discovered an ancient manuscript which they, in their role, deemed to be of great value. Her teaching strategy was "mantle of the expert,"[1] in which she metaphorically draped over the young children a cloak that connoted that they were able and dedicated members of their intentional religious community. In the course of just a few days, in a stifling summer classroom that was a far-from-ideal setting, the children moved from ordinary, everyday language to diction they sensed was appropriate to monks who have experienced a significant moment in their communal life, the moment reflected in the excerpt quoted above.

Most observers of writing in the classroom note that the major hurdle writing teachers face is creating a genuine purpose for writing[2] since children see more point in talking. Yet, the children in the drama described here came to a moment of genuine awe in seeing a written manuscript, and cared enough about that event to record it in carefully selected words.

I was struck by the children's awareness of the significance of their role as preservers of history, as well as the authenticity of voice, clarity of image, and richness of sensory detail that characterized their accounts of their experience during the drama. Heathcote's own formal and precise language, the careful preparation of the "ancient" manuscript they would later find, and the slow pace of the drama to enable imagemaking and reflection—these were the critical elements leading to an appreciation of written records and the careful wording of the accounts dictated to the adult "scribes" (actually 35 adults who alternately observed the drama sessions and wrote down the accounts the children dictated). These adults, in role as acolyte monks, copied the reports in a careful, round italic hand. Seeing their stories thus presented as a beautiful permanent record provided pressure for even more precise diction, dignity of language, and seriousness of tone.

During the first five days of the 10-day sequence, the teacher had the children become a contemporary monastic order that discovered a priceless, old manuscript, preserving a story written long ago. This scroll was to take them back to the time of King Arthur and became the focus for the last five days of the drama. The first five days were devoted to creating the everyday tasks of a group of monks—keeping bees, making cider and honey, and planning, executing, and writing about the day they accidentally discovered an ancient legendary tale. The events of these five days can be divided into 10 distinct episodes:

1. brainstorming what the group thinks, believes, and knows about King Arthur;
2. making a topographical map;
3. revising and labeling the map;
4. drawing pictures of the abbey in which they live;
5. checking the thatch for swallows' nests;
6. holding vespers;
7. engaging in tasks as monks (repairing bee hives, cleaning, preparing the guest house, maintaining the cider press, repairing the thatch, etc.);
8. deciding how to find the sacred object;
9. freeing a bull, finding the hidden treasure, and dictating an account of how it happened;
10. viewing the manuscript and deciding what to do with it.

The first two episodes (brainstorming and making the map) occurred the first day; episodes three through six, the second day; seven, the third day; eight and part of nine, the fourth day; and the rest of nine and ten, the fifth day.

Contemporary experts in the art of composition point out that a number of different types of activities are involved in the writing process.[3] The most common processes mentioned are those that characterized the five drama sessions that are the focus of this study. They are:

- collecting data and trusting one's own first words;
- making choices;
- focusing and clarifying an image;
- becoming aware of senses and feelings;
- using appropriate diction;
- organizing;
- revising and editing.

All of these activities were a part of the drama. The first three—collecting data, making choices, and clarifying an image—were a prominent part of each of the 10 episodes. Awareness of the senses and feelings was increasingly stimulated after the fourth episode. The pressure for appropriate diction was mildly applied during the third episode when Heathcote suggested giving the places on the map old-sounding names, but the heaviest pressure began in the ninth episode with the dictation of their accounts. At this point, Heathcote provided a set of 10 headings, both to stimulate formal language and to help the participants reflect on their experience and organize the segments of their account. The final activity—revising—began orally when the place names were revised on the map. On the last day, the children revised and edited their written records.

The children began to sense the importance of a written record at the beginning of the seventh episode. Heathcote formally introduced a special scriptorium and an adult in role as the leading scribe. We look here, in turn, at each of the types of activities common to drama and writing, and show how each was stimulated. Organizing is omitted because the children did little beyond responding to the way Heathcote organized both the drama and their own written accounts. Finally, we look at the way Heathcote helped the group come to value writing and old manuscripts.

COLLECTING DATA AND TRUSTING ONE'S OWN
FIRST WORDS

To insist that students write before they have accessed what they know or have collected some material is to court trivial inauthentic response. In the drama of the abbey, the monks did not begin to compose their accounts until the fourth and fifth days. By that time, the attitudes they could project had been bred through their slow discovery of what a monk's daily life in an abbey must be like. In the precise pantomiming of repairing hives and picking apples, each child had time to contemplate what it would mean to live as part of a religious order, where the quality of one's work mattered, and where there was a long tradition of living in terms of one's vows and the needs of others. That attitude is reflected in this account:

> I looked at the box and there was a gold sword on it. I figured that the sword was guarding something holy. I wasn't sure whether the whole thing was Christian or pagan. Because if it was pagan, it might be an idol that I wouldn't want to see. If it was Christian I would want to.

The children decided that the old manuscript they were to "find" had been hidden away in the trunk of a tree. They thought that if their prize bull were to have slipped off a rock ledge and had landed in the branches of a tree next to the ledge, they would have to go rescue him, and then they would find the manuscript. The tasks in the monastery that they had made real for themselves were reflected in their accounts of the moment they realized the bull was in trouble, as these two excerpts show:

> I was picking apples in the orchard and I heard a bull whining very loudly. So I started climbing up the hill while looking through my binoculars, and I saw something brown caught in the tree. I studied it carefully and noticed that it was making lots of noise.

> The first thing I remembered was that I still had a knife in my hand from cutting apples at the cider press. I used the knife to cut some branches...

Because starting a composition is a hurdle for many students, composition teachers have devised a number of different strategies for helping them leap over initial blocks. Such strategies include free writing, meditation, talking with people and taking notes, keeping a journal, exploring analogies, making lists, and clustering.[4] Heathcote did all of these in the early stages of the drama. She deliberately began with rubrics that were nonthreatening: "This I Think," "This I Believe," and "This I Know." These were listed at the top of each of three sheets of newsprint that covered long tables. There was no opprobrium if some children had nothing to put down under "This I Know," and it was equally acceptable if they just put checks or question marks beside the entries others had made, depending on whether they agreed or questioned the item. The children were told that whatever they knew or didn't know was not the issue; it was expected that they begin with what they had. The categorizing of their thoughts helped them discover questions as well as their own information.

Heathcote provided a model for the children by withholding her own expertise and deliberately seeming to be puzzled, musing over what she knew or thought. While the children filled the three long pieces of blank paper, she was never in the familiar role of teacher as director and information-giver, except when she noticed and congratulated them for gathering their own material about King Arthur. The children were building up their confidence and independence, and at the same time they were adding information to their store of knowledge.

When Heathcote introduced information, she did it in a casual "by the way" manner, as when she clustered the elements of the drama in a loose array around a central circle that had "Our Drama" printed in the middle. This invited a response because it looked unfinished. Heathcote's stance was one of fellow explorer, as if to say, "Let's see what we can discover by creating this life for ourselves." This stance is a way of giving children what Donald Graves (1983) describes as "turf." One of the children—as reflected in a thank-you letter he wrote to her after the drama was over—recognized that Heathcote was trying to get him to express his own feelings: "You helped me and the rest of us to learn how we should express our feelings toward drama and not just to stand there thinking, 'Now what does this teacher know that I don't?'"

MAKING CHOICES

Over and over, the teacher asked the children to decide among alternatives. This began on the first day when they had to decide how to categorize what they knew, thought, or believed about King Arthur, and also when they were creating a land in which to live. As they made a choice, the teacher fed in the implications of that choice. Students must select among alternatives and then follow out the implications of each choice if they are to achieve focus and coherence in their thinking or their communication. At least since Aristotle, rhetoric has been defined in part in terms of the choices a speaker or writer makes. Studies of writers by such researchers as Linda Flower and John Hayes (1981) show how writers make a series of decisions, employing problem-solving strategies as they work.

Some of the choices were reflected in the children's dictated accounts.

> I think that we should all collaborate our ideas so we can get the full story. I think that we should recopy it [the ancient manuscript], hang it in the church in a square version so it won't be as long and re-roll the original and have the prior re-hide it, but we should let the prior come and see the original.

Although the children were not used to making decisions in the presence of a teacher, Heathcote would not let them off the hook. During the fourth episode, when they were drawing pictures of the abbey on the blackboard, one of the girls suggested they needed a guest house. Heathcote repeated the suggestion so that everyone could hear. "Someone suggested we should have a guest house. Do you want a guest house?" The children started discussing types of guests they might have, such as hikers. Heathcote picked up on this suggestion and pressed again, "Do you want hikers?" She then asked them a second time about the guest house, forcing a group decision.

FOCUSING AND CLARIFYING AN IMAGE

The children's imagemaking began with episode two when they created a land with their hands, using a square of green silk stretched over wads of newspaper to form the topography. Then Heathcote had them move from the bird's-eye view they had just created to visualize the land again from the perspective of one who actually dwelt there. They revised the map from that stance.

During episode seven the children were pushed to even more precise private imagemaking. Each chose a task in the abbey that was critical to the success of their mutual enterprise as an ongoing competent brotherhood, and they spent all of the third hour-long session doing that task. No teaching strategy paid off more obviously in the quality of the children's accounts than the slowing of the pace, and the pressure to visualize and kinesthetically realize each action, slowly pantomiming their work in the air about them. By the ninth episode, when they were all looking at a bull in a tree, they could make the image come alive in their own minds, as these excerpts from their accounts show:

> One of the branches seem to be ripping his leg. We see that his legs are slashed by the branches, and each time he tries to move them the branches keep going deeper and deeper into his legs.

> We slowly opened it [the box in which the manuscript was hidden] and found a bundle the size of a newborn baby.

The words came because the picture was clear in the child's mind. The injured legs of the bull, which did not exist except as a mental image, came through as clearly as the bundle, a material object in the drama. The image of a newborn baby evokes the gentleness with which the monks treated the sacred object they found.

BECOMING AWARE OF SENSES AND FEELINGS

Identification and belief in a drama grow in the seedbed of sensory experience and feelings. Heathcote consciously cultivated this rich soil well. The fifth episode marked the beginning of her teaching in role as a fellow monk. This effected a transition from a teacher and class looking down on a topographical map and up at pictures drawn on a blackboard to becoming denizens of their abbey. Heathcote accomplished this largely through appeals to their senses: "I can see buildings behind us [as she stood in front of the children's pictures on the blackboard]. If you look now you can see the sun is just touching the waterfall."

Out of role, she smiled and asked for commitment: "Are you good at seeing like that?" They nodded. "Good! I'll address you as monks as if we are looking round the monastery to check that everything is well and no repairs are needed. Shall we do that?" More nods. "I'm sure I saw a swallow in the bell tower. Who rang the bell this morning?" A hand went up. Heathcote looked directly at her. "Have you seen swallow droppings up there?" The girl nodded. "Is the bell rope in need of repair?" And so the imagemaking continued. The child who timidly decided to be the bell ringer was pushed to create a bell tower and a rope in her mind.

When the children first began to go to the bull in trouble, Heathcote appealed to their auditory sense as she set up a bellowing that was to lead them slowly to the image of the bull caught in the tree. That incessant noise was mentioned by several of the monks in their accounts. The kinesthetic experience of pulling on ropes amid the pained bellowing of the bull helped the children sense the size and weight of its body, as reflected in this excerpt:

> We took a rope on the top of the cliff and lowered it to tie around the bull. During the time that I did that a brother ran down to the abbey and got a tranquilizer. Then we slowly lowered the rope as the rest of the brothers pulled the branches away. I hope the bull will be all right. He seems to be badly hurt.

USING APPROPRIATE DICTION

During episode three, Heathcote encouraged the children to give names to the places on their topographical map. She copied the names they made up onto strips of paper, the children placing these as labels on their map. When one child suggested "River Winding," Heathcote noted, "Now local people tend to shorten names." When the teacher wrote it on a strip of paper, it was "The Wynde," using an old spelling to nudge them back to the 6th century.

When a child suggested "Ruby Falls," Heathcote asked, "Is that because the sun sets on it there?" The child nodded. "Good, you've just given us due west then. That's useful, isn't it? Then which will be south? East? North?" Before long labels went onto the low places: North Flaatts and South Flaatts, again in the old spelling.

Heathcote joined in the naming process, labeling a mountain Giant's Tor, explaining that *tor* was the ball he played with. "It's...the kind they'd tell legends about," she mused, to stimulate their sense of living in a place with a history and to foreshadow the story they were to discover later. She was also preparing them for the old Celtic names they would read in the "ancient" manuscript they would discover (Gwalchmai, Medraut, Agravain, etc.). Thus, although the language of the children was quite casual at this point, they were being prepared, through the seemingly simple task of naming places, for the diction that would be required when they went back to the time of King Arthur.

The children dictated an entry into their record for each of the ten episodes in their experience of finding the manuscript. These episodes took place over the five days of the drama. From the first to the tenth entry, the children's language changed in most cases. For example, "Brother Adrian" briefly wrote his first entry: "I saw the tree, the rocks around it. But I couldn't see it very clearly because of the water." The next two "chapters" were far more elaborate and included such precise diction as "thrashing," "flank," and "slash."

> *I sight the bull* [this title and the next were listed on the blackboard]. We were hiking up the hard trail. When I came to the tree, I saw something thrashing wildly. I thought it was the bull because the noise came from that direction.

> *I see the problem clearly.* The bull was sort of suspended on the large branches and the bull was moving around it, trying to get out. And little branches were falling, and it had some scratches on its flank and a slash down its leg, but it didn't look hurt, only stunned.

As the drama proceeded and the children saw their words transformed from sound on the breath to ink on paper, they began to grow a language to match the drama of their experience. As they saw their accounts become part of a permanent record, their choice of what to say and how to say it was, in Lee Odell's terms, "guided by their awareness of the audience and purpose" (1981, p. 100).

REVISING AND EDITING

More revising and editing occurred than I was able to record on tape. It began orally when the children revised the place names for their map. One child suggested "South Side Valley" and another commented that it sounded "too Chicagoish." Heathcote's model of old-sounding names for old places was beginning to take hold. Whenever the children were making choices, they also may well have been revising their contributions as they reflected on the consequences of each choice.

Revising was easier to see once the children started dictating their accounts. Some modification occurred when the account was first dictated, as when one child started with, "We will try to fix him up," but then changed it to, "We are going to attempt to rescue him and heal up his wounds." The presence of the "acolyte monk," or adult scribe, taking care to record his story precisely provided the pressure he needed to revise the diction toward greater formality.

SENSING THE IMPORTANCE OF A WRITTEN RECORD

In addition to leading the children in activities common to both drama and writing, Heathcote worked deliberately to make the act of writing significant and to help the children appreciate the value of an ancient written artifact. The main focus of the drama from the second through the fifth day was a promised sacred object. On the second morning, the teacher showed the children what they would be finding as a treasure. "We've created a truthful sacred object," she said, showing them the outside of a bundle, carefully tied with yarn. On the fifth day they discovered the bundle, and upon opening it, found it to be a scroll of an ancient legendary tale—prepared by the adult class members—which was wrapped in a piece of rough-woven cloth. By making the finding happen only after an arduous rescue of a bull in the sacred oak, the teacher built up the suspense and prepared the children for something of great value.

The manuscript pages looked impressive; they had been carefully lettered in italic script on ecru vellum, resembling parchment, with illuminated letters and hints of illustration. The edges of the pages had been singed to simulate the effects of a Saxon raid, so that the children could readily imagine them to be very old.

When the monks were opening the bundle, Heathcote, in role as Brother Doric, admonished them: "Open carefully. We do not know what damage might be done." She suggested that it must have been wrapped so well because it mattered to someone that it be preserved. After they opened the first wrapper, they found this message:

> To all who may find this:
> This story of Gwalchmai and the Light was discovered in the year of our LORD CMXI and was restored by the loving hands of those who still serve the LORD near Kirkby Water.

This message plunged them into the brotherhood of all those who preserve words from the past for those who come after them. The children's response to their newly felt responsibility is reflected in this account:

> We should get a big glass case and put it in so no one can touch it. Use heavy glass. Place the case at the top of the church where the priest stands so no one can hurt it. We should not pin it back together because it was made a long time ago. That would be modern and this is ancient.

Although, from the second day of the drama, the children knew they were to find something valuable "by accident," their opening up of the manuscript was accompanied by genuine, soft "ohs" of wonder. After puzzling over the script for a few moments, one of them shouted excitedly, "It has to do with King Arthur!"

The children's appreciation for the manuscript's value came through again in their discussion. They were concerned that the heat from photocopying might damage the parchment. They were in a quandary as to whether it was worth the risk to let the public view their find. The teacher mused and nodded as they debated what to do. To their questions, she added this one: "Are the old stories of the world important, I wonder?"

Finding the ancient manuscript became a lever to raise the value of their own account in their eyes. They, like the monks of old, had created a manuscript, a work that should be preserved. Thus, the most significant distinction between writing and speaking—the permanence of a written record—was heralded. The children saw that their accounts were part of a significant document when they were presented with 90 pages of their own carefully lettered stories, along with a cover sheet, stating:

Archives

These are the collected accounts of the discovery of the ancient scroll by the monks at Kirkby Water Abbey on the twenty-fifth of July in the year of our Lord MCMLXXXIII.

COMMON ELEMENTS IN DRAMA AND WRITING

Most research in composition begins either at the point when writers are at a thinking stage for a particular piece of writing, or even later, at the point of utterance. The implication of this observational study of drama is that the process of writing begins far earlier and that improvisational drama can provide the types of experience that writers must have if they are to be successful. By moving into role, teachers can invite children to join them in discovering what a particular perspective might be like. In other words, a class becomes engaged with the teacher in the task of developing understanding. The talk and tasks enacted in bodily gestures are tailored toward activating the children's tacit knowledge, toward helping them create images and invent behaviors to suit an unfamiliar context. The teacher creates a setting in which learners feel responsible for what happens next. In the drama in the abbey, the creation of a record became for the children what Janet Emig (1977) terms a "responsible and committed act," maybe even one with "an aura, an ambiance, a mystique" (p. 124).

This would be difficult to measure, but one wonders if the children didn't experience the drama differently after they saw that what they said was going into a permanent record. Does the fact that one is going to write about an event change what one sees? Are the acts of drama and writing reciprocal? Does giving words to experience make it resonate more completely?

To summarize, both improvisational drama and writing entail these activities:

- collecting data and trusting one's own first words;
- making choices;
- focusing and clarifying an image;
- becoming aware of senses and feelings;
- using appropriate diction;
- organizing; and
- revising and editing.

We have seen how one particular drama made writing important by casting the children as a brotherhood of monks with an honored scriptorium, by having them report their tasks with precision, by finding an ancient manuscript of inestimable worth, and by seeing their own account of this discovery transformed into a scroll written in italic script. They not only had a rich context for twriting, but they had an experience of what it means to affect future generations. They had built together a moral community. In the process, they became archetypal, in the tradition of all those who keep and value records.

NOTES

[1] See Heathcote and Bolton's *Drama for Learning: Dorothy Heathcote's Mantle of the Expert Approach to Education* (1995) for an explanation and illustrations of this approach. See especially pages 117–168 for an explanation and analysis of a similar drama.

[2] See, for example, Moffett and Wagner's (1992) discussion of the differences between home and school learning, pp. 43–44, and Chapter 9, "Writing."

[3] See, for example, Murray's (1997, pp. 9–10) list of parts of the process.

[4] See, for example, Elbow (1981); Moffett and Wagner (1992); and Rico (1983).

REFERENCES

Elbow, P. (1981). *Writing with power.* New York: Oxford University Press.
Emig, J. (1977). Writing as a mode of learning. *College Composition and Communication, 28,* 122–127.

Flower, L. S., & Hayes, J. (1981). A cognitive process theory of writing. *College Composition and Communication, 32*, 365–387.

Graves, D. (1983). *Writing: Teachers and children at work*. Portsmouth, NH: Heinemann.

Heathcote, D., & Bolton, G. (1995). *Drama for learning: Dorothy Heathcote's mantle of the expert approach to education*. Portsmouth, NH: Heinemann.

Moffett, J., & Wagner, B. J. (1992). *Student-centered language arts and reading, K-12* (4th ed.). Portsmouth, NH: Boynton/Cook Heinemann. (Original work published 1968)

Murray, D. (1997). *Write to learn* (5th ed.). New York: Holt, Rinehart, and Winston.

Odell, L. (1981). Defining and assessing competence in writing. In C. Cooper (Ed.), *The nature and measurement of competency in English* (pp. 95–138). Urbana, IL: National Council of Teachers of English.

Rico, G. (1983). *Writing the natural way*. Los Angeles: J. P. Tarcher.

Wagner, B. J. (1985). Elevating the written word through the spoken: Dorothy Heathcote and a group of 9 to 13-year-olds as monks. *Theory Into Practice, 24*(3), 166–172.

OTHER RESOURCES

Dyson, A. H. (1997). *Writing superheroes: The social and ideological dynamics of child writing*. New York: Teachers College Press.

Edmiston, B. W. (1994). More than talk: A Bakhtinian perspective on drama in education and change in understanding. *Journal of the National Association for Drama in Education, 18*(2), 25–36.

Edmiston, B. W. (1995). Discovering right actions: Forging ethical positions through dialogic interactions. In P. Taylor & C. Hoepper (Eds.), *Selected readings in drama and theatre education: The IDEA '95 papers* (pp. 114–125). Brisbane, Queensland, Australia: National Association for Drama in Education Publications.

Heathcote, D. (1970). How does drama serve thinking, talking and writing. *Elementary English, 47*(8), 1077–1081.

Heathcote, D. (1978). Of these seeds becoming. In R. Shuman (Ed.), *Educational drama for today's schools* (pp. 1–40). Metuchen, NJ: Scarecrow Press.

Heathcote, D. (1980). *Drama as context* (M. Barrs, Ed.). Aberdeen, England: National Association for Teaching of English.

Heathcote, D. (1983). Learning, knowing, and languaging in drama: An interview with Dorothy Heathcote. *Language Arts, 60*(6), 695–701.

Hoetker, J. (1969). *Dramatics and the teaching of literature*. Champaign, IL: National Council of Teachers of English.

Macrorie, K. (1980). *Searching writing*. Rochelle Park, NJ: Hayden.

Moffett, J. (1967). *Drama: What is happening: The use of dramatic activities in the teaching of English*. Champaign, IL: National Council of Teachers of English.

Moffett, J. (1983). *Teaching the universe of discourse.* Boston: Houghton Mifflin. (Original work published 1968)

Neelands, J., Booth, D., & Zeigler, S. (1993). *Writing in imagined contexts: Research into drama-influenced writing.* Toronto, Ontario, Canada: Toronto Board of Education. (ERIC Document Reproduction Service No. ED 355 576)

Read, B., & Cherry, L. (1978). Preschool children's production of direct forms. *Discourse Processes, 1,* 233–245.

St. Clair, J. P. (1991). Dorothy Heathcote as philosopher, educator and dramatist (Doctoral dissertation, University of North Carolina at Greensboro, 1991). *Dissertation Abstracts International, 57*(02), 394A.

Smagorinsky, P. (1995). Constructing meaning in the disciplines: Reconceptualizing writing across the curriculum as composing across the curriculum. *American Journal of Education, 103*(2), 160–184.

Sutton, J. (1998, Spring). Setting the stage: Creative drama in the writing classroom. *Stage of the Art, 9*(7), 11–15.

Wagner, B. J. (1978a). Educational drama and language development. In R. B. Schuman (Ed.), *Educational drama for today's schools* (pp. 87–96). Metuchen, NJ: Scarecrow Press.

Wagner, B. J. (1978b). Educational drama and the brain's right hemisphere. In R. B. Schuman (Ed.), *Educational drama for today's schools* (pp. 133–154). Metuchen, NJ: Scarecrow Press.

Wagner, B. J. (1983). The expanding circle of informal classroom drama. In B. A. Busching & J. I Schwartz (Eds.), *Integrating the language arts in the elementary school* (pp. 155–163). Urbana, IL: National Council of Teachers of English.

Wagner, B. J. (1990). Dramatic improvisation in the classroom. In D. L. Rubin & S. Hynds (Eds.), *Perspectives on talk and learning* (pp. 195–211). Urbana, IL: National Council of Teachers of English.

Wagner, B. J. (1994). Drama and writing. In A. C. Purvis (Ed.), *The encyclopedia of English studies and language arts, vol. 1* (pp. 403–405). New York: National Council of Teachers of English and Scholastic.

Wagner, B. J. (1999). *Dorothy Heathcote: Drama as a learning medium.* Portland, ME: Calendar Islands Publishers. (Original work published 1976)

chapter 8

Creating a Context for Persuasive Letter Writing*

Betty Jane Wagner
Roosevelt University

I n this chapter, I present a quasi-experimental study that examines the effect of role-playing on writing. In today's accountability climate, studies of this kind, which are scientifically controlled, are reliable, and can be replicated, are often more convincing to educational policymakers than the more richly detailed studies, such as others presented in this book. Because the results can be generalized with confidence to a larger population, studies of this nature have their place as evidence that drama does indeed have an impact on the development of skills, such as writing, that the larger public deems valuable. Those of us who know from experience that drama tends to build moral communities among its participants need to find ways to demonstrate this potency to the public at large. In quasi-experimental studies, it is advisable to examine as wide a population as feasible and to control as many factors as possible, so the effects can be attributed to the cause one is testing. In this study, the cause I chose is 30 minutes of role-playing, and the effect is the persuasive strength of written letters.

Like six other investigators,[1] I set out to test the often-repeated claim that drama improves writing.[2] Like five of these investigators—Karen Lee Dunnagan (1991) is the exception—I found that drama does have a statistically significant positive effect on the quality of students' writing. I compared three different circumstances: (a) oral role-playing, (b) a class discussion and presentation of models and rules for persuasion, and (c)

---

*Summarized from Wagner (1986), *The Effects of Role Playing on Written Persuasion: An Age and Channel Comparison of Fourth and Eighth Graders.*

no instruction at all. I had 84 comparable fourth graders and 70 comparable eighth graders write three letters to their school principals on three different topics in one of these three instructional conditions before writing: role-playing, discussion, and no instruction. I analyzed variance with the following independent variables: three modes of instruction, two grade levels, three topics, and sex. I had the letters the students wrote scored to measure the degree to which the students took into account the perspective of the person they were trying to persuade and showed an understanding of that person's point of view. The dependent variables were (a) Highest Level of Target Orientation and (b) Variety of Levels of Target Orientation.

Role-playing in this study is limited to a 30-minute improvised, unrehearsed oral interaction in a simulated context. This is not a full-scale drama as described in the other studies presented or reviewed in this book. Of course, drama in the classroom should not be limited to such a short time period, but I felt that if I could show an impact from even this brief introduction to role-playing among a group of students who had no other experience with drama, the results would make an even more powerful case for drama than if the drama had been longer. Limiting the actual time of the drama experience made it easier to control the effect of other influences, such as ongoing writing instruction during the school year when I was not conducting the study. By choosing a large number of students (158 in 6 classrooms) and limiting the drama time to 30 minutes, I was able to achieve results that could be more reliably generalized to other groups of students.

I set up the role-playing by having students work in pairs to create a dialogue in an imagined situation in which one partner assumed the role of a student and the other the role of the school principal. The goal was for the student-in-role to persuade the principal-in-role to change his or her mind about something. After I introduced the situation with a guided meditation, primarily to help them get into role as a busy school principal, all of the pairs of students role-played simultaneously without any direct teacher intervention. The effect of this role playing on the persuasive letters written afterward was compared with the effect of (a) a class discussion and a presentation of models and rules of good persuasion and (b) no instruction.

I focused on fourth and eighth graders, in part because none of the previous studies tested the claims of drama's effectiveness with students at these grade levels. I also wanted to study an instructional strategy that solidly embeds learning in its social context and thus might contribute toward building an integrated social-cognitive theory of writing. This theory has been informed by decades of studies by developmental psychologists who have shown oral language growth reflects development in social cognition.

I chose persuasion because the findings of several studies show written persuasion to be significantly harder for students to produce than other types of discourse.[3] This seems puzzling since even preschoolers use oral language to persuade, often quite effectively, particularly in their spontaneous play.[4]

A second reason for this focus is that the quality of student persuasive writing seems to have declined since 1973, according to the National Assessment of Educational Progress. The percentage of 13-year-olds writing a successful persuasive letter has declined (Mullis, 1985); although 69% were able to do a marginal job in 1973, the proportion dropped to 64% in 1978, and 14% in 1984. During this same period, when persuasive writing sharply declined in quality, descriptive, expressive, and informative writing of 13-year-olds showed little change. The situation has gotten worse since then, according to an analysis of student portfolios (Gentile, Martin-Rehrmann, & Kennedy, 1995). Students at the three grades tested (fourth, eighth, and twelfth) had considerable difficulty producing persuasive responses that were beyond minimally developed, with 3% or less across grade levels writing elaborated or better responses. This is in contrast to informative writing, for which at least 75% of the students of the three grade levels produced at least a minimally developed level. In the Portfolio Study conducted by NAEP (Gentile, et al.), only 4% of the papers submitted by fourth graders, and 9% of those submitted by eighth graders were persuasive in aim. The rest of the papers were mainly narrative or informative. At fourth grade, three-quarters of the students' persuasive portfolio papers merely represented various ways of writing about an opinion; only 25% "of the papers made attempts at presenting an argument rather than just stating an opinion and reasons to support it, and only 1% contained enough discussion of the opinion to be considered a presentation of an argument" (p. 78). By eighth grade, 61% "were attempts at argumentation, but only 4% succeeded in presenting an argument" (p. 78).

I am concerned about this decline in persuasive writing ability, especially in light of children's obvious oral persuasive skills. I felt that rehearsal, in the form of role-playing, should help students access their oral persuasive competence and thus write better persuasive letters. In other words, role-playing would be more effective as prewriting than class discussion and a presentation of models. Two students opposing one another in role would provide a familiar conversational setting and social pressure to develop appropriate arguments, enabling students, through role-play, to root their writing task in what Vygotsky (1978) sees as basic, namely gesture and symbolic play.

Studies of the writing process show writers of all ages muttering to themselves or composing aloud as they write, even when such oral rehearsals are not deliberately evoked as in the composing-aloud proto-col research strategy. Talking especially surrounds writing events of young writers who "only gradually move from immediate action-related, talk-related contexts for composing toward sustained composing without frequent reference to and reliance upon the non-textual context to facil-itate communication of meaning" (Birnbaum, 1981, p. 569).

Because Birnbaum (1981) found that less proficient fourth and sev-enth graders still require an immediate audience and the support of oral language to see a purpose for writing, I thought fourth and eighth graders would benefit from role-playing. An immediate audi-ence, especially one who has been coached to play the role of someone who is hard to persuade, would probably stimulate an elaboration of an argument. I also thought talking about a topic would help generate ideas. In his case study of their writing processes, Rucker (1981) found composing aloud to be the most frequently used strategy of sixth grad-ers. One of them always had to talk out her ideas before she could write alone.

METHOD

I selected a school district that was implementing a fairly standard writ-ing curriculum, that had no ongoing drama program in the schools, and that assessed writing samples annually at grades 2 through 8.

Students in the Study

The subjects of this study were 42 boys and 42 girls at the fourth grade level and 35 boys and 35 girls at the eighth grade level. They were ran-domly selected from 11 comparable heterogeneous classes in a school district in a middle-class suburb changing demographically from a pre-dominantly Jewish population to a mixed population, 25% of which were Asian students, as well as a few from India. Typically, at least one parent had some post-high school education. To control for the effect of previous drama training, I screened out of my sample any students who had been studying drama in out-of-school programs or who had had drama in previous schools.

Instructional Conditions

To control for teacher effect, I conducted both instructional sessions and administered all of the writing tasks, using the same written assignments for each topic and in each instructional condition. Students wrote three persuasive letters to their school principals on three different topics in three instructional conditions: (a) role-playing prior to writing; (b) direct instruction prior to writing, consisting of a class discussion, story, models of a persuasive letter, and rules for persuasion; and (c) no instruction.

In the experimental or role-playing condition, all students simultaneously role-played with a partner and then wrote on the same topic after a break of between 10 and 15 minutes for the fourth graders, or until the same class period the next day for the eighth graders. The school schedule made it impossible to schedule the sessions the same way at both grade levels. Each student in the experimental condition role-played twice, taking a turn as the persuader for approximately 15 minutes, and as the target for the persuasion for another 15 minutes; the same topic was used, but the partners changed roles. I paired the students with a partner of the same sex, since most observers of children of these ages suggest children feel freer to communicate if they are not talking across gender lines (Mitchell, 1974).

The direct-instruction condition was introduced, in part, to avoid confounding the results with the effect of time on task. This instruction also provided an opportunity to assess the effectiveness of an approach to persuasion that is typically advocated in school textbooks and is common in practice. First, I told a story of a trial lawyer who needed to get a group of U.S. Marines to act as witnesses. Then students read together, discussed, and analyzed typed copies of two models of good persuasion: one, the trial lawyer's persuasive speech and the other, a persuasive letter to a principal on a topic similar to the one on which they were subsequently to write. I went over a list of eight rules of good persuasion[5] and showed how the models reflected these rules. Five minutes before the end of the period, I passed out and then collected the topic for the subsequent writing task and asked the students to think about what they would say when they wrote their persuasive letters (later the same day for the fourth graders; the next day for the eighth graders).

In the no-instruction condition, students saw the assigned topic for the first time right before they wrote. All three writing sessions were conducted in the same way. I gave production signals, or simple promptings, to write as much as possible; these were adapted from those used by Scardamalia, Bereiter, and Goelman (1982). Their goal, like mine, was to discourage the brevity that is common in children's essays.

Writing Topics

Because the quality of writing, including its level of persuasiveness, varies depending on the assigned topic or writing task,[6] I chose three topics that were as similar as possible to promote greater reliability of the testing instrument. All three called for a persuasive letter on a subject on which the students had some familiarity, and in the same setting, the school; all were addressed to the school principal.

The first topic was to argue that students their age be allowed to select their own subjects in school; the second, to argue for a school-sponsored party during school time once a month; and the third, to argue for a change in the school cafeteria.

Scale for Level of Target Orientation

The three persuasive letters, written by each of 84 fourth graders and 70 eighth graders in response to three different writing prompts, provided the data for this study. The 462 persuasive letters (three letters, one on each topic, written by each student) were coded, then scored blindly and independently by two scorers on a seven-interval scale for two features: Highest Target Orientation Level and Variety of Levels of Target Orientation. The scale was adapted from one developed by Delia, Kline, and Burleson (1979). See Appendix A at the end of this chapter for the scale I developed to measure this sensitivity to audience, titled "Target Orientation." Each level on the scale represents a greater adaptation to the perspective of the principal.

In traditional rhetorical theory, a major feature of effective persuasion is a sensitive awareness of, or empathy with, the needs and desires of the person or persons one is trying to persuade, or at least an imagined identification with this audience. This insight—whether or not the persuader is conscious of it—facilitates generating the types of appeal that are likely to influence another person to believe or do what the persuader intends. The art of persuasion is rooted in empathy and identification with others, qualities that characterize sensitivity to moral nuances in a community. Unless a persuader can at least imagine what it is like to hold a view other than his or her own, she is likely to come across as doctrinaire or polemic, and so is more likely to alienate than to persuade.

The Pearson inter-rater reliability of the two scorers was $r = .82$ on Highest Level, and $r = .78$ on Variety of Levels of persuasive assertions. Even when the inter-rater reliability was refigured using Cohen's kappa to take account of the probability that the scorer's agreement occurred by chance, the reliability is still at the $p < .001$ level for both measures.

Scoring

The scorers distinguished each discrete persuasive assertion on the writing samples and assigned it a number from 0 to 6, using the Scale for Level of Target Orientation. To determine what a persuasive assertion was, I set up a system for parsing the texts that was as descriptive (as opposed to evaluative) as possible. The persuasive unit used here is a semantic, not a linguistic, one: the smallest discrete persuasive unit that cannot be subdivided into two separate units without altering its meaning. This parsing scheme follows the system Delia, Kline, and Burleson (1979) used and is similar to one Scardamalia, Bereiter, and Goelman (1982) employed, having scorers segment discourse samples into units that can function as requests or reasons. A persuasive assertion is a request, reason for a request, or an attempt to put the principal in a receptive mood. It can be a part of a sentence (usually one clause in a compound sentence), a whole sentence, or a unit that, if punctuated conventionally, would be a complex sentence. The only exception is a student letter that has no request or reason at Level 1 on the scale. In that case, one request and one reason was scored as two persuasive assertions, so the student was given credit for having a Level 1 assertion (a simple request with no reason given) when the Variety of Levels of Target Orientation was tallied. In all other cases, if a complex sentence consisted of a single request *and* a single reason, that sentence was scored as one persuasive assertion.

If, however, any sentence contained words, phrases, or clauses that constituted more than one reason, each reason was scored as a separate persuasive assertion. The quality of a reason was not evaluated; even if it were not a particularly convincing reason, it was still counted. As long as the student had generated a unit that might conceivably be considered a persuasive request, reason, or attempt to get the principal in a receptive or cooperative mood, it was treated as a persuasive assertion. If not, it was scored with a 0 as a nonfunctional unit.[7] Each separate assertion was categorized, even if it were an assertion at the same level as one of the subcategories in the Scale for Level of Target Orientation.

The scorers used the examples for each subcategory taken from student writing samples as a guide for determining the Level of Target Orientation. Neither of the scorers was aware of the scores the other one had assigned until inter-rater reliability could be determined. Any assertion that clearly met the guidelines on the Scale for Level of Target Orientation was assigned its appropriate number, even though that level was not consistent with adjacent units or with the general level of the piece. The highest score assigned to any persuasive assertion was recorded as the first score on each writing sample, a score for the dependent variable, Highest Target Orientation Level.

The assumption underlying this scoring system was that although it was obvious students would differ in the highest level they exhibited, any given paper, including the best paper, would probably show a range of levels of target orientation. A student capable of using a high-level strategy might choose to use a lower one, but a student who was not yet capable of a higher-level strategy would not produce one. Thus, failure to use a strategy reflecting a higher-level of target orientation could not definitively be interpreted as lack of skill. The student might simply have chosen not to use a high-level strategy. My scale tests performance, not competence. It is modeled on categorizations developed by psychologists Kohlberg and Perry to measure stages of moral, intellectual, and ethical development (Blasi, 1976).

The second score on each student sample was a measure of the Variety of Levels of Target Orientation. To determine this, the scorers counted the number of different levels of assertions, which they had recorded in the margins of the papers. The scores ranged from 1 to 6 on any one writing sample. For example, if a student used only unelaborated statements of personal desire or need (Level 1 on the scale above) and reasons that show only how it is necessary, desirable, or useful for the persuader (Level 2), her score was 2. In other words, persuasive assertions were considered different only if they represented different categories, from 1 through 6 on the scale. See Appendix B at the end of this chapter for a sample letter of a student who made an effort to understand the perspective of the principal.

The independent variables were the three modes of instruction (role playing, direct instruction, and no instruction), the two grade levels (fourth and eighth), the two sexes, and the three topics (student selection of subjects, in-school party, and changes in the cafeteria). The two dependent measures were Highest Target Orientation Level and Variety of Levels of Target Orientation.

I compared the scores on the two dependent measures for each of the three writing samples of the 154 subjects in each of the instructional conditions, at both grade levels, for each of the three topics for persuasion, and for both sexes. I tested results for significance at the .05 level. Means and standard deviations of the dependent variables by the levels of the independent variables are shown on Table 8.1, Table 8.2, and Table 8.3 at the end of this chapter.

The effect of each mode of instruction was assessed using a counterbalanced, quasi-experimental, four-way randomized groups design, as shown in Figure 8.1 at the end of this chapter. I used an analysis of covariance (ANCOVA), with length as the covariate, and post-hoc Newman-Keuls tests.

RESULTS

Findings show:

a. Role-playing in partners is significantly more effective in helping students write persuasive letters that are oriented toward their target than is direct instruction consisting of a class discussion and examples of model persuasive letters, or than no instruction.
b. Direct instruction is not significantly more effective than no instruction.
c. Eighth graders significantly outperform fourth graders.
d. Topic has a significant effect.

A significant two-way interaction between sex and instruction ($p < .048$) on the Variety of Levels measure shows role-playing to be more effective with girls, who also write longer letters.

Because the correlations between the number of words in each student letter and both dependent variables were significant, I included length as a covariate in the ANCOVA. The correlation between length and the Highest Target Orientation Level score was $r = .50$; between length and the Variety of Levels score, $r = .57$.

The four-way analysis of covariance showed that mode of instruction and grade level exerted a significant main effect ($p < .0001$), as predicted, on the Highest Target Orientation Level and Variety of Levels of Target Orientation measures. Topic had a significant main effect on both dependent variables, but sex did not on either measure.

Highest Level of Target Orientation

For the measure of Highest Target Orientation Level, an analysis of covariance with the covariate of length showed a main effect for mode of instruction ($F_{2,425} = 10.925$; $Adj.\ M_{ni} = 4.00$, $Adj.\ M_{di} = 3.96$, $Adj.\ M_{rp} = 4.38$); for grade level ($F_{1,425} = 12.988$; $Adj.\ M_8 = 4.30$, $Adj.\ M_4 = 3.96$; and for topic ($F_{2,425} = 6.759$; $Adj.\ M_1 = 4.12$, $Adj.\ M_2 = 4.29$, $Adj.\ M_3 = 3.93$). See Table 8.1, Table 8.2, and Table 8.3 at the end of this chapter. Significance was at the $p < .0001$ level for the main effect of grade and instruction, and at the $p < .001$ level for topic. Sex exerted no significant main effect, nor were there any significant interactions that affected Highest Target Orientation Level.

A post-hoc Newman-Keuls test on the adjusted means showed role playing to be significantly better than direct instruction in improving persuasive letter writing ($p < .01$, Newman-Keuls). Role-playing was also significantly more effective than no instruction ($p < .01$, Newman-Keuls).

There was no significant difference between direct instruction and no instruction.

There was a significant difference between persuasive letters written on the choosing-subjects topic 1 and the cafeteria topic 3 ($Adj.\ M_1$ 4.12 – $Adj.\ M_3$ 3.93 = .19; $p < .05$, Newman-Keuls). There was an even more significant difference between the party topic 2 and the cafeteria topic 3 ($Adj.\ M_2$ 4.29 – $Adj.\ M_3$ 3.93 = .36; $p < .01$, Newman-Keuls). There was no significant difference between topics 1 and 2.

Variety of Levels of Target Orientation

For the Variety of Levels of Target Orientation, an ANCOVA with the covariate of the total number of words showed—as with the Highest Level of Target Orientation measure—that mode of instruction, grade level, and topic all have significant main effects, but sex does not.

The main effect for mode of instruction is at the $p < .003$ level ($F_{2,425}$ = 5.755; $Adj.\ M_{ni}$ = 3.74, $Adj.\ M_{di}$ = 3.77, $Adj.\ M_{rp}$ = 4.02 [see Table 8.1]). The Newman-Kuels test shows that role-playing is significantly more effective ($p < .01$) than either direct instruction or no instruction, and there is no significant difference between direct instruction and no instruction. Eighth graders outperform fourth graders on the Variety of Levels produced per 100 words ($F_{1,425}$ = 16.108, $p < .001$; $Adj.\ M_8$ = 4.03, $Adj.\ M_4$ = 3.69 [see Table 8.2]). Topic has a main effect at the $p < .001$ level ($F_{2,425}$ = 8.068; $Adj.\ M_1$ = 3.81, $Adj.\ M_2$ = 4.05, $Adj.\ M_3$ = 3.69 [see Table 8.3]). The performance on the party topic 2, when corrected for length, is significantly better than on either of the other two topics ($p < .01$, Newman-Keuls), between which there is no significant difference.

The Newman-Keuls test on the adjusted means showed that, on the Variety of Levels of Target Orientation measure, role-playing was significantly more effective ($p < .01$) than either direct instruction or no instruction, but there was no significant difference between direct instruction and no instruction. A paired comparison between role-playing and direct instruction showed $Adj.\ M_{rp}$ 4.02 – $Adj.\ M_{di}$ 3.77 = .25; a paired comparison between role-playing and no instruction showed $Adj.\ M_{rp}$ 4.02 – $Adj.\ M_{ni}$ 3.74 = .28.

The ANCOVA with the covariate of length showed a significant interaction between sex and instruction ($F_{2,425}$ = 3.056, $p < .048$). To test the effect of mode of instruction for boys and for the girls, I did an ANCOVA for each sex. Instruction showed no significant effect on the boys, but for girls the effect was significant at the $p < .002$ level ($F_{2,227}$ = 6.599; $Adj.\ M_{ni}$ = 3.95, $Adj.\ M_{di}$ = 3.80, $Adj.\ M_{rp}$ = 4.25).

A post-hoc Newman-Keuls test on the adjusted means showed role-playing to be significantly better than direct instruction in its effect on the girls' persuasive letter writing (*Adj. M_{rp}* 4.25 − *Adj. M_{di}* 3.80 = .45; p < .01, Newman-Keuls). Role-playing was also significantly more effective than no instruction for girls (*Adj. M_{rp}* 4.25 − *Adj. M_{ni}* 3.95 = .30; p < .01, Newman-Keuls). Surprisingly, girls performed significantly worse after direct instruction than with no instruction (*Adj. M_{ni}* 3.95 − *Adj. M_{di}* 3.80 = .15; p < .05, Newman-Keuls).

I also analyzed the sex difference for each mode of instruction. Only in the role-playing condition was there any significance for sex. Girls significantly outperformed boys after role-playing (p < .024, $F_{1,151}$ = 5.191; *Adj. M_g* = 4.23, *Adj. M_b* = 3.93); surprisingly, boys showed a non-significant trend of performing worse in the role-playing condition than in the other two conditions.

Other Findings

A Pearson's correlation of the scores on the two dependent variables showed that Highest Target Orientation Level and Variety of Levels correlate well with one another (r = .89, p < .001).

There was no significant fatigue effect. To test for it, I compared the role-played scores with the written ones for a subsample of 14 students who first wrote and then role-played, using a one-tailed t test. Transcripts of their oral persuasion were scored the same way the writing samples were scored. The subsample produced significantly better oral than written persuasion on the two dependent measures (p < .001). On the Highest Target Orientation Level, $t(13)$ = 3.93, M_{rp} = 4.75 (*SD* = .872), M_{wr} = 3.29 (*SD* = 1.18); on Variety of Levels, $t(13)$ = 4.61, M_{rp} = 4.57 (*SD* = .829), M_{wr} = 3.04 (*SD* = 1.12).

Summary of Findings

Thus, the main effects, interactions, and post-hoc analyses of covariance and Newman-Keuls tests on both the Highest Target Orientation Level and the Variety of Levels measure show that fourth and eighth graders who role-play produce persuasive letters that are more oriented toward their target than either students who have had a discussion of, and models and rules for, persuasion, or those with no instruction. There is no evidence to confirm that students who were presented with models and rules produce better persuasive letters than those with no instruction. After a discussion, instead of writing better than in the no-instruction condition, the total group of subjects actually wrote slightly worse per 100 words, as measured by the Highest Target Orientation Level measure.

Topic had a significant main effect on both measures. Students wrote their best persuasion on party topic 2, and they wrote more persuasive assertions per 100 words on the cafeteria topic 3 after direct instruction than with either role-playing or no instruction. On the two measures, eighth graders significantly outperformed fourth graders.

REFLECTION

This study convincingly demonstrates that role-playing, but not a discussion with examples and rules, significantly affects persuasive letters written by fourth and eighth graders. When children role-play in partners, taking turns trying to convince an intransigent target, they are on familiar social ground. Even young children are competent oral language users, with a sensitivity to their listeners' status differences and with the capacity, at a very early age, to adapt their discourse to different audiences in both actual and role-played conversations.[8] Moreover, even young children have been shown to use argument effectively to resolve a conflict or solve a problem (Genishi & Di Paolo, 1982). It is not surprising then that role-playing helps students access their oral competence.

Fourth and eighth graders probably feel freer to experiment with persuasive strategies when facing only one other person, especially a same-sex peer, than when writing on their own. As children imagine their way into the stance of a persuader, first in role-playing and then in writing, they are more likely to tap into an unconscious sense of real-world contexts for persuasion and adapt their discourse to it. Conversational exchange, though not simple, feels natural, in part because of the emotional overtone that accompanies a social act. It is this tone that is probably the most difficult for students to conjure up in a classroom writing situation. It is critical that a writer imagines his or her audience in creating a written product that is appropriate and effective (Flower & Hayes, 1980). Unless a writer can intuit another person's reasons for denying a request, he or she is hampered in the ability to write persuasion sensitive to that person's perspective.

Since much of our general knowledge of how to use language is personal or unconscious (Polyani, 1962), our understanding of appropriate persuasive strategies is probably largely tacit. My findings show children can produce effective persuasion, orally and in writing, even though they may not yet be able to apply a teacher's analysis of persuasion to their own writing task. By the time they reach fourth grade, children have at least rudimentary social cognition and schemata for persuasion, as this study shows. Role-playing requires something more than superficial imitation of another person's behavior. A role-player needs to have

at least an implicit theory of another person's beliefs and needs to operate according to that "theory" (Bereiter & Scardamalia, 1983). Specific
information about audience adaptation is not as useful as imagined oral
dialogue.

My findings confirm those of Troyka (1973): Role-playing significantly
affects persuasive writing. These findings are consistent with both Florio's (1978) and my ethnographic study reported in the Chapter 8 of
this book: role-playing and writing are closely associated. In a classroom where students are encouraged to assume roles, writing in role
spontaneously arises.

My findings do not confirm eight other studies[9] that show that dramatic activities affect the language of boys more than girls. However, my
findings are consistent with those of Ingersoll and Kase (1970), who
found that creative dramatics has a greater effect on the learning and
retention of fifth and sixth grade girls than on boys. In my study, girls,
after role-playing, produced a significantly greater Variety of Levels of
Target Orientation than did boys. Girls who produced the fewest, or a
medium number, of words benefit the most from role-playing on the
Variety of Levels measure, whereas boys who produced an average number of words were significantly more affected by direct instruction than
by role-playing.

Explanation of Topic Effects

In choosing three similar topics I hoped to minimize topic effects, but
this study confirms the common assumption that the quality of writing,
just like the quality of a drama, is largely dependent on the importance
of the subject to the writer (Keech & McNelly, 1982). Thus, it is possible
that there may be no such thing as a "repeated measure" in drama or
writing research. As psycholinguistic studies of speech production have
shown, when children have something to say, they demonstrate the use
of structures they previously seemed not to be able to produce (Slobin &
Welsh, 1973). Thus, it may be impossible to design a set of writing topics
students will find equally engaging.

The one topic on which students at both levels performed best on
both measures was topic 2, the assignment to persuade the principal to
have a school-sponsored party (see Table 8.3 at the end of this chapter).
Perhaps students felt this was a request the principal would have many
good reasons for denying and thus sensed they would have to come up
with unusually good arguments to make a case for it, or this might have
been a request they really wanted to have granted.

How can we explain the poorest performance on the first two measures on the change in the cafeteria? One possibility is that writers did

not have spelled out in the assignment a single request they were to support, in contrast to the written directions for the other two topics. When asked to present a case for something they wanted changed in the cafeteria, they tended to come up with a string of complaints and requests, including pleas for their favorite foods, rather than making a good case for any single change, as most did for the other two topics. This could explain why only on the cafeteria topic students wrote more persuasive assertions in the direct instruction condition than in role-playing. In the direct instruction, I emphasized the importance of focusing on a single request and presenting a clear case for it as appropriately as possible. A second explanation for the poor performance on topic 3 is that students might have felt that the principal would be more likely to comply with this request than student choice of subjects or a school-sponsored party, so they saw no need to come up with as many or as good reasons. If so, my subjects felt more like the children in a study by Clark and Delia (1976, 1977), who posited that their subjects produced fewer arguments for an intimate target than for a stranger because they felt their request would be granted anyway. A fourth possible explanation is that the students were tired of writing persuasive letters to the principal by the time this topic was introduced, since it was presented last to all of the classes of students.

An audiotape of two pairs of fourth graders who argued for a change in the cafeteria showed a surprising consequence. When these four children wrote their subsequent persuasive letters, half of them switched to arguing for the changes their partner had advocated. For example, one child argued that fourth graders should be allowed to put their coats on the stage in the cafeteria (which also doubled as an auditorium) in order to keep them from getting food on them, as was likely when they had to take them to their chairs. Her partner argued for two lines at the steam tables to speed up the process of getting food. Evidently, the challenge of opposing these changes—in their role as principal—convinced them that their partner's case was so persuasive that they now believed and could argue for it in a letter.

Implications for a Social-Cognitive Theory of Writing

We are still a long way from understanding how children draw on their oral language resources when they write. At no point do children seem to think that writing is the same as talking. Emergent literacy studies[10] suggest that a child begins to write by imitating writers and written products. However, beginning writers also surround writing with talk and somehow find reasons to substitute written symbolization for oral. They eventually make a transition from talking to writing. Numerous examples of children's written persuasion and letters in a non-narrative mode[11] suggest that persuading and informing are, for some children, at least as important an impetus for writing as is telling a story, which Britton (1983) assumes to be primary.

The focus on cognition in research on the writing process has often been too narrow, paying little attention to social processes. My findings provide another brick toward the building of an integrated social-cognitive theory of writing. All are connected: cognition, language, and context. Social cognition is a concept that encompasses intuitive or logical representations of others; these representations make it possible to develop inferences about another person's covert, or inner, perceptions, thoughts, and feelings, and so to act more appropriately.

Learning to write effective persuasion is not simply skill acquisition. Target orientation, or specific audience sensitivity, is critical to its success. It is through oral interaction that social cognition and schemata for persuasion are developed and honed.

My study is consistent with Vygotsky's (1978) concept of learning through social interaction. A persistent problem of school writing is the difficulty of getting students to consider the rhetorical context. Especially in persuasive discourse, student writers need to make guesses about the potential reaction of a reader other than the teacher.

In order to succeed in the task posed to students in this study, they had to recognize the status difference between the student and principal and to intuit how that should influence the tone and register of their role-played and written persuasion.

Limitations of this Study

The most serious limitation of this study is that the role playing experience provided an oral rehearsal, or "drafting," that the more passive listening to a discussion and analyzing models did not. If role-playing were compared with another type of rehearsal, such as free writing or small-group discussion, we might have better control over the variable of practice. Also, the role-playing session included a bit of guided imagery and contemplation, which is considered to play a significant role in the composing process (Moffett, 1991), and so, may have contributed to the quality of the students' writing.

Other limitations are that the topics were not comparable and the instructional time of 35 minutes was very short. A comparative study over a longer period of time might show a greater effect, especially at eighth grade. Because students at that age seemed hesitant to role-play, perhaps a longer practice period would have helped them feel more comfortable and might more positively affect their writing.

EDUCATIONAL IMPLICATIONS

The most obvious implication for teaching is that role-playing in partners is a significantly more effective prewriting heuristic for fourth and
eighth graders for developing audience-adapted persuasive letters than
the presentation of information with an analysis of models and a set of
rules. The time-honored, typical teacher instruction, the method
reflected in the current traditional paradigm (Berlin & Inkster, 1980),
is only slightly more effective than no instruction. The findings of this
study show fourth and eighth graders have rudimentary schemata for
persuasion and an unconscious audience sense that they can adapt to
writing.

Because persuasion is one of writing's significant functions in the
world of the workplace, it is important that students learn how to write
in a way that takes account of their audience. Of course, if teachers are
to be successful with role-playing, they will need to be trained to control
it in the classroom so peer dialogue does not degenerate into nonpro-
ductive interaction or lack of belief. Kaaland-Wells (1993) found, on the
basis of a questionnaire, that only 31% of elementary teachers have had
even so much as a single course in creative dramatics; this is an
improvement over the decade before, however. She compared her survey of 224 elementary classroom teachers in a large urban school district
with that of Stewig (1984). She found more teachers had been exposed
to drama than Stewig had found 10 years earlier.

The rhetorical aspect of written persuasion, which includes target orientation, is not different in kind from oral persuasion, although oral
and written arguments can be radically different in organizational structure. Persuasive letters may help students link the two. It is probably easier to write such letters than argumentive essays because the letter is
closer to familiar real-world oral persuasion. The audience is easier to
imagine, so the challenge to social cognition is not at as high a level of
complexity as conjuring up an anonymous and distant audience, as is
usually expected for argumentation. Also, as Pringle and Freedman
(1985) have noted, presenting only one side of an issue and reasons for
it is considerably less complex than choosing a side to present, showing
arguments on both sides, and then making a case for the side one has
chosen, as is often required in essays presenting a logical argument.

Writing persuasion, especially when it is evoked by genuine situations
that provide a purpose—situations in which writers have a real stake in
the outcome—should help prepare students for the kind of reasoned
logical argumentation that characterizes much academic writing in secondary schools and colleges. Persuasive writing, because of its demand
for audience adaptation, may be especially appropriate for students

who have seen very few models of effective argumentation, are not familiar with its formal organization, and are not yet able to abstract and conceptualize at a mature enough level to discover or create a rigorously logical structure to unify and order their written arguments.

Because the performance on my two dependent variables correlated significantly with length, it follows that if students write more, they are very likely to produce more reasons for their request and to elaborate on those in ways that increase the effectiveness of their persuasion. Other researchers have shown that longer tends to be better in children's writing.[12] Encouragement, such as discussion before writing or conferencing during the process, are likely to help students produce longer, and thus probably more effective, writing.[13] The findings of this study lend support for rhetorically motivated writing programs such as Moffett and Wagner's (1976/1992), characterized by writing for real or clearly imagined purposes and audiences.

Persuasion in School

One of the problems students may have faced with the assignments I gave was sorting out the real from the pretend. I told them that the principal was really going to read their letters, and in so doing I set up a situation they could perceive to be real-world persuasion. But when I told them that I had told the principal that I had given them this assignment, they realized the principal would know their letter was in some sense "phony."

One eighth grader met with me outside of class to discuss a real persuasive challenge he faced. He wanted to take what he had learned about writing persuasion and apply it to a letter to the principal about a teacher who was being mean and unfair to the students. I ended up advising him to *talk* instead with the principal, ideally with one of his parents present, inasmuch as some particulars are best not committed to writing. Thus, even when a student has a genuine reason for writing a persuasive letter to a principal, the nuances of the power relationship make the task unusually complex.

Another insight into the problem of distinguishing the real from the pretend came from a preliminary pilot study I did before the study reported here. A group of eighth graders who had just finished reading *Huckleberry Finn* took the role of Huck and argued for freeing the slave Jim. Their target was a woman dressed as Miss Watson, an unyielding and determined slave owner. The persuasion they developed in the role-playing in this totally simulated scene seemed to be less fraught with ambiguity and complexity than the role-playing they did for a scene closer to home, namely, a dialogue with the principal. Perhaps both oral and written persuasion in role as a character far removed from the time and place of the actual school setting is easier for students because they are not caught in the confusion of whether they are engaging in an imaginary or a potentially real-world encounter with its concomitant power differential.[14] Thus, at least for fourth and eighth graders, the school principal may not be an appropriate target for persuasive letters.

Some of the best letters, in terms of target orientation, conveyed the sense that the student was writing from conviction, presenting a case in an authentic voice, implying a belief that he or she had a genuine stake in the outcome of the response to his persuasion. One fourth grader's letter was tangential to the topic of choosing school subjects, but written with the passion of pleading a case; he wanted an after-school tackle football team. Another argued eloquently for having the principal decide on school subjects because the writer thought most children would choose gym and art, and how could a bunch of athletes and artists ever run a society?

To quote one eighth grader's opening line, "School is an important and long part of a student's life." How can teachers make this long and important time meaningful and at the same time expect students to repeatedly write persuasion that is not part of a genuine interaction? In order to succeed as a writer in school, a student "must learn to maintain certain pretenses—chiefly that topics are self-initiated when in reality they are teacher-imposed, and that one's audience is an undifferentiated adult public when in reality it is just one's teacher or, at best, one's teacher and a few classmates," as Mellon (1978, p. 262) reminds us. Writing in school is, in part, a game of pretend. Thus, it tends to be inauthentic. Yet, for most of us, school is the place where writing is primarily learned. Perhaps it will help if students see that persuasive writing in the classroom is in a sense playing a role, and that success is dependent in part on the same phenomenon on which success in the theater is based, namely at making the present real setting *disappear*.

The young of society are socialized in school for the "necessary impersonal life," as W. H. Auden puts it. Perhaps we should make it clear to students that part of the school writing-of-persuasion game is laying aside personal convictions at times in order to try on the convictions of others; the goal is greater sensitivity to, and understanding of, the world outside oneself and the world of the past. Classroom role-playing, whether it be oral or written, can be effective in eliciting language that is appropriate for a wide variety of real-world occasions. Such role-playing may help students demonstrate their competence without implying to them or us that an assignment, especially when it is administered as a writing test, is an authentic persuasion event.

APPENDIX A:
SCALE FOR LEVEL OF TARGET ORIENTATION[15]

I. NO DISCERNIBLE RECOGNITION OF, AND ADAPTATION TO, THE TARGET'S PERSPECTIVE

    0   Utterance that is not a desire or request, a reason or support for request, nor an attempt to put the principal in a receptive mood

       a.   Opening[16]

       b.   Introductory or transitional utterances

       c.   Closing that is not a repetition

    1   Unelaborated request or statement of personal desire or need, including pleas or begging; if the only time it appears is in a sentence with a reason, it should be marked as a Level 1 assertion so the paper is distinguished from the one that has no persuasive assertion at this level

       a.   Question used as an indirect request

       b.   Simple statement of desire used as an indirect request

       c.   Plea

       d.   Wrapup conclusion and request

II. IMPLICIT RECOGNITION OF, AND ADAPTATION TO, THE TARGET'S PERSPECTIVE

    2   A reason for the request, showing only how it is necessary, desirable, or useful for the persuader (demonstrating an awareness that the principal needs a reason; or simple recognition of the social convention of politeness)

       a.   Elaboration of the problem

       b.   Elaboration of persuader's need

       c.   Elaboration of how persuader would like to see the request granted, but with no implied awareness of the target's perspective

       d.   Egocentric justification of reason

       e.   Recognition of effect of politeness

    3   Elaboration of persuader's or persuasive target's need, plus minimal dealing with anticipated counterarguments; reasons for the request that imply some awareness of the questions or concerns that would come to the principal's mind

       a.   Implied recognition that the target of the persuasion may not automatically be interested in the request

       b.   Implied refutation of anticipated counterargument

       c.   Elaboration of need from the perspective of an involved party other than the persuader or principal

      d.   Appeal to general principles or mutual values, but implied rather than explicit

      e.   Acknowledgment that counterargument has merit, but the persuader disagrees with it

      f.   Example of analogous case or facts to support request

      g.   Strategy for implementation that may show no awareness of the principal's perspective

      h.   Minimal anticipation of principal's counterargument

III. EXPLICIT RECOGNITION OF, AND ADAPTATION TO, THE TARGET'S PERSPECTIVE

    4 Obvious but truncated effort to show relevant consequences to the principal of accepting, or rejecting, the persuasive request, an effort that reveals awareness of the principal's perspective and problems

      a.   Explicit attempt to identify with the target's situation, or the values shared by the persuader and the target—to "soften her up"

      b.   Recognition of consequences of granting, or failing to grant, the request

      c.   Unelaborated statement of advantage to principal

      d.   Effective bribes or "sensible" threats

      e.   Effective rhetorical questions

    5 Elaboration of the consequences of complying, or not complying, with the persuasive request; or elaboration of specific ways to implement the request that would mitigate the problem a principal would consider important

      a.   Ways to solve a logistical problem

      b.   Ways to involve target in solving a logistical problem

      c.   Ways to avoid a problem created by the proposal

    6 Explicit attempts by the persuader to take the target's perspective in articulating an advantage to the target, or proposal of a genuine compromise

      a.   Advantage to the target

      b.   Proposal of a genuine compromise, so both parties have something to gain

APPENDIX B

Dear Mr. Smith,[17]

3[18]   I have been chosen by a few of my classmates to write you a letter

1   regarding the parties one Friday a month. We all think this is a good idea.

2   Most of us live so far away that it's hard for us to socialize with
2   our friends. This way we could see our friends during school hours and
3   make plans there, so our phone lines won't always be tyed up.

         I heard that there is some discussion about if it should only be for
         8th, 7th & 8th, or 6th, 7th, & 8th grade students. I'm a fellow eight grade
2   myself, but my classmates and I have talked to 7th & 6th graders and
3   most of them agreed that it should only be for 8th graders as long as
3   they get to have them, too.

4   I know you are wondering about it affecting our school work. We
6   think that you should give it a trial run, say 2 parties this & next
        month. If a good percent of the school work drops, stop the program
        and apologize

5 6   to the 6th & 7th graders. If not, put it on trial for the same reason every
3   year. At least that will give each class a fair chance.

4   You are probably wondering what advantages this has in store for
2 2 you. A lot of us have friends in other places. We would tell them about it.
5   Maybe the wing schools or local high schools will use this idea. I'm sure
5 5 they already heard about it. They may pick up on the idea and use it.
6   Then those principles would get all the credit. If you don't make your de-
6   cision fast, they'd get all the credit. If you decide to do it, and make the
6   party soon, you'll get the credit for it.
3   2 This may sound bizarre but, this just might be a new school fad.
1 6 3 Think about it. Your picture on the front of magazines. Don't laugh. It
3 6 just might happen. You and your school would be famous.
1   4 Please Mr. Smith, think about it. This may be your only chance.

                  Sincerely yours,
                  Stephanie Childs
3   on behalf of the eight grade
                  students here at North Junior High

3   P.S. Thank you for taking the time to read through this letter. SC

TABLE 8.1
Main Effect of Mode of Instruction with
Covariate of Number of Words
Means

	No Instruction	Direct Instruction	Role-Playing	Level of Significance
	Means for Highest Target Orientation Level			
Main Effect Instruction	4.00	3.96	4.38	$p < .0001$
	Means for Variety of Levels of Target Orientation			
Main Effect Instruction	3.74	3.77	4.02	$p < .003$

TABLE 8.2
Main Effect of Grade Level with Covariate of Number of Words
Means

	Grade 4	Grade 8	
	Means for Highest Target Orientation Level		
Main Effect Grade Level	3.96	4.30	$p < .0001$
	Means for Variety of Levels of Target Orientation		
Main Effect Grade Level	3.69	4.03	$p < .0001$

TABLE 8.3
Main Effect of Topic with Covariate of Number of Words
Means

	Subjects Topic 1	Party Topic 2	Cafeteria Topic 3	
	Means for Highest Target Orientation Level			
Main Effect Topic	4.12	4.30	3.93	$p < .001$
	Means for Variety of Levels of Target Orientation			
Main Effect Topic	3.81	4.05	3.69	$p < .003$

FIGURE 8.1.   Counterbalanced Design

	Group 1	Group 2	Group 3
Topic 1	RP*	DI**	NI***
Topic 2	NI	RP	DI
Topic 3	DI	NI	RP

  * Role playing
 ** Direct instruction
*** No instruction

NOTES

[1] Dunnagan (1991); Moore and Caldwell (1990); Pellegrini (1984); Ridel (1975); Roubicek (1983); and Troyka (1973).

[2] Britton (1970); Britton, Burgess, Martin, McLeod, and Rosen (1975); Dixon (1967/1975); Heathcote (1981); Hoetker (1969); Moffett and Wagner (1992); and Plowden (1967).

[3] Crowhurst (1980, 1983); Fowler (1982); Freedman and Pringle (1984); Hidi and Hildyard (1983); and Matsuhashi (1987).

[4] Genishi and Di Paolo (1982).

[5]a. Know exactly what you want the other person to do, think, believe, or feel.

b. Make what you want clear.

c. Give as many reasons as you can for your position.

d. Tell why you think these are good reasons.

e. Show the other person you understand his or her point of view.

f. Try to convince the other person that you are fair and honorable and that your point of view is a good one.

g. Assume the other person does not agree with you, and try to help him or her see why he should change his mind.

h. Show how the other person would benefit by changing his or her mind and adopting your position.

[6]Clark and Delia (1976, 1977); and Kinzer and Murphy (1983).

[7]The only units not included as persuasive assertions were those that were neither requests nor reasons, nor elaborations of these reasons, nor attempts to put the principal in a receptive mood; these were scored as 0.

[8]Cook-Gumperz and Corsaro (1977); Cook-Gumperz and Gumperz (1981); Cooper (1979); Eisenberg and Garvey (1981); Garvey (1979); Kroll and Lempers (1981); Maratson (1973); Martlew, Connolly, and McCleod (1978); Pellegrini (1982); Read and Cherry (1978); Sachs and Devin (1976); Sachs, Goldman, and Chaille (1984); Scarlett and Wolf (1979); and Wellman and Lempers (1977).

[9]Burns and Brainerd (1979); Dunn (1977); Galda (1984); Rosen (1974); Smilansky (1968); Sommers (1972); Wright (1974); and Youngers (1977).

[10]See, for example, Clay (1982); Dyson (1983); Ferreiro and Teberosky (1982); and Teale and Sulzby (1986).

[11]See case studies, such as those of Bissex (1980); Collerson (1983); and Gundlach (1981).

[12]Grobe (1981); and Hidi and Klaiman (1984).

[13]Calkins (1980); and Graves (1983, 1994).

[14]See Chapter 5 in this book for an example—in the tradition of Heathcote—of selecting an imaginary setting far removed from the problems in the classroom.

[15]To avoid confusion or the cumbersomeness of the phrase *he or she*, on this scale I am using the pronoun *she* to refer to both sexes.

[16]The illustrative types of assertions (a to h) under each of the headings were used as guiding examples.

[17]The names of the principals, students, and school are pseudonyms; otherwise, this letter is verbatim with none of the spelling or punctuation changed.

[18]The numbers in the margin represent the score assigned to each persuasive assertion.

REFERENCES

Bereiter, C., & Scardamalia, M. (1983). Levels of inquiry in writing research. In P. Mosenthal, L. Tamor, and S. A. Walmsley (Eds.), *Research on writing: Principles and methods* (pp. 3–25). New York: Longman.

Berlin, J. A., & Inkster, R. P. (1980). Current-traditional rhetoric: Paradigm and practice. *Freshman English News, 8*, 1–5, 14.

Birnbaum, J. C. (1981). A study of reading and writing behaviors of selected fourth grade and seventh grade students. *Dissertation Abstracts International, 42*, 152A–153A. (University Microfilms No. 81-15176)

Bissex, G. L. (1980). *Gns at wrk*. Cambridge, MA: Harvard University Press.

Blasi, A. (1976). Issues in defining stages and types. In J. Loevinger (Ed.), *Ego development: Conceptions and theories* (pp. 182–202). San Francisco: Jossey-Bass.

Britton, J. N. 1983. Writing and the story world. In B.M. Kroll and G. Wells (Eds.), *Explorations in the development of writing* (pp. 3–30). New York: John Wiley and Sons.

Britton, J. N., Burgess, T., Martin, N., McLeod, A., & Rosen, H. (1975). *The development of writing abilities, 11-18*. Urbana, IL: National Council of Teachers of English.

Burns, S. M., & Brainerd, C. J. (1979). Effects of constructive and dramatic play on perspective-taking in very young children. *Developmental Psychology, 15*, 512–521.

Calkins, L. M. (1980). Children's rewriting strategies. *Research in the Teaching of English, 14*, 331–341.

Clark, R. A., & Delia, J. G. (1976). The development of functional persuasive skills in childhood and early adolescence. *Child Development, 47*, 1008–1014.

Clark, R. A., & Delia, J. G. (1977). Cognitive complexity, social perspective taking, and functional persuasive skills in second- to ninth-grade children. *Human Communication Research, 3*, 128–134.

Clay, M. M. (1982). *Observing young readers: Selected papers*. Exeter, NH: Heinemann.

Collerson, J. (1983). One child and one genre: Developments in letter writing. In B. M. Kroll & G. Wells (Eds.), *Explorations in the development of writing* (pp. 71–93). New York: Wiley.

Cook-Gumperz, J., & Cosaro, W. (1977). Social-ecological constraints on children's communicative strategies. *Sociology, 11*, 411–434.

Cook-Gumperz, J., & Gumperz, J. J. (1981). From oral to written culture: The transition to literacy. In M. F. Whitemen (Ed.), *Writing: The nature, development, and teaching of written communication, volume 1: Variation in writing: Functional and linguistic-cultural differences* (pp. 89–109). Hillsdale, NJ: Lawrence Erlbaum.

Cooper, M. (1979). Verbal interaction in nursery schools. *British Journal of Educational Psychology, 49*, 214–225.

Crowhurst, M. (1980). Syntactic complexity and teachers' quality ratings of narrations and arguments. *Research in the Teaching of English, 14*, 223–231.

Crowhurst, M. (1983, April). *Persuasive writing at grades 5, 7, and 11: A cognitive-developmental perspective*. Paper presented at annual meeting of the American Educational Research Association, Montreal, Ontario, Canada. (ERIC Document Reproduction Service No. ED 230 977)

Delia, J. G., Kline, S. L., & Burleson, B. R. (1979). The development of persuasive communication strategies in kindergartners through twelfth graders. *Communication Monographs, 46*, 241–256.

Dixon, J. (1975). *Growth in English*. Urbana, IL: National Council of Teachers of English. (Original work published 1967)

Dunn, J. A. (1977). The effect of creative dramatics on the oral language abilities and self-esteem of Blacks, Chicanos, and Anglos in the second and fifth grades. *Dissertation Abstracts International, 38*(07), 3907A. (University Microfilms No. 77-29908)

Dunnagan, K. L. (1991). Seventh-grade students' audience awareness in writing produced within and without the dramatic mode. *Dissertation Abstracts International, 51*(12), 4043A. (University Microfilms No. 91-11695)

Dyson, A. H. (1983). The role of oral language in early writing processes. *Research in the Teaching of English, 17*, 1–30.

Eisenberg, A., & Garvey, C. (1981). Children's use of verbal strategies in resolving conflicts. *Discourse Processes, 4*, 149–170.

Ferreiro, E., & Teberosky, A. (1982). *Literacy before schooling*. Portsmouth, NH: Heinemann.

Florio, S. (1978). *The problem of dead letters: Social perspectives on the teaching of writing* (Research Series No. 34). East Lansing, MI: Michigan State University. (ERIC Document Reproduction Service No. ED 163 492)

Flower, L. S., & Hayes, J. (1980). The cognition of discovery: Defining a rhetorical problem. *College Composition and Communication, 31*, 27–43.

Fowler, L. M. (1982). Descriptive and persuasive writing skills of children (Doctoral dissertation, University of Georgia, 1981). *Dissertation Abstracts International, 42*, 4362A.

Freedman, A., & Pringle, I. (1984, Summer). Why children can't write arguments. *English in Education, 18*, 73–82.

Galda, L. (1984). Narrative competence: Play, storytelling, and story comprehension. In A. Pellegrini & T. Yawkey (Eds.), *The development of oral and written language in social contexts* (pp. 105–117). Norwood, NJ: Ablex.

Garvey, C. (1979). An approach to the study of children's role play. *The Quarterly Newsletter of the Laboratory of Comparative Human Cognition, 1*, 69–73.

Genishi, C., & Di Paolo, M. (1982). Learning through argument in a preschool. In L. C. Wilkinson (Ed.), *Communicating in the classroom* (pp. 49–68). New York: Academic Press.

Gentile, C. A., Martin-Rehrmann, J., & Kennedy, J. H. (1995). *Windows into the classroom: NAEP's 1992 writing portfolio study* (Report No. 23-FR-06). Washington, DC: National Center for Education Statistics, Office of Educational Research and Improvement, U.S. Department of Education.

Graves, D. H. (1983). *Writing: Teachers and children at work*. Exeter, NH: Heinemann.

Graves, D. H. (1994). *A fresh look at writing*. Portsmouth, NH: Heinemann.

Grobe, C. (1981). Syntactic maturity, mechanics, and vocabulary as predictors of quality ratings. *Research in the Teaching of English, 15*, 75–85.

Gundlach, R. A. (1981). On the nature and development of children's writing. In C. H. Frederiksen & J. F. Dominic (Eds.), *Writing: The nature, development, and teaching of written communication, vol. 2: Writing: Process, development and communication* (pp. 133–151). Hillsdale, NJ: Lawrence Erlbaum.

Heathcote, D. (1981). Drama as education. In N. McCaslin (Ed.), *Children and drama* (2nd ed.; pp. 78–90). New York: Longman.

Hidi, S., & Hildyard, A. (1983). A comparison of oral and written productions in two discourse types. *Discourse Processes, 6,* 91–105.

Hidi, S., & Klaiman, R. (1984). Children's written dialogues: Intermediary between conversation and written text? In A. Pellegrini & T. Yawkey (Eds.), *The development of oral and written language in social contexts* (pp. 233–241). Norwood, NJ: Ablex.

Hoetker, J. (1969). *Dramatics and the teaching of literature.* Champaign, IL: National Council of Teachers of English.

Ingersoll, R. L., & Kase, J. (1970). *Effects of creative dramatics on learning and retention of classroom material* (Grant G-1-9-08055-0105 010). Washington, DC: National Center for Educational Research and Development.

Kaaland-Wells, C. E. (1994). Classroom teacher's perception and use of creative drama. *Dissertation Abstracts International, 55*(02), 214A. (University Microfilms No. 94-18, 311)

Kaaland-Wells, C. E. (1994). Classroom teachers' perception and use of creative drama. *Youth Theatre Journal, 8*(4), 21–26.

Keech, C., & McNelly, M. E. (1982). *Effects of variation in a writing test prompt on holistic scores and composing process, part two.* Technical Report No. 2 of the NIE Writing Assessment Process (Grant No. NIE-G-80-0034). Berkeley, CA: Bay Area Writing Project.

Kinzer, C., & Murphy, S. (1983). *Beyond the field test of writing prompts: A preliminary investigation of the nature of response variation to selected field-tested prompts.* Unpublished report. Berkeley, CA: Bay Area Writing Project.

Kroll, B. M., & Lempers, J. D. (1981). Effect of mode of communication on the informational adequacy of children's explanations. *The Journal of Genetic Psychology, 138,* 27–35.

Maratson, M. P. (1973). Non-egocentric communication abilities in preschool children. *Child Development, 44,* 696–700.

Martlew, M., Connolly, K., & McCleod, C. (1978). Language use, role, and context in a five-year old. *Journal of Child Language, 5,* 81–89.

Matsuhashi, A. (1987). Revising the plan and altering the text. In A. Matsuhashi (Ed.), *Writing in real time: Modeling production processes* (pp. 197–233). Norwood, NJ: Ablex.

Mellon, J. C. (1978). A taxonomy of compositional competencies. In R. Beach & P. D. Pearson (Eds.), *Perspectives on literacy* (pp. 250–272). Minneapolis, MN: College of Education, University of Minnesota.

Mitchell, J. J. (1974). *Human life: The early adolescent years.* Toronto: Holt, Rinehart and Winston.

Moffett, J. (1991). Writing, inner speech, and meditation. In J. Moffett (Ed.), *Coming on center* (pp. 133–181). Montclair, NJ: Boynton/Cook.

Moffett, J., & Wagner, B. J. (1992). *Student-centered language arts and reading, K-12* (4th ed.). Portsmouth, NH: Boynton/Cook Heinemann. (Original work published 1968)

Moore, B. H., & Caldwell, H. (1990). The art of planning: Drama as rehearsal for writing in the primary grades. *Youth Theatre Journal, 4*(3), 13–20.

Mullis, I. V. (1985, March-April). *NAEP perspectives on literacy: A preview of the 1983–84 assessment results, the young adult literacy assessment and plans for 1986.* Paper presented at annual meeting of the American Educational Research Association, Chicago. (ERIC Document Reproduction Service No. ED 260 096)

Pellegrini, A. D. (1982). The construction of cohesive text by preschoolers in two play contexts. *Discourse Processes, 5*(1), 101–108.

Pellegrini, A. D. (1984). Symbolic functioning and children's early writing: The relations between kindergartners' play and isolated word-writing fluency. In R. Beach & L. S. Bridwell (Eds.), *New directions in composition research* (pp. 274–284). New York: Guilford.

Plowden, L. B. (1967). *Children and their primary schools.* London: HMSO.

Polyani, M. (1962). *Personal knowledge: Towards a post-critical philosophy.* Chicago: University of Chicago Press.

Pringle, I., & Freedman, A. (1985). *A comparative study of writing abilities in two modes at the grade 5, 8, and 12 levels.* Toronto: Ontario Ministry of Colleges and Universities.

Read, B., & Cherry, L. (1978). Preschool children's production of direct forms. *Discourse Processes, 1,* 233–245.

Ridel, S. J. H. (1975). An investigation of the effects of creative dramatics on ninth grade students. *Dissertation Abstracts International, 36,* 3551A. (University Microfilms No. 75-26, 811, 238)

Rosen, C. E. (1974). The effects of sociodramatic play on problem-solving behavior among culturally disadvantaged children. *Child Development, 45,* 920–927.

Roubicek, H. L. (1983). An investigation of story dramatization as a pre-writing activity. *Dissertation Abstracts International, 45*(02), 403A. (University Microfilms No. 84-12051)

Rucker, G. H. (1981). The composing process of gifted and average sixth grade students: A case study (Doctoral dissertation, University of Colorado, 1981). *Dissertation Abstracts International, 42*(08), 3481A.

Sachs, J., & Devin, J. (1976). Young children's use of age-appropriate speech styles in social interaction and role-playing. *Journal of Child Language, 3,* 81–98.

Sachs, J., Goldman, J., & Chaille, C. (1984). Planning in pretend play: Using language to coordinate narrative development. In A. Pellegrini & T. Yawkey (Eds.), *The development of oral and written language in social contexts* (pp. 119–128). Norwood, NJ: Ablex.

Scardamalia, M., Bereiter, C., & Goelman, H. (1982). The role of production factors in writing ability. In M. S. Nystrand (Ed.), *What writers know* (pp. 173–210). New York: Academic Press.

Scarlett, W., & Wolf, D. (1979). When it's only make-believe. In E. Winner & H. Gardner (Eds.), *Fact, fiction, and fantasy in childhood* (pp. 485–496). San Francisco: Jossey-Bass.

Slobin, D. I., & Welsh, C. A. (1973). Elicited imitation as a research tool in developmental psycholinguistics. In C. A. Ferguson & D. I. Slobin (Eds.), *Studies of child language development* (pp. 119–128). New York: Holt, Rinehart and Winston.

Smilansky, S. (1968). *The effects of sociodramatic play on disadvantaged preschool children*. New York: John Wiley and Sons.

Sommers, M. W. (1972). The effects of creative drama on person perception. *Dissertation Abstracts International, 33*(04), 1876A. (University Microfilms No. 72-277823)

Stewig, J. W. (1984). Teacher's perceptions of creative drama in the elementary classroom. *Children's Theatre Review, 33*(2), 27–29.

Teale, W. H., & Sulzby, E. (Eds.). (1986). *Emergent literacy: Writing and reading*. Norwood, NJ: Ablex.

Troyka, L. Q. (1973). A study of the effect of simulation-gaming on expository prose competence of college remedial English composition students. *Dissertation Abstracts International, 34*, 4092A. (University Microfilms 1985, No. 73-30, 136; ERIC Document Reproduction Service No. ED 090 541)

Vygotsky, L. S. (1978). *Mind in society: The development of higher psychological processes* (M. Cole, V. John-Steiner, S. Scribner, & E. Souberman, Eds.). Cambridge, MA: Harvard University Press.

Wagner, B. J. (1987). The effects of role playing on written persuasion: An age and channel comparison of fourth and eighth graders. *Dissertation Abstracts International, 47*(11), 4008A. (University Microfilms No. 87-05196)

Wellman, H. M., & Lempers, J. D. (1977). The naturalistic communicative abilities of two-year-olds. *Child Development, 48*(3), 1052–1057.

Wright, L. (1974). Creative dramatics and the development of role taking in the elementary classroom. *Elementary English, 51*, 89–93.

Youngers, J. S. (1977). An investigation of the effects of experiences in creative dramatics on creative and semantic development in children. *Dissertation Abstracts International, 39*, 117A. (University Microfilms 1978, No. 7810 405, 922)

OTHER RESOURCES

Dyson, A H. (1981). Oral language: The rooting system for learning to write. *Language Arts, 58*, 776–784.

Dyson, A H. (1989). *Multiple worlds of child writers: Friends learning to write*. New York: Teachers College Press.

Dyson, A H. (1990). Talking up a writing community: The role of talk in learning to write. In S. Hynds & D. L. Rubin (Eds.), *Perspectives on thought and learning* (pp. 99–114). Urbana, IL: National Council of Teachaers of English.

Dyson, A H. (1993). *Social worlds of children learning to write in an urban primary school*. New York: Teachers College Press.

Dyson, A H. (1995). Writing children: Reinventing the development of child-hood literacy. *Written Communication, 12*, 4–46.

McNaughton, M. J. (1997). Drama and children's writing: A study of the influence of drama on the imaginative writing of primary school children. *Research in Drama Education, 2*(1), 55–86.

Wagner, B. J. (1988). Research currents: Does classroom drama affect the arts of language? *Language Arts, 68*(1), 46–55.

Wagner, B. J. (1991). Imaginative expression. In J. Flood, J. M. Jensen, D. Lapp, & J. R. Squire (Eds.), *Handbook of research on teaching the English language arts* (pp. 787–804). New York: Macmillan.

Wagner, B. J. (1995). A theoretical framework for improvisational drama. *Journal of the National Association for Drama in Education, 19*(2), 61–70.

Wagner, B. J. (1996). Research matters. *Drama Matters, 1*(1), 28–31.

Wagner, B. J. (1998). *Educational drama and language arts: What research shows.* Portsmouth, NH: Heinemann.

part IV

Teacher Development

I n the final part of this book, we present two very different chapters. The first is one of the last contributions by the late Richard Courtney to his rich legacy of reflections and research in the field of educational drama. What has characterized his work is a commitment to improve self-expression, creativity, and responsible social interaction among students of all ages. Over the years, he has not only been a premier practitioner of what he termed "developmental drama," but also a theorist and advocate for its use in schools. As David Booth (Barnard, 1998) wrote in his tribute:

> No matter where I traveled—Great Britain, the United States, Australia—Richard was known by everyone connected with the arts, with theatre, with educational drama; his impact on our knowledge of the theory and practice of arts education was phenomenal. He gave each of us who knew him background and frameworks for developing and extending our personal philosophy of teaching. (p. 10)

Courtney's many books and his research, and that of his graduate students, have created a rich discourse community in which to define, clarify, reflect on, and improve the practice of drama in schools. We are very grateful to this unique and highly productive professor who has enriched our understanding of drama's role in developing moral communities.

Joe Norris's final chapter shows us how to incorporate drama into teacher education. If we want this powerful instructional technique to become a critical force in every classroom, we need to show teachers its value.

One of my own favorite strategies in graduate classes is to invite the students on the first night of class to cluster, in small groups, around a large photo of an author of one of our required texts. For example, on the first night of a seminar entitled Language, Linguistics, and Literacy, I set up photos of Mikhail Bakhtin, Jerome Bruner, Stephen Pinker, and

Lev Vygotsky. In front of each, I had a card that succinctly listed 10 of the most salient ideas of that theorist. I told the students to group themselves around the photos and decide which one of them would assume the role of the scholar, and which his wife, assistant, graduate student, or whomever. Then I gave them a few minutes to read the major ideas of that writer, a paragraph or two of biographical information, and the table of contents of one of the four texts they had just purchased before class. I turned around, donned my jacket and glasses, and, in role, thanked them all for agreeing to spend the next month working together to write a textbook for the course they in reality had signed up for. I asked them if their rooms at the Hotel Nikko were comfortable. "Did you get either the Japanese style or the American style bathtub you ordered? How about your computer? Did you get the right Mac, Dr. Bakhtin? You realize we shall be exchanging chapters, so it is crucial we all have e-mail. Are there any problems with that?" And so it went as they reported on various frustrations, becoming more comfortable in their new roles as the discussion continued. Then we introduced ourselves in role, and I asked them to tell us which issues must be covered in the new textbook. Of course, they stayed fairly close to the list on their cards at this point, but as soon as Dr. Pinker insisted that we need to stress the biological basis for language acquisition, I asked Dr. Bruner how that fit with his notion of scaffolding, and then asked Dr. Vygotsky to enlighten the debate with his views on the zone of proximal development. Dr. Bakhtin was soon arguing with Dr. Pinker's colleague about the need for dialogue, and we were off. Although the students had not yet read much of any of these writers, they were soon debating their ideas, just from looking at the lists I had given them and the table of contents of the four books they had brought to class. By the end of the first class, the students had a glimpse of what was in store for the course, and they found it easy to decide which of the authors they would choose on the night they were to lead the seminar discussion.

As you can see, I strongly agree with Joe Norris that drama is adult's work. Moral communities are grounded in a climate of openness and mutual respect. Nothing creates this faster than educational drama.

REFERENCE

Barnard, J.-B. (1998). Tribute to Richard Courtney. *Research in Drama Education*, 3(1), 9–11.

chapter 9

A Lifetime of Drama Teaching and Research

Richard Courtney*

SCHOOL EXPERIMENTS

I t all began for me in January 1948, when I was demobbed from the Royal Air Force; with nine months to spare before going to the university, I taught as an unqualified teacher in a rural village elementary school in England. The headmistress took the five- to seven-and-a-half-year-olds and I had 27 seven- to ten-and-a-half-year-olds. I enjoyed it, except for math, where I had 27 levels in that one class and could never get around to all of them within the hour. Quite quickly I discovered drama. In geography, we were studying wheat on the Canadian prairies, but it hardly related to the British children's experience. So, in a field belonging to the school, the children and I created the prairies— a virtual reality in miniature size. We grew real wheat on our prairies, dug out the Great Lakes and the St. Lawrence River, filling them with water, and shipped the grain on model boats to Montreal and over the Atlantic. We collected the grain in small sacks, passed them on to mothers who volunteered to bake it, and had the bread for lunch the following day. By the end of the project, all 27 children had dramatically experienced Canadian prairie wheat and trading patterns. The success of this experiment led me to use drama "across the curriculum" for most subjects—although I still had not succeeded in teaching 27 math levels simultaneously!

The chairman of the school board, the vicar, heard from the children how they liked drama, so he asked me up to the manse for a cup of tea.

---

*Richard Courtney died on August 16, 1997.

205

("A great honor," confided the headmistress with a wink.) In response to his questions, I replied, with youthful enthusiasm, about how children really learn through drama, about how it vastly increases their motivation, self-concept, and confidence, and how it is a natural therapy for increasing psychic health. I should have stopped while I was ahead. At the word *therapy*, the vicar went quite pale, saying thinly: "None of my children are mad, y'know!" I had learned the importance of using the receiver's language when reporting research, particularly in an advocacy role. (The reader should not think, because this was 1948, that it couldn't happen today—it was also said to me by a senior administrator at a drama therapy conference in 1988!)

At the university where I did my teaching practicum, I was at "a blackboard jungle"—an urban secondary school for boys, where a 15-year-old boy six inches taller than I attacked me with a switchblade. I jutted my knee into his groin, bent his arm behind his back, and marched him off to the headmaster, who said there was little he could do: "The boy is already on probation for stabbing a man in the back—the magistrates go easy on ex-evacuees!" (I watched this boy's later career through the crime reports in the newspapers.)

In the same school, I taught a class in history and we began with the Renaissance voyages of discovery. On the first day, the headmaster took me aside, saying, "You're the drama man, I hear? Well, we don't do drama here. It's a meat-and-potatoes school, this, so no 'fancy stuff,' okay?" But the students in the class were floundering in history, so we dramatized all the voyages, from Prince Philip of Portugal to Christopher Columbus. One boy, Harry, had a twisted leg and arm, spoke with a severe lisp, and frightened the others when he fell down in epileptic fits. The others would not accept him in any improvisational group. He solved his problem by being "the fish" that swam under all the explorers' ships, and he went everywhere—down the coast of Africa, around the Cape of Good Hope to Goa, and even to the West Indies—witnessing everything that happened. Then the headmaster paid us a surprise visit. "Here," he whispered to me angrily, "I thought I told you that we don't do drama here!" I said it was history, but he sneered. "Do you think I fell off a Christmas tree?" he hissed. "I know drama when I see it—and *that's* drama!" So he questioned the boys about what they had learned and was astounded to find their replies rich and fluent. His eyes nearly popped out of his head when the usually silent Harry told him all he had seen while acting as "the fish"—he knew it all, because he'd been there! When I returned to the school the following Fall, I found I was teaching this "drama across the curriculum" the majority of the time. I was then asked by the headmaster to teach there permanently.

A couple of years later, the incident with Harry led to my joining Kenneth Lovell in the development of his postgraduate Education Diploma course on "backward children" for teachers at Leeds University. The teachers visited my school, and I also instructed them onsite in their schools. For this diploma, I conducted my first genuinely designed research, showing that: a) drama encouraged reticent backward students to join activities with others and learn well, b) drama discouraged physically handicapped students from disturbing the drama activities of others, and c) backward students learning through drama had an achievement rating at about 12-15% above their norm. But it was at this time, also, that I became highly skeptical of using objective research methods on human subjects because I discovered that measurement could not answer questions about *quality*. What makes one improvisation "good" compared with another is not something that can be scientifically measured.

Almost simultaneously, I was designing architecture for educational drama and theater and discovered that all 20th century British theaters had been built with audience risers (until The Mermaid at Puddle Dock) based on the *average* eye height of those seated—which meant that roughly 51% could see the stage clearly, but that 49% could not. Little wonder, then, that I became wary of averages and statistics in designing for human need.

In 1956, I became Master for Drama at Yorkshire's second comprehensive school, the new Colne Valley High School. It was huge—the entering class of 11-year-olds was 500 students. Both my growing team of teachers and I each taught a class once a week in improvisation and creative dance, while I also worked with other teachers to stimulate "drama across the curriculum." We undertook many research studies showing that: a) drama was an effective teaching/learning method in English and other subjects, and b) an increased exposure to creative drama and creative dance improved both students' learning and social behavior. Increasingly, we used qualitative research methods, specifically case studies.

At the same time, I was also responsible for the production of plays outside of school time. We made it a cooperative task between all the teachers, with a production committee that supervised the whole process, from choosing plays to the final performances. The research that occupied me, however, was on play choice. We discovered that there was a high correlation between a) plays chosen specifically for students' needs (in age range, interests, etc.), b) the enjoyment of the student players, and c) the educational satisfaction of the teachers. What did not correlate, we discovered, was the view of the parents who wanted "a more professional approach"—that is, more slickness, more musicals, and a more Hollywood-type of production, which had a low priority for the teachers.

At the same time, I began the Four Valleys Youth Theatre, the first youth theater in Britain designed as a single-purpose youth club. It was designed for students who were not continuing in school but who were interested in staging productions for local elementary schools, as well as for adult audiences. We conducted some research, particularly of audience response, but we found this difficult to achieve while we were in production. This experience demonstrated that research for a theater company should usually be an independent endeavor.

RESEARCH IN DRAMA TEACHER-EDUCATION

In 1959, I was appointed Senior Lecturer in Drama at Trent Park College, in London, one of the government's two leading drama teacher-education colleges. While there, I conducted five types of research, consisting of:

* **Drama therapy.** From 1959 to 1968, I was a part-time adjunct to a distinguished psychotherapist at The Tavistock Clinic, in London. Together we engaged in practical research, preparing a series of guidelines for drama therapists, which I used in my subsequent work. These included:
  a) a distinction between drama therapy for psychic health, as in education; and for diagnosis, treatment, and cure, as in psychotherapy;
  b) a list of a range of dramatic activities, both unique to therapy and drawn from educational drama, along with their common therapeutic effects;
  c) specific problems with the psychological and physically disadvantaged, along with useful dramatic techniques for this group; and
  d) an annotated bibliography.
* **Spaces and equipment for educational drama.** I conducted this research with the Ministry of Education, as well as groups of architects designing such spaces within counties (equivalent to provinces or states). This work resulted in my 1966 book, *The Drama Studio*.
* **The efficacy of various teaching methods.** We were surprised to discover that the depth of the drama experience differed little according to the method used. Judging from the criteria used by teachers (e.g., what has now become known as "the play way" of Caldwell Cook [1917], "sincerity and absorption" of Peter Slade [1954], the "exercise" approach of Brian Way [1967/1972], "the mantle of expert" of Dorothy Heathcote [Heathcote & Bolton,

1995], the improvisation of Viola Spolin [1963/1985], and the "creative dramatics" of Winifred Ward [1930], and others), each method seemed to have its advantages and disadvantages, but teachers disagreed as to the criteria used for judging its efficacy. "True believers" in the different camps, of course, drew different conclusions, but *in research terms* there appeared little difference in the quality of the experience.

- **Drama activities with deprived youth.** These I supervised for about 10 years for the boroughs of Smethwick and Stockport—for two nights a week in the actual boroughs, and three weeks residentially in the Easter holidays. The key to the residential courses was improvisation—based on the aesthetic criteria of student choice and judgment—leading to an improvised production, with student designed and executed settings and costumes, performed before an invited audience of parents and educators. We wanted to know how theatrically effective independent choice could be. The results showed that the highest caliber theater could be achieved, provided there was good social cohesion. This was documented in a film of the students creation: An improvised medieval mystery play, with the audience on swivel chairs in the center, and the players on different stages all around the perimeter (including a gigantic Hell's mouth that the students had based on *The Book of Kells*).

- **The spontaneous drama of babies.** After finding my 10-month-old son sitting in the living room pretending to be (impersonating) his mother as he went to sleep, we did a pilot study and discovered that the first full dramatic act with all children appeared at the same age—they all initially pretended to be, that is impersonated, their mother. Starting in 1959, I persuaded my students at Trent Park, together with those at other London colleges, where I was an examiner, to observe 9- to 10-month-old babies, and found the trait to be universal. In 1968, in Canada, we found the same thing in Canadian, American, Amerindian, Chinese, Fijian, Australian, aboriginal, and other babies. We considered the research complete in 1971 and ceased observations. Over this long period of time, we also observed older children and found a series of steps in dramatic action according to maturation, which I published later in *The Dramatic Curriculum* (1980/1982).

UNIVERSITY RESEARCH

When I became a Canadian in 1968, I first taught graduate students in a theater department in a Faculty of Fine Arts. Zina Barnieh was my first

Masters of Fine Arts student. Her research project was a production for young people of Eric Nicol's *Clam That Made A Face,* about an Indian potlatch, with a total Amerindian cast; it was performed in the longhouse at the Provincial Museum, in Victoria. In this, Barnieh explored the Indian content and the participational method in a spectacular production. Other research in the arts that I supervised included a team who did improvisations working with a local TV station, trying various techniques to increase the participation of children watching in their homes.

The most extensive educational research was conducted in The Victoria Project (1968–1971); we wanted to see if there were differences in creativity among White, Amerindian (Coast Salish), and Chinese elementary school children (a dangerous topic because we might be accused of not being 'politically correct' in assuming that there might be differences between races). To avoid cultural biases among leaders, the children engaged in free play with their own cultural peers, in different classes of 5, 7, 9, and 11 years. Analysis of the data from trained observers showed that White children were the best achievers in verbal expression, and Amerindian in bodily expression. Chinese children, as they matured, required increased adult direction to be expressive. These findings with Chinese children in Canada were replicated in a subsequent study by Jay Chen in Toronto in the 1980s.

This led to a number of practical research studies in various cultures outside Canada, particularly in tribal societies—with Pueblos and the Hopi in the United States, on various Pacific islands, and with Australian aboriginals—all of which amplified the findings of The Victoria Project. We also found that the content of dramatic expressions was directly infused with a culture's ritual-myth, but it was less so in agricultural societies, and least so in industrial and post-industrial societies. When the latter cultures had a rich folklore (as in rural Britain or rural Bulgaria), this influenced improvisational content more than when folklore was not so rich (as in rural North America).

RESEARCH IN A RESEARCH INSTITUTION

For over 20 years, I taught graduate students and conducted research in The Ontario Institute for Studies in Education, in Toronto. I strongly believe that doctoral candidates need to identify the research questions most important *for them,* and of which they have practical background experience. Because most of my students were teachers, the concerns they persued in their theses included:

a) the improvement of learning in subject areas (e.g, reading, writing, oral language, social studies, music, and visual art) through drama;

b) comparisons among drama experts from observations, interviews, and texts;

c) studies of theater for young audiences and Theater in Education (TIE) companies; and

d) explorations of theory developed from practice.

Some examples are:

- the learning of generic skills in a "co-op" grade 12 drama class that transferred to work contexts;
- how psychic health improved through drama and affected students' achievements;
- the effect on school students of theater-for-young-audiences and Theater in Education (TIE) companies, using various kinds of followup;
- the effect on students of the specialty arts secondary schools now emerging in North America; and
- comparisons among various African experiments in the use of drama for social development (e.g., for political awareness, for working toward developing a school in the community, etc).[1]

Simultaneously, I conducted large-scale research projects where graduate students had an opportunity to learn research skills. Two projects, conducted with colleagues for Ontario's Ministry of Education, addressed issues in elementary schools: children's learning through drama and the arts, and drama and arts teachers' "practical knowledge." The final reports confirmed what drama teachers already knew from experience, but needed to make explicit in times of fiscal restraint. Enthused, the Ontario drama and arts associations distributed them free to all their members.

The research showed that children in drama and arts classrooms improved in their self-confidence and self-concept, in their perception and self-awareness, in their thinking styles and self-expression, and in their motivation and transference of knowledge and experience—which varied with maturation. Meanwhile, elementary drama and arts teachers operated by personal knowledge (tacit, unconscious) as well as explicit knowledge (mostly conscious, and often in words). Because a large part of their abilities were tacit, they could stimulate the children to do their best work. An indirect effect of the research was to show that elementary drama and arts teachers were doing a good job and to show others *how* they were doing it. This raised their status in the education community.

In the past decade, I have, based on my experience, put forward a new notion that has begun to affect research as I retire from the field. For years we have been restricted because social science has classified research as *either* objective, which means counting or measuring, *or* as subjective, which indicates entirely the view of the observer with no checks to see if it is valid. This has always proved difficult, if not impossible, for post-Kantian aesthetics (i.e., aesthetics as qualities of thinking, and *not* as the study of beauty). The work of art is subjective as the artist creates it but, seemingly, objective as the audience perceives it—although the audience allows for the subjectivity of the artist.

This difficulty occurs with all media, that which "stands in the middle" between the artist and audience, or *mediate*, like an improvisation or a painting. There is, in fact, a *mediate object* (e.g., a picture or an improvisation) which provides *mediate knowledge* that is distinct from objective and subjective objects and knowledge.

In this context, I have put forward the Comparative-Emergent Qualitative Research Method (CEQRM), in Part 2 of my book *Drama and Feeling* (1995), which has begun to be used successfully by drama and arts researchers. Without attempting to explicate it fully here, I will give an example. For the question, "What learning happens when creative drama is taught to first graders compared to sixth graders?," data is collected from:

- the literature for first grade and sixth grade
- teachers of creative drama (experts at a practical level) for first grade and sixth grade
- consultants and advisors (experts at a further practical level) for first grade and sixth grade.

This data is analysed, in the Grounded Theory mode, separately into six different groups, which are then compared first grade to sixth grade. The CEQRM does *not* give absolute results applicable to all children (which quantitative research claims to achieve but does not in the arts), but it *does* provide comparative results for a specific group of children and a specific group of teachers—and in that context, *it works*.

DEVELOPMENTAL DRAMA

In 1968, at the University of Victoria, British Columbia, I reconceptualized the field of educational drama as developmental drama—"the study of human development in dramatic action both personally and also socially and culturally, and in two parts, which were distinguished by the use of logical classes:

a) undergraduate work in practical fields (e.g., educational drama, drama therapy, drama in social work, drama in life, educational theater) based on experiential learning plus some academic work; and

b) graduate work (e.g., research and theory) about practical fields, using a variety of theoretical frameworks, including philosophy, psychology, sociology, and anthropology.

The basis of this discipline is practical experience in dramatic action. To act gives us, the players, "a coming to know." It is a unique method of knowing, quite different from experience in the actual world (as in Dewey's "learning by doing"), or from reading or listening (learning based on indirect experience). Drama consists of a double process (imagining plus action) which is on-going—it exists primarily in space and time, or the here and now. It is reflected upon *after* the act; but we learn to operate *within the action*--"as if" we are a different entity. Drama creates "a fictional world" (e.g., "the play world" of the child, and "the aesthetic world" and "the theater world" of the adult), the purpose of which is to compare it to the actual world, resulting in our own unique perspective on reality within our own context. Fundamentally, this is a life operation which also functions in most practical fields where it has many similar and different purposes.

Despite the long record of research indicated in this chapter, I do not feel myself to be primarily a researcher, but more a teacher who uses research to help my teaching. This is because research by itself proves very little. In order to affect what happens in classrooms, *advocacy* is far more important. In the final analysis, drama teachers must not only learn how to do research, but also how to use this research as authority to increase and improve educational drama.

NOTES

[1] Graduate students whose theses have a high reputation include: Peter McLaren (now at UCLA), whose thesis became an international best-selling book, *Schooling as a Ritual Process* (1985); Dennis Mulcahy, who now directs teacher education at Memorial University, in Newfoundland; Robert Gardner, who now directs the radio/television department at Ryerson Polytechnical University and is a renowned TV "doctor" of existing programs and series; Poranee

Guratana, who wrote the first book in Thai on creative drama; Graham Scott, who became the founding director of The Drama Resources Centre, Melbourne, Australia; together with many theater directors, writers, film and TV makers, as well as teachers, consultants, etc.

REFERENCES

Cook, H. C. (1917). *The play way.* London: Heinemann.

Courtney, R. (1966). *The drama studio: Architecture and equipment for dramatic education.* London: Sir Isaac Pitman.

Courtney, R. (1982). *The dramatic curriculum.* London and Ontario: Althouse Press, University of Western Ontario. (Original work published 1980)

Courtney, R. (1995). *Drama and feeling: An aesthetic theory.* Montreal and Kingston, Canada: McGill-Queen's University Press.

Heathcote, D., & Bolton, G. (1995). *Drama for learning: Dorothy Heathcote's mantle of the expert approach to education.* Portsmouth, NH: Heinemann.

McLaren, P. (1985). *Schooling as a ritual process.* London: Routledge and Paul Kegan.

Slade, P. (1954). *Child drama* (B. Way, Ed.). London: University of London Press.

Spolin, V. (1985). *Improvisations for the theater: A handbook of teaching and directing techniques.* Evanston, IL: Northwestern University Press. (Original work published 1963)

Ward, W. (1930). *Creative dramatics.* New York: Appleton.

Way, B. (1972). *Development through drama.* New York: Humanities. (Original work published 1967)

OTHER RESOURCES

Booth, D., & Martin-Smith, A. (Eds.). (1988). *Re-cognizing Richard Courtney: Selected writings on drama and education.* Markham, Ontario, Canada: Pembroke.

Courtney, R. (1982). *Re-play: Studies of human drama in education.* Toronto: Ontario Institute for Studies in Education Press.

Courtney, R. (1985). The dramatic metaphor and learning. In J. Kase-Polisini (Ed.), *Creative drama in a developmental context* (pp. 39–64). New York: University Press of America.

Courtney, R. (1987). *The quest: Research and inquiry in arts education.* Lanham, MD: University Press of America. (Original work published 1984)

Courtney, R. (1989a). *Drama and intelligence: A cognitive theory.* Montreal and Kingston, Canada: McGill-Queen's University Press.

Courtney, R. (1989b). *Play, drama and thought: The intellectual background to dramatic education* (4th rev. ed.). Toronto: Simon and Pierre. (Original work published 1968)

Courtney, R., Booth, D. W., Emerson, J., & Kuzmich, N. (1988). *No one way of being: The personal knowledge of elementary arts teachers.* Toronto: Ontario Ministry of Education. (ERIIC Document Reproduction Service No. ED 305 296)

Courtney, R., & Park, P. (1982). *Learning through the arts* (Vols. 1-4). Toronto: Ontario Ministry of Education.

Courtney, R., & Schattner, G. (1981). *Drama in therapy* (Vols. 1 and 2). New York: Drama Book Specialists.

Johnson, L., & O'Neill, C. (Eds.). (1984). *Dorothy Heathcote: Collected writings on education and drama.* London: Hutchinson.

Wagner, B. J. (1999). *Dorothy Heathcote: Drama as a learning medium.* Portland, ME: Calendar Islands Publishers. (Original work published 1976)

chapter 10

Creative Drama as Adult's Work

Joe Norris
University of Alberta

THE PLAY'S THE THING

I n February of 1996, a petition was delivered to the Alberta Legisla-
ture asking the government to reinstate a full kindergarten. It consisted of over 1,500 paper dolls strung together, upon which were the
signatures of young children and their parents. The Speaker of the
House refused to accept it, claiming that it did not conform to government standards. According to him, it was messy and disorderly and
could not be easily archived as a government document. Crayon signatures were inappropriate. The Conservative government in power
mocked and jeered at the petition in legislative assembly, much to the
dismay of many Albertans. This was not a way to welcome our very
young into the democratic process. What they were indeed learning was
that democracy means conforming to the dominant epistemology and
that color of any sort was not acceptable.

The terms *child* and *adult* are too often used not just to describe, but to
evaluate. The word *child* connotes something less or negative, as when
we slip into usage such as "childish" versus "mature." Childish defines
behavior deemed inappropriate in the adult world, and even "child" can
be used in a pejorative sense, as in "don't act like a child." The adult
world is much more valued than the world of a child. The Alberta government could not appreciate the efforts of their young constituents.
The petition format appeared playful, and thus trivial.

Culler (1982) reminds us of the logocentricism of our culture. He, as
well as other deconstructionists, claim that many terms are based upon
binary opposites. Words tell us what something is by telling us what it is
not. Without "night," "day" would have no meaning. Not only are
terms linked in such a binary way, but one of the terms connotes a

217

higher status than the other. One term becomes dominant, while the other is subordinate. Beneath our language, lies an epistemological bias that drives everyday thinking and creates a bias toward bi-polarity. In order to achieve a just and balanced society, these epistemological assumptions need to be made evident. Without this understanding, language can be a tool for oppression.

Consequently, in creative drama, process drama, theater, and other arts, the language we use can work to defeat us. An alignment with the "child's world" is understood by those who see that learning can be playful, but an emphasis on this may do little to gain support from those who believe that learning is serious business. In the arts we "play" the piano and put on a "play." "Play" is opposite of "work," work being the dominant term. For many, work is important, and play is frivolous.

Cottrell (1979) boldly states that "Play is the work of young children" (p. 2). Such a statement is a battle standard around which to rally. It gives justification to what many in the arts truly believe. By saying that what we do is serious and rigorous, Cottrell gives us a giant step up the credibility ladder. Unfortunately, she did so at a great cost. Our work as drama teachers is still aligned with "the child." What we do is important, but only at the subordinate level.

King (1983), in a study of young children, found that they had a different concept of work and play. For many, work was something they do for someone else, while play is something they do for themselves. King's study clearly showed that the terms have very little to do with an activity, but more with the attitude one brings to the activity. One can "work" rather than "play" the piano, a painful experience for both the performer and the audience.

Play and work then function not as verbs at all, but as adverbs. They describe an inner attitude toward an action. If people believe that what they are doing is either serious or forced, they would be "working." If one is doing an activity for oneself or doing it frivolously, one would be "playing."

But need it be this way? In a post-modern era, could not these terms become complementary rather than opposite? In a mutualistic classroom (Maruyama, 1974) or office, where "team" is the norm, would one not be doing an activity for both oneself and others? Should not going to work be a fulfilling and rewarding experience? If so, why cannot one say, "I am going to play today"? The thought of it, however, still makes it appear that someone is being paid for doing nothing. The terms *work* and *play* are deeply embedded in our collective subconscious, and the way they are presently held works against the valuable "work" those in drama education perform.

It is my belief that drama has proven itself, time and time again, as a valuable learning experience. Not only do students enjoy the process, they leave with a richness and depth that comes from a shared experience. By being one of many participants, they learn that knowledge is contextual and that multiple perspectives are not only allowed, but celebrated (Neelands, 1984). Recent qualitative studies (Edmiston, 1991; Norris, 1989; Taylor, 1993) attest to the value of drama as a learning medium. The question, then, is why it is relegated almost exclusively to the young. The only extensive documentation of creative drama with adults is in realms drama therapy and popular theater. Again, it is used with "perceived" subordinate segments of the population—the ill and the disadvantaged.

If drama is the powerful learning medium we claim it is, we must use it with all ages and with all peoples. Imagine a board meeting that spontaneously breaks into a role-play to help its members understand customer dissatisfaction, or a legislative assembly forming tableaus to determine a new way of structuring the cabinet. The tools we use as drama teachers are underutilized and misunderstood. Until we bring them out of the cupboard with the banner "All play is work," we are denying our society the rich potential our art form has to offer in improving the human condition.

Play is Adult's Work

With the belief that drama as a learning medium could be applicable to all ages, I have embarked on a lifelong self-study to find ways where I could use drama to teach drama, use drama to teach the teaching of drama, and use drama to teach curriculum theory. I believe that if I only profess its value without ever employing it in my own teaching at the tertiary level, I am defeating my own beliefs. Drama as a learning medium has its place in university classrooms.

The following are activities I have used in my university teaching over the past seven years to demonstrate to teachers of drama and other subjects not only that the concepts they need to know could be learned through drama, but that the dramatic frame provides insights that cannot be obtained through other media. I believe that if I can demonstrate the use of drama in "higher" education, teachers are much more likely to try it in elementary and secondary classrooms. For drama majors it is easier, as they are used to playing; however, at times it takes a while to break their "performance only" syndrome. Many believe that "performance," not "play," is the thing, and initially cannot see the purpose drama serves in the learning process. However, over the years, they have left the course claiming they did not realize how powerful and meaningful drama could be without a performance. For graduate students, with little or no drama background who enroll in a curriculum course, I start by gently easing them in. Even here, students have left claiming, "I cannot teach the same way again." They recognize that drama can simultaneously reach the hearts, minds, and bodies of students, making learning relevant, rigorous, and fun.

ICE BREAKERS

It is my firm belief that significant drama and learning can only take place when one is willing to place one's personal beliefs in juxtaposition with others. It is the space between oneself and others where true understanding resides. There, one recognizes that one cannot truly know, as all knowing is framed by one's personal constructs. Education provides opportunities for people to examine themselves in the face of others (Levinas, 1984), and educational drama provides rich meeting places for such occasions.

The willingness to disclose and publicly question what is central to one's understanding is underpinned by trust. Without trust, one is not able to place oneself openly before another, making communion impossible. Ice breakers, and other drama education methods that foster the building of trust, are necessary to create a playful atmosphere. This allows the participants to know that this classroom is a safe place where their beliefs can be examined without blame. Only then can drama and learning become significant as fear, the major obstacle to understanding (Nachmanovitch, 1990), is lessened. Significant cognitive activity can take place once it is underpinned by the necessary affective state of trust.

I begin my graduate education classes with an affirmation of my belief in ice breakers, admitting that, like any tool, they can be used, misused, or abused—and that my students have likely experienced the full range. I provide my rationale in the form of a name game, which gently invites each student to place a bit of himself or herself before the class. I provide them with a rationale for ice breakers: They are necessary to build the sense of community that a seminar class like this requires. Then I introduce a form of a name game that gently invites students to place a bit of themselves before the class. I then explain a concrete poetry activity I often used when I taught in a junior high school; the example I draw on the board is one of a ninth grader.

"Joey" was into sports. He easily made the letter "J" into a hockey stick, the "O" into a soccer ball, and the "Y" into the uprights of a football goal post, but he had trouble with the letter "E." He came up to me a few times asking for help (which he seldom did), and finally I found the question to help him find his own solution. I asked him, "What do you wear?" His eyes lit up and he scurried back to his seat only to return a short time later with a drawing of hockey shoulder pads turned sideways. The arms were the top and bottom lines of the capital letter "E" and the chest portion was the middle. He was proud of himself.

After providing Joey's example, as well as a couple of others, I pass out file cards and colored markers and ask my students to draw their names. I prepare them with a simple guided-imagery exercise. I have them close their eyes; I side-coach with questions like: Where do you live/work? What are your hobbies? What is your most pleasant experience in school as a student, as a teacher? Who are the most significant people in your life? Where is your favorite place? These questions assist them in finding the "lived-experience" of themselves, which is the foundation of classroom stories, drama, and curricular understanding.

Each student then explains his or her name card to the class. Usually questions are asked and a lot of appreciative "hmms" and "ahs" are heard as we each witness the significance another brings to her or his life. Although not actively dramatic, each student, by telling vignettes, assists in creating a classroom culture of storytelling. The classroom is filled with significant stories. I point out that the cards themselves have charted a part of their own personal curriculum which makes up who they are, and that in this course we will be looking at a much broader definition of curriculum than what is normally associated with schooling.

This ice breaker successfully sets the tone for the course. It helps to demonstrate that curriculum is more than the objectives found in guides and textbooks. It is the "lived-experiences" of teachers and students as they commune together (Aoki, 1996) Curriculum, then, is the relationship among teacher, students, and subject matter.

Students often give spontaneous feedback to this activity, either after class or at the start of the next week. A few had even rushed back to their own classes and tried it. They were amazed at how it facilitated conversations between teacher and student. The students were able to recognize that classrooms are not only places of knowing and doing, but places of "being" (Morris, 1981). They were now ready to begin a course in curriculum theory and to explore the "lived-experiences" of classroom life, using drama as a tool to access such an understanding.

IN ROLE AS JOURNALISTS

The current positivistic model of curriculum is so pervasive that its inertia alone is tyrannical. Its reduction of education into technical terms needs to be questioned, even though its hegemony makes such questioning seem ludicrous. I needed an activity that would enable my graduate students to understand that all curriculum orientations are points of view that are underpinned by the philosophical beliefs of various power groups. Role-play was a way in.

Students were put in groups of two or three and handed a card with the names of a fictional educational journal, magazine, or newspaper. They were to be members of an editorial board who would chart the future of the publication. I urged them to use the tone given in the title to assist in developing a character for themselves, assuming that certain types of individuals would be attracted to a particular journalistic style and approach. Some of the journal titles I provided to insure a variety of approaches: *Parent's Quarterly, Teacher's Digest, Education's Watch Dog, Innovations and Triumphs, The Teacher, Living and Learning, IDEAS, Raising Children, Better Teaching/Better Learning, Report of Business, Educational Inquirer,* and *Our Great Province Weekly.*

To help each group co-construct the members of an editorial board, I hand out character-development sheets. I have found that sometimes it is better to create characters as a group, rather than as individuals, because the group process helps students recognize that identities are indeed co-created and that the relationships one has with others contributes to a definition of oneself. In a group they are able to design not only an identity, but an identity in relationship to other identities.

The character development sheet asks:

- What is your character's name, age, marital status, educational history, and employment history?
- How long have you been with this journal?
- Describe your job interview, your relationship with your boss and coworkers, and your office and place of employment.
- Do you plan to stay in this job, or do you have your sights set elsewhere?
- What is your idea of a great vacation?
- What hobbies and outside interests do you have?
- What means of transportation do you use?
- Describe your living quarters and home life.

These prompts help to focus the group and provide a sense of belief for the subsequent activities. I have found the half-hour or so spent on this well worth the time. It tends to move the students away from the general and stereotypical into the particulars needed for belief. If rushed into too soon, role-play can result in superficial action.

Then I gather the class in a circle and have each member assume the role of their character and introduce themselves in role. There is lots of laughter as we witness the emergence of new characters, and I take this opportunity to ask further questions to get to belief through the particular.

After the characters have introduced themselves to the class, they meet, in role as editorial boards, in their small groups and discuss the nature and history of their publication, using the following questions:

- What is the mandate of this newspaper/journal/talk show/news report?
- How long has this journal been in operation?
- What special interest groups does it serve?
- What kind of advertisements are in it?
- How many subscribers does it have?
- How many people are employed?
- What are the titles of three articles during the last five issues, or planned future issues?
- What do the covers look like? Design one. (You may change the title but keep the general intent.)

The groups then report back, defining their publication. Again, there is laughter, and additional questions are asked in order to bring depth to the publication.

For the final activity in this stage of the process, the class is asked to examine the course outline as if it were a press release. In role, they are asked to create a series of interview questions to ask me regarding the course, which they will use for an article they are cowriting. Yes, some of their own questions, as students, find their way into the interview that will follow; however, they must be worded from the character's point of view. Once a series of questions is constructed, I take the "hot seat."

The questions are thoughtful, insightful, and challenging. Each year, this activity pushes me to find a rationale for why I do what I do and to defend it in a roomful of people with varying interests. It is my opportunity to explain to my new students why I am doing what I do, but the role-play removes the power structure of a teacher talking down to his/her students. Rather, it is the students, in role as journalists, who have the power. Through the role, they can ask questions they might not normally ask as students. Through the role, we are able to make explicit early in the course the legitimate undercurrents which never become evident in some courses.

I enjoy the challenge, but most often my students come up to me after they are finished, concerned for my emotional health. They consider the act a brave one, recognizing the stress it places upon an individual, but grateful for my providing my vision for the course. In the debriefing that follows, we return to our "everyday" selves, filled with the insights that the role-playing has given us. We discuss how the process of role-playing does not take us away from reality, but closer to it, as it enables the participants to examine the course from many perspectives. We discuss curriculum theory as a perspective, not a truth, recognizing that education is indeed a political arena full of many points of view.

The role-play helps build playful connections between otherwise strangers. By cobuilding characters, publications, and an interview, we have become engaged with one another in a "fantastical world." We have begun to work as a team in what can be perceived as a "low-risk" activity, since the activity was (a) not graded, and (b) beyond the everyday self. The play built a stepping stone to more significant work and conversations with one another.

Later in the course, the students conduct a survey of educational journals and use this activity and other course materials to examine the epistemological and ideological orientations of existing journals. This publication exercise helps them to see beyond the articles to the inherent biases of all publications. The drama ushers them into the lived-experience of critical theory, as they are now astutely aware that curriculum is more a matter of perspective than truth. They have lived this through the role-play.

Few of these graduate students had any previous creative drama and/or theatrical experience. Consequently, the course design recognized where they were, while at the same time demonstrated that drama could be significant as a tool for both understanding and the dissemination of that understanding. The course reinforced that drama activities can enhance understanding as do journal entries, class discussions, research reports, and essays.

Subsequent classes also incorporated drama where appropriate. Students were asked to become prominent educators in order to debate educational issues. They recognized that the role, by distancing one from his or her own point of view, assists one to (a) place his or her own point of view in juxtaposition with others, and in so doing, (b) provide one with a tool for critiquing oneself. The aim of this graduate course was to enable students to see curriculum not as a fixed and predetermined set of objectives, but to see instead the multiple perspectives that underpin those objectives, often serving to privilege, or even exclude, other stake holders. Curriculum was then seen as a lived-experience (Aoki, 1996), and drama allowed us to experience it. It does have its place as a learning medium in graduate schools.

Some took this activity a step further by incorporating drama into class assignments: A few students wrote papers in a script format; one did a curricular reading of a movie, writing it in a play program format; and some used role-play and simulations in their final class presentation. I even received a few watercolors and one oil painting, accompanied by a written explanation. They were able to take what they had learned from the class and apply it to their own work, both in their classrooms and in the fulfillment of course requirements. For many, creative drama became as legitimate as other traditional forms of instruction and assessment.

WELCOME TO TRAFALMADOR

Besides my work with graduate students in the teaching of curriculum theory, I have used drama to teach the teaching pedagogy. My drama majors and minors come to education methods classes after a number of courses in the drama department. This portion of their program is understandably performance oriented. I wanted my students to make a quick shift from drama as a medium for performance to drama as a learning medium (Wagner, 1976/1999). I wanted them to begin the course using the anthropological construct of teacher as stranger (Greene, 1973)and question their own beliefs.

I have always been impressed with the work of Heathcote (Heathcote, 1980, 1983; Wagner, 1976/1999). I find it courageous, exciting, and frightening. The thought of meeting a group of strangers, as Heathcote does, and asking them "What would you like to make a play out of?" was not anything I felt comfortable doing. As both a student and a teacher, I found the structure of a script provided a nice safety blanket. Yet, I did not want to meet my drama education students for the first time with the traditional, "hand out the course outlines and describe the assignments" routine. I wanted to meet them dramatically; Greene provided a theory and Heathcote provided a model for my way in.

On the first day of class, the drama education majors find themselves milling around the hallway. Some know each other from other classes, but it is seldom that one person knows everybody. They find it strange— usually, they enter a classroom, sit down, and wait for the instructor to begin. Today, however, is different; there are signs on both doors to the room, each stating:

> Drama Majors
> Do Not Enter
> Until
> Instructed To Do So

Inside, the room is arranged in different stations. The lights have been dimmed and the center of the room has been cleared. Around the walls are stations, each with a set of instructions. If one were to enter by the main door, one would see a quotation colored by a green gel, projected on a wall opposite the entrance. It reads, "Before we learn how to teach in such a way, we must learn how to learn in such a way" (Pinar, 1975, p. 412). To the left is a TV playing a tape of teachers teaching drama, to the right, a stack of books on educational drama. Other centers around the room are a puppet box, a collection of teacher-prepared documents dealing with the teaching of drama, a tape recorder with a collection of tapes, an assortment of curriculum guides from various provincial agencies, and a small hat and props box. To assist them with the centers, suggestion sheets are provided at each station.

At the designated time for the start of class, a caped and hooded figure carrying a clipboard emerges from one of the doors and enters the hallway.

> "Would the drama education majors gather around. *(They gather.)* I have just received this memo from my superiors and have been told to welcome you to the planet Trafalmador. *(A look of surprise appears on most faces, followed by a knowing smile.)* I understand that this is your first visit to the planet. *(Some nod, some do nothing.)* Please correct me if I'm wrong. *(Pause)* If memos on your planet Earth are anything like the memos on Trafalmador, you're guaranteed to have errors." *(Laughter.)*
>
> I look around the group, asking, "First visit?" *(Heads nod, yes.)* "Amazing. The memo was right for a change."
>
> "I also understand that you have come here through various means of transportation and that many do not know one another. Am I right?" *(Again, heads nod in agreement.)*
>
> "My name is Joe Norris and I'll be your tour guide during your visit." I turn to a student who seems to have been engaged so far and ask, "How did you get here? Did you come on the new shuttle or did you pilot your own ship?"
>
> "The shuttle."
>
> "Oh, the new XK-1000. How did you find the shift into hyper drive?"
>
> A student responds, "Smooth."
>
> *(I respond according to the answer.)* "Great. They were having problems with that. Nothing life-threatening but a little nausea, so I have been told."

We begin to improvise a role-play where I ask them their names and questions regarding their trips to Trafalmador. There is laughter as more buy into the drama. I plant ideas to help scaffold them into the role, but ask them to correct me if my memo is in error in any way. In this way, we negotiate the drama. People pass us in the hall and look at us sideways. The cape, however, gives them a clue that something is up.

Once a bit of playfulness and rapport is established, I move back into focus.

> "So I understand you are here to research Trafalmadorian classrooms." *(Heads nod in agreement.)*
>
> "As I mentioned earlier, I'll be your guide for this tour. If you have any questions, feel free to approach me. We shall enter the classroom now. Please note that for the first part of your visit, there will be no students. We would like you to examine the physical layout of Trafalmadorian classrooms and the materials we use. You may find this quite different than classrooms on Earth. Make some notes and I'll answer questions after you have time to explore."

I raise my hand using the Vulcan handshake and say, "I give you the Trafalmadorian form of welcome, 'Gweep.'" As they enter the classroom, I repeat the greeting to each student, most responding back. They are each handed a general instruction sheet to guide them from center to center, and from time to time I side-coach with questions and instructions. The exploration takes about 30 minutes.

During this time, students browse the collection of drama education books, making a list of which ones they would like to purchase. They peruse the various curriculum guides and compare the approaches taken. They listen to music, determining which types of activities the various pieces might supplement. They watch the tape of teachers teaching and try to identify the teaching strategies employed.

After the students have had enough time to visit at least three stations, I place them into groups of three or four and have them discuss their visit, coming up with questions from what they have seen so far and questions regarding their upcoming extensive visit to Trafalmador. I then explain that we use the "hot seat" convention on Trafalmador and that I will take the hot seat to answer questions after they have some time to prepare.

After ample time, I ritually place a chair in a central position, asking them to gather around. Their questions are fast and furious and, like those of the graduate students, I find they challenge me to question my own beliefs and assist me in articulating what I implicitly believe in. Through the course of the hot seat I, in role, articulate to my students many of my beliefs about teaching drama, enhanced with Trafalmadorian anecdotes. By the end, the students know what to expect and I have been able to be much more open and passionate about the course as a result of the role. I find that a teacher's passion can be intimidating to new students. This role frames my intensity in such a way that my enthusiasm is transformed into play, making it a much more palatable form of passion.

Once the questions begin to wind down, I stand up, turn my back, take off the cape, give a visible physical shudder or two, and say, "Welcome to EDSEC 324. It is good to see you. We'll take a 10-minute break and come back and talk about your recent visit to Trafalmador."

After the break, the students go off, either on their own or in small groups, to make a list of the various events that took place during the visit, then we meet to debrief the activity. I observe their progress, read over their shoulder, and make some comments. Once most have finished, I reassemble the entire class. We explore the activities, their sequence and nuances, to determine the advantages and disadvantages each possesses. We discuss the effect of beginning the first class the way I did. We discuss what worked and didn't work for some. We notice that there are various perspectives, all of which are legitimate. This will relate nicely to a subsequent lecture which uses the term *conspectus* (Neelands, 1984, p. 40). We begin to see that students come with many styles of learning and that no one activity is best for everyone.

Through the discussion and my modeling of my own decision making process, I begin to move them from thinking of themselves as participants to thinking of themselves as leaders. I often refer to this as "the teacher brain." For the drama minors, this is their first methods class, and I need to quickly make them aware that shortly they will no longer live in classrooms where they are one of 30 being carried by a teacher, but that *they* will be carrying 30. For many, this is a big shift. The drama majors have had only a semester of education courses with a four-week practicum before coming to this class, and many have at least one semester of arts and sciences courses between their education courses and this term. This opening warms them back up to the teacher's perspective.

By the end of the session, we have discussed many concepts of lesson planning, but through the context of a shared experience. Through the insights and notes we take, we reconstruct the plan I have used for this opening day. I also hand them a copy of my plan to demonstrate that improvisational teaching is not just a gimmick, but is supported by a firm foundation. Through the opening drama, the students begin to understand group or educational drama, specific teaching techniques such as contracting and side-coaching, my expectations for the course, how to plan a lesson, and the role of drama as a learning medium for all ages. We begin to build rapport as we work as a team through the construction of the group drama and through the discussions which follow.

The Visit to Trafalmador drama lesson provides the opportunity for connections at many levels.

To conclude this class, I point out that for the first class we have created a play—not a play in the sense of a performance, but a play which O'Neill (1995) refers to as "process drama" and Alberta education labels "group drama." I point out that we have used drama activities to help us understand educational issues and, as a quote on the overhead projector suggested, we learned to learn in such a way. Rather than "talking about" or "looking at examples" of group drama, we experienced one and then reflected upon that experience. Hence, this first class modeled the basic premise of drama education, learning by doing and reflecting on that doing (Bolton, 1993). I explain that much of the course will be based upon this approach.

LIVE MARIONETTES: LESSONS IN LEADERSHIP

Many of the dramas I have constructed over the years have their origins in my students' needs. I listen to conversations and search for creative drama activities from my own repertoire, or create a new one that will help us to better understand the phenomenon. Sometimes a general activity provides surprise insights and I file it for future use. While teaching a mini-unit on puppetry, a class and I suddenly had an "a-ha moment," providing profound insight into leadership. Whenever the need emerges in a particular class, I resurrect this one to help increase our understanding of power in the classroom.

One need not cite sources to know that the number one concern of beginning teachers is control. The fear of losing it is pervasive, and books on classroom management abound. Many place the teacher in the center, expecting power to be distributed from the top down. While there is some truth to this perspective, this hierarchical approach does not readily suit itself to the drama classroom. Concepts of negotiation, contracting, and student voice fill the literature (Bolton, 1979; Heathcote, 1983; Neelands, 1984; O'Neill, 1995; O'Neill, Lambert, Linnell, & Warr-Wood, 1976). However, current classroom management strategies become problematic when one moves from a hierarchical to a more mutual classroom perspective (Norris, 1996). The teacher's leadership style is far less hierarchical and far more responsive in the drama classroom, and this not only needs to be made explicit, but is better understood if experienced. Reflection on this particular marionette exercise has made this evident.

To start, I divided the students into partners, making one a marionette and the other a puppeteer. They both faced in the same direction with one standing on a chair behind the other. The person on the floor was to be a marionette and, rather than using string, the puppeteer would give verbal instructions to the marionette. However, the puppeteer would move his or her hands as if they were moving actual strings. First, they were to work on precision, exploring the three dimensions of height, breadth, and width. Later, speed would be added, and finally, activity cards were given with instructions like "fly fishing" and "oil painting." The marionette was not to know the activity, was not to think or talk, but was merely to follow instructions.

After a while precision was reached and the activity was debriefed (reflected on). We talked about precision and accuracy and the difficulty to maintain it when speed increased. We talked about communication and how the visual feedback helped the sender fine-tune instructions. From this, we discussed how any form of student evaluation can be a form of teacher evaluation, as student achievement lets the teacher know what the students need. From this, I asked the questions, "Who is the leader? Who is in control?"

At first, the responses were the puppeteer, of course. But slowly the responses reversed. By looking at the marionette, instructions were fine-tuned; therefore, even in this very controlled environment, the near-to-powerless marionettes exercised power. When instructed to raise a hand distance and speed often varied, thus the marionette led and the puppeteer had to mirror the movement to maintain precision. Even in leadership, there is a dimension of following.

The conversation then shifted to the classroom. We used the puppeteer/puppet metaphor to discuss the student/teacher relationship. We looked at the concept of leading from behind and, like the adage "the best acting is reacting," we concluded that "the best teaching is reacting." The marionette exercise gave us many insights into teaching and helped us to understand that leading and following is a mutual and recursive activity, and that effective leadership is determined as much by the followers as it is by the leader. Teaching, for us, became a little clearer.

TRUST FALL

During a discussion about their practicum experiences, one student exclaimed that he felt boxed in. He felt that both his cooperating teacher and his faculty supervisor weren't giving him enough freedom; he wanted more space. As a teacher, I understood his perspective, yet knew that there was more than one side to the issue. I searched for an activity that would help us all understand this phenomenon better.

Often, I don't know what insight I am searching for, but intuitively know that a particular exercise might help us find it, and it usually works.

I chose the form of trust fall, where everyone forms a circle, with one person in the center. The person in the center falls in one direction, is caught by two or more persons in the circle and returned to center and falls again, usually in another direction. Slowly the falls become larger and larger, according to the comfort level of the person falling.

There was a small group of three in this discussion. I asked them to form a circle and I took the center. As I became comfortable, I began using the student's words, "Give me more space." The catchers seemed reluctant at first. However, over time they began to move back and I fell further and further. Upon another instruction, I was slowly returned to the center and the exercise ended.

During the debriefing, the student who was concerned with freedom spoke first. He said, "I didn't realize how much work I was imposing on my support system by asking for freedom." He recognized that I represented him and labeled the three catchers as the teacher, the faculty supervisor, and his wife. Our discussion on this short exercise was lengthy, and it helped us all to better understand the practicum experience. Through this, we all realized that each of the three parties feels "caught" between the other two. The creative drama opened the door for these insights to occur.

THE TEXTBOOKS

Textbooks, although often necessary, can be tedious to cover. They, however, contain a lot of useful information, which students can assimilate themselves. The practice of covering them chapter-by-chapter may not be an efficient use of time when there are many hands-on activities to cover as well. I ask my students to read their texts and set a day in the course to cover them. I inform them that they will be continually assessed in the course and in teaching, as I believe that the texts have valuable insights into teaching. I also tell them that to cover them chapter-by-chapter in some ways is a lack of trust in (a) their abilities, because I don't think they'll understand it without my help, or (b) I don't trust that they will actually read it, so to make certain, I make them accountable in class. I ask them to help me to trust them.

The two books I have used in the past, in addition to curriculum guides and exercise books, are *Free Play: The Power of Improvisation in Life and the Arts* (Nachmanovitch, 1990) and *Making Sense of Drama* (Neelands, 1984). I ask that they make notes as they read the texts and incorporate their insights into class discussions, journals, and written assignments. For *Free Play*, I also ask them to keep a list of meaningful quotations.

On the designated day, I place students in groups of three or four and provide them with large sheets of paper and markers. They are to go through *Free Play* and their notes and write down meaningful quotes. As a quote is written, the group is to discuss it; the conversations are usually rich and insightful. Once they have had ample time to discuss a number of quotes, we move to the second stage of the exercise. It refocuses them and helps them to recollect their thoughts on the book.

I dim the lights, but keep them bright enough for people to read their quotes. I remind them that the best acting is reacting, so listening is very important for this exercise. We will be creating a quote collage. I start, and if my quote calls for a quote one of them has written down, someone is to read it. If someone begins speaking before another, the second person's quote may no longer fit, so that person needs to wait for another opportunity. Listening is the key, as they are permitted to repeat quotes, echo quotes, and explore the text with their voices.

The next 15 minutes are spiritual. Each year, the substance of the text floats on our voices as we listen and respond to the messages beneath the words. The class is a symphony, with many movements as the form of speech and the content of Nachmanovitch's words blend. His book is very much a spiritual artistic journey, and this exercise is in keeping with the tone of the book. I listen for an appropriate time to conclude. The class usually remains in silence.

Feedback is often, "There was no better way to cover the book." *Free Play* calls for art, and we have responded to it in an artistic way. At times I wonder if we should be spending more time reading practical activity books, and I debate abandoning this book. I have asked former students, and their response is usually an emphatic "no." The book and the way we cover it returns us to the soul of our art form and they believe that this too is practical. They believe that we need more time to return to our roots. For many, this is a significant class and *Free Play* is one text that they now say they plan to read again.

My trust has worked. They don't read the text because I manipulate them into it—they read it because they want to. Finding activities that make the material relevant is our task as teachers. This drama activity enabled students to see beyond the text to the treasures which lay within.

The day continues with a change of pace as we turn our attention to *Making Sense of Drama*. Keeping the same groups (usually five to six, depending upon the numbers), I individually go to each group and assign them a task. Two groups are advertising executives who have been asked to create a quote-of-the-day desk calendar for drama teachers and are to go through the book finding appropriate quotes. Two other groups are assigned the task of creating a set of classroom posters to inspire drama students. They are to find quotes and think of visuals that may accompany them. The third set of two groups become government officials who are to design a checklist of knowledge, skills, and attitudes drama teachers must possess, and they are to use *Making Sense of Drama* in designing this list.

Leaving them to their tasks for a while, I then return to the groups in role, with variations depending upon the task of the group. For example: "Who's in charge here?"

After they respond, I announce, "As you all know, we are in a process of downsizing and I have both some good and bad news for you. The bad news is there are going to be more layoffs. The good news is that it doesn't have to be you. The head office has asked me to inform you that there is one other team working on the same project and the team that presents the best package will keep their jobs, while the members of the other team will be laid off. Please note that our criterion will not be only artistry; you must also evidence a thorough understanding of Neelands' message. We have our academic integrity to protect as well."

After a short discussion, they get back to work; some groups are renewed and more focused due to the intervention. Some ask for paper and markers, others rehearse their presentation. They play with Neelands' ideas, using new forms and debating their significance. Through role, the text now has a different but equally as meaningful a life.

The presentations are entertaining and informative. They summarize the book by highlighting useful segments which can guide practice. Neelands' words provide a lot of information on the knowledge, skills, and attitudes needed by teachers and students in a drama classroom. In this exercise, they are not presented in a hierarchical fashion which can produce resistance. The activity permits us to deal with the material without the power structures inherent in hierarchical modes of instruction. Through the play, Neelands' insights become accessible as certain forms of resistance are removed. For one class, the icing on the cake was a presentation they made directly to Jonathan Neelands, during a visit to the university.

WHAT CREATIVE/EDUCATIONAL DRAMA CAN DO

Through the examples provided, I trust it is evident what creative drama can do, not in the form of statistical proof, which often obscures our art form, but in the people who leave a dramatic exercise a little bit more insightful due to the experience. I conclude by highlighting some of the concepts on which this approach is founded.

First and foremost, creative drama can enable people to be comfortable and to trust one another. Play is not the opposite of work; it is essential for work, as it produces a high degree of trust required by working teams. Creative drama frames an activity in such a way that risk is minimized and insights are maximized. The activities presented here demonstrate that creative drama provides a platform upon which open conversations can take place. Without these, significant work cannot be accomplished, as the real concerns get buried. In my classrooms, I have found an openness to discussion and a willingness to publicly question oneself. The drama exercises assisted us in achieving a relationship that fostered this openness and reflection.

With trust established, different points of view can now be seen as necessary. Rather than believing that different opinions are adversarial, the students could see that most often they represented different perspectives or portraits of the same phenomenon. With this understanding, group discussions took on a new character as the willingness to expand one's perspective replaced the drive to convince others that you were right and they were wrong. Like the wise people of Indostan, we accepted that we were looking at different parts of the same elephant.

We also recognized that we were looking with different eyes. By accepting the opinions of others, we were able to look at things from many angles. Through the exploration of self in juxtaposition with self-in-role, we came to know that meaning cannot be separate from the giver of meaning. Meaning then became post-modern in that it was understood that meaning not only lies in the thing itself, but the medium or instrument used to portray that thing, as well as the interpretations of the people involved. Knowing then became ambiguous and problematic. Knowing also became political, as we began to notice that certain power structures exist which impose meaning onto others. Creative drama has much to offer in the understanding of hermeneutics and axiology.

Reality also became a questionable phenomenon as it became recognized as, in part, politically constructed. The imaginary roles we used provided useful but different insights; consequently, the separation of reality and fantasy became problematic as the creative drama also made sense. Through this juxtaposition of reality and fantasy, we could see the epistemological assumptions of the hegemonic practices we use. Reality and fantasy became complementary rather than polarized terms. Through drama, we come to recognize that the dominant practices we label as reality can be as fantastical as the dramas we play. Quoting Shakespeare, we are indeed "such stuff as dreams are made on." When we realize that our construct of reality can enslave and stifle, the imagination can once again be set free to serve self and others. Creative drama has the potential to continually renew the world in a peaceful but energetic fashion.

Creative drama, then, is a tool to take us beyond the constraints of our own limited perspective by providing us with not only a tool to look differently, but an attitude through which diversity is valued and celebrated. Through role-play, one distances oneself and can therefore see oneself and one's vision of the world differently.

But creative drama is not only doing and displaying. The discussions which precede and the reflections which follow the activities are essential. Through them we recognize that living and learning is beyond doing, that the state of being, which underpins the doing, is essential. Only with trust and acceptance can significant conversations and meaning take place. Like action research (Kemmis & McTaggart, 1988), creative drama goes in cycles of distance-near (doing) and distance-far (reflecting). The distance-far can, in some ways, bring one closer to a phenomenon by revealing another perspective, and the distance-near bring one along further as the range is limited. With one you get depth, with the other breadth. The concepts subjective and objective also become complementary as do the particular and the universal. Creative drama provides polyocular vision (Maruyama, 1974).

Creative drama then not only has its place in the education of the young, but in the education of all adults. It is a powerful tool to determine and create meaning at various levels, albeit a greatly underutilized tool. It has the power to change hearts and minds; perhaps that is why some resist it. Drama will always be a political tool, and for those who either wish to maintain their status or resist change, it is threatening. But for those who embrace it, it will improve understanding in both school and in life. Its additional benefit is that while it is building meaning, it is simultaneously building community. Creative drama is an integrative discipline which continually operates at the cognitive and affective levels. It is indeed adult's work.

REFERENCES

Aoki, T. (1996). *Spinning enspiriting images midst planned and lived curricula*. Paper presented at the meeting of the Fine Arts Council, Edmonton, Canada.

Bolton, G. (1979). *Towards a theory of drama in education*. London: Longman.

Bolton, G. (1993). Drama in education and TIE: A comparison. In T. Jackson (Ed.), *Learning through theatre* (pp. 39–47). New York: Routledge.

Cottrell, J. (1979). *Teaching with creative dramatics*. Skokie, IL: National Textbook Company.

Culler, J. (1982). *On deconstruction*. Ithaca, NY: Cornell University Press.

Edmiston, B. W. (1991). "What have you traveled?" A teacher-researcher study of structuring drama for reflection and learning. *Dissertation Abstracts International*, *52*(05), 1624A. (University Microfilms No. 9130469)

Greene, M. (1973). *Teacher as stranger: Educational philosophy for the Modern Age*. Belmont, CA: Wadsworth Publishing.

Heathcote, D. (1980). *Drama as context*. Aberdeen, England: The National Association for the Teaching of English.

Heathcote, D. (1983). Learning, knowing, and languaging in drama: An interview with Dorothy Heathcote. *Language Arts, 60*(6), 695–701.

Kemmis, S., & McTaggart, R. (1988). *The action research planner* (3rd ed.). Victoria, Australia: Deacon University Press.

King, N. (1983). *Work and play contexts and curriculum practice*. Paper presented at the American Educational Research Association Annual Meeting, Montreal, Quebec, Canada.

Levinas, E. (1984). Emmanuel Levinas. In R. Kearney (Ed.), *Dialogues with contemporary continental thinkers* (pp. 47–70). Manchester, England: Manchester University Press.

Maruyama, M. (1974). Hierarchists, individualists and mutualists. *Futures, 6*(2), 103–113.

Morris, E. (1981). *Being and doing*. Los Angeles: Ermor.

Nachmanovitch, S. (1990). *Free play*. Los Angeles: Jeremy P. Tarcher.

Neelands, J. (1984). *Making sense of drama*. London: Heinemann.

Norris, J. (1989). Some authorities as co-authors in a collective creation production. *Dissertation Abstracts International, 50*(11), 3417A. (University Microfilms No. 031555634X)

Norris, J. (1995). The use of drama in teacher education: A call for embodied learning. In B. Warren (Ed.), *Creating a theatre in your classroom* (pp. 179–305). North York, Ontario, Canada: Captus Press.

Norris, J. (1996). *Implementing a mutualist curriculum in a teacher education program: A beginning teacher educator's story*. Paper presented at the American Educational Research Association Annual Meeting, New York.

O'Neill, C. (1995). *Drama worlds: A framework for process drama*. Portsmouth, NH: Heinemann.

O'Neill, C., Lambert, A., Linnell, R. & Warr-Wood, J. (1976). *Drama guidelines*. London: Heinemann.

Pinar, W. (1975). Curerre: Toward reconceptualization. In W. Pinar (Ed.), *Curriculum theorizing*. Berkeley, CA: McCutchan Publishing.

Taylor, P. (1993). Our adventure of experiencing: Drama structure and action research in the grade seven social studies classroom (Doctoral dissertation, New York University, 1992). *Dissertation Abstracts International, 53*(09), 2759A.

Wagner, B. J. (1999). *Dorothy Heathcote: Drama as a learning medium*. Portland, ME: Calendar Islands Publishers. (Original work published 1976)

OTHER RESOURCES

Bentov, M. (1974). Creative drama in education: Rationale, curriculum applications and teacher training (Doctoral dissertation, Harvard University, 1974). *Dissertation Abstracts International, 34*(09), 6858A.

Camerota, E. C. (1981). The effect of dramatic improvisation on the attitudes of high school teachers toward students (Doctoral dissertation, Rutgers University, 1981). *Dissertation Abstracts International, 41*(09), 197A.

Coppens, H. (1993, July). *Teaching teachers to act in role: A drama method to teach behavioural leadership during teachers training courses.* Paper presented at the International Conference on the Work and Influence of Dorothy Heathcote, Lancaster University, England.

Feinberg, R. M. (1977). *The modification of sex-role attitudes of students through teacher in-service education using creative dramatics.* Unpublished doctoral dissertation, Boston University School of Education.

Karowski, L. (1988). The effects of roleplay on changing attitudes of preservice elementary social studies teachers toward reflective inquiry (Doctoral dissertation, Pennsylvania State University, 1988). *Dissertation Abstracts International, 49*(11), 3254A.

McCammon, L., Norris, J., & Miller, C. (1998). Cacophony and fugue: Pre-service narratives create conversation about drama education. *Research in Drama Education, 3*(1), 29–44.

O'Neill, C. (1991). Training teachers. *Teaching Theatre, 2*(4), 5–6.

Weeks, T. M. (1993). Role playing: A video production for teacher training. *Dissertation Abstracts International, 54*(04), 1312A. (University Microfilms No. 93-24261)

We learned through the play.... We learned through the parts we were given. It is something not easy to explain. I am new to playing but it has seemed to me like dreaming. The player is himself and another. When he looks at the others in the play he knows he is part of their dreaming just as they are part of his. From this come thoughts and words that outside the play he would not readily admit to his mind.

Barry Unsworth, author of *Morality Play*,
a novel published in 1995 by Doubleday

About the Authors

Richard Courtney
A foremost theorist in the field of drama in education before his death on August 16, 1997, Courtney was Professor Emeritus at the Ontario Institute for Studies in Education at the University of Toronto. He was born in Suffolk, England, on June 4, 1927, and educated at Leeds University. He studied with Shakespearean scholar G. Wilson Knight and Pirandello director and translator Frederick May. In the 1960s, while training drama teachers at Trent College, in London, he wrote a book that linked the discipline of educational drama with the then-current thinking in psychology, philosophy, anthropology, and theater history. This book, titled *Play, Drama, and Thought*, established his reputation as a foremost drama theorist. At age 40, Courtney emigrated to Canada from Great Britain, where he taught at the Universities of Victoria, Calgary. He also taught at the University of Toronto, where he had a joint appointment in the Ontario Institute for Studies in Education and the Graduate Drama Centre. Among Professor Courtney's over 50 books, those in print in addition to *Play, Drama and Thought* (4th ed., 1989), include *Drama and Intelligence* (1989), *Drama and Feeling* (1995), eight books in *The Director's Shakespeare* series, and *The Birth of God: The Moses Play and Monotheism in Ancient Israel* (1996). Courtney has also published poetry and plays. He and his wife, the lexicographer, Rosemary Courtney, lived on Salt Spring Island, British Columbia.

Holly Giffin
Giffin has written and taught in the fields of communication, developmental psychology, conflict resolution, and educational drama for over 25 years. She studied with Virginia Koste and Thelma McDaniel in the Drama/Theatre for the Young Program at Eastern Michigan University, where she received her Master of Arts degree. Giffin earned her Ph.D. at the University of Colorado, where she worked closely with Elise Boulding, a Nobel Peace Prize nominee. In 1988, she received the Outstanding Research Award from the American Alliance for Theatre and

Education. She was elected First Vice President of the AATE in 1995, overseeing research, publications, and standards. For 11 years, Giffin developed and implemented the conflict resolution progam at the Gold Hilll Elementary School in Boulder, Colorado, estensively incorporating drama as a learning medium. Most recently, she is co-director of the Colorado branch of the Children's Creative Response to Conflict, as well as an instructor in educational methods at the University of Colorado.

Shirley Brice Heath

A Professor of English and Linguistics at Stanford University, she has also been co-principal investigator (with Milbrey W. McLaughlin) of a multi-year project studying the out-of-school learning environments young people choose for themselves. Serving as linguistic anthropologist on the project, Heath has focused on the language acquisition and practical skills of reasoning and relating that young people derive particularly from arts programs. Drama projects and conflict resolution programs appear more frequently than any other kind of arts program among those identified by youth as highly useful for negotiation of their daily lives and planning for their futures. Heath is co-author (with McLaughlin) of *Identity and Inner-city Youth: Beyond Ethnicity and Gender* (1992), and author of *Ways with Words: Language, Life and Work in Communities and Classrooms* (1983).

Karen Hume

A full-time elementary school teacher in a school district just outside of metropolitan Toronto, Hume is also a doctoral student at the Ontario Institute for Studies in Education. She has been teaching for 12 years, working with students in grades 1 through 8, as well as serving occasionally as a teacher librarian and technology specialist. In recent years, Hume has been involved in action research in her classroom. Her current areas of interest for classroom research are: community development, knowledge construction, the affective curriculum, science, history, and the processes involved in inquiry and in co-researching issues with her students.

Joe Norris

Norris is an associate professor with the Department of Secondary Education at the University of Alberta in Canada. He teaches drama methods to drama education students, a Theatre in Education (TIE) troupe course, general education methods to undergraduate students, and curriculum theory to graduate students. Professor Norris divides his research interests into the areas of teacher education, mutualist curricula, drama in education (both as a separate subject and as an integrator),

and TIE. He has served as president of the Educational Drama Association of Nova Scotia, president of the Fine Arts Council of Alberta, and research chair for the American Alliance for Theatre in Education.

Paula M. Salvio

Salvio is an associate professor of education at the University of New Hampshire. Her scholarship is in curriculum theory, with a focus on performance theory, narrative ethics, and autobiography. She has published widely in journals such as the *Cambridge Journal of Education*, *English Quarterly*, *Journal of Teacher Education*, *Language Arts*, *Journal of Curriculum Studies*, and the *Journal of Curriculum Theorizing*. Professor Salvio is currently a Gustafson Fellow at the University of New Hampshire, where she is currently writing a book on the teaching life of the Pulitzer Prize winning poet, Anne Sexton.

Peter Smagorinsky

An associate professor of English Education at the University of Georgia, he taught high school English in the Chicago area from 1976 to 1990, while earning his M.A.T. and Ph.D. at the University of Chicago. Through the National Research Center on English Learning and Achievement (CELA), funded by the Office of Educational Research and Improvement, Professor Smagorinsky is currently studying the transition that English teachers make from preservice to the workforce. He is co-editor of *Research in the Teaching of English*, a trustee of the Research Foundation of the National Council of Teachers of English, past co-chair of NCTE's Assembly for Research, and past chair of NCTE's Standing Committee on Research.

Betty Jane Wagner

Wagner is internationally recognized as an authority on the educational uses of drama in the classroom and on writing instruction. In 1998, she received two awards: the Judith Kase-Polisini Honorary Research Award from the Allliance for Theatre and Education for her contribution over the years to international drama/theatre research and the Rewey Belle Inglis Award from the National Council of Teachers of English for Outstanding Woman in English Education. Her best-known books are *Dorothy Heathcote: Drama as a Learning Medium* (1976/1999), considered a classic in the field; *Student-Centered Language Arts, K-12*, co-authored with the late James Moffett (1992); *Situations: A Case Book of Virtual Realities for the English Teacher*, co-authored with Mark Larson (1995); and *Educational Drama and Language Arts: What Research Shows* (1998). She has written several curriculums, including *Interaction* (1973), *Language Roundup* (1997), and *Books at Play* (1997), a drama and literacy program. Professor

Wagner has also written numerous chapters in books, such as the *Handbook of Research on Teaching the English Language Arts* (1991/1999) and *Perspectives on Talk and Learning* (1990), as well as articles for National Council of Teachers of English journals. Wagner is a professor in the College of Education at Roosevelt University and director of the Chicago Area Writing Project.

Gordon Wells

Wells is Professor of Education at the Ontario Institute for Studies in Education at the University of Toronto. As a member of the Curriculum Department and of the Centre for Teacher Development, he researches and teaches in the fields of language, literacy and learning, and sociocultural theory. Professor Wells's specific interest is in dialogic inquiry in the classroom. In recent years, all these professional interests have come together in a number of collaborative action research projects that he has conducted with teachers in Ontario and other regions. He is currently engaged in a project entitled, "Developing Inquiring Communities in Education," which is funded by the Spencer Foundation. Wells has lectured and consulted in Europe, Latin America, Asia, and Australia, as well as in Britain and North America. His publications include: *The Meaning Makers* (1986), *Constructing Knowledge Together* (1992), *Changing Schools from Within: Creating Communities of Inquiry* (1994), and *Dialogic Inquiry: Towards a Sociocultural Practice and Theory of Education* (1999).

Jennifer Lynn Wolf

A teacher in the Cotati-Rohnert Park Unified School District, in California, Wolf has taught English and drama for the past eight years at the high school level in city and suburban schools. Since 1990, she has served as a senior research associate with the Learning for Anything Everyday project, focusing on effective school and community theater partnerships, and on how drama can be used as an effective teaching technique across the curriculum. Wolf has an undergraduate degree in English, Theater, and Education from Northwestern University and an M.A.T. from Stanford University. Much of Wolf's learning came from the theater program at Northwestern. Her chapter, "Balancing Act: Using Drama to Even the Exchange of Information in the Classroom," in the *Handbook for Literacy Educators: Research on Teaching the Communicative and Visual Arts*, illustrates how drama levels the relationship between teachers and students. Massen has also co-authored a book with Jan Mandell titled *Performing On and Off Stage* (in press).

Katherine Rose Yaffe

Yaffe received her M.A. in Child Drama/Theatre from the University of Denver and is a licensed elementary school teacher. She continued her training in educational drama with Dorothy Heathcote at the University of Newcastle Upon Tyne, in England. In 1979, Yaffe founded the Colorado Educational Theatre (CET) and currently serves as the company's Artistic/Educational Director. In collaboration with CET actors-teachers, she created the Building Bridges™ program, which has been implemented in over 250 schools throughout Colorado since 1988. From 1993 to 1998, CET worked as artists-in-residence for Adams County School District 14, where Yaffe trained teachers and taught prosocial skill drama programs for at-risk children. Yaffe has written teacher handbooks, including *Building Bridges, Creative Conflict Management for Primary and Intermediate Grades,* and is currently developing a new drama-based curriculum and manual on gender equity training for young people.

Author Index

Subject Index